SKILLS FOR CONSUMER SUCCESS

MARY QUEEN DONNELLY

St. Mary's Dominican High School
New Orleans, LA

2d Edition

Published by

H11 **SOUTH-WESTERN PUBLISHING CO.**

CINCINNATI   WEST CHICAGO, IL   DALLAS   LIVERMORE, CA

CONTENTS

UNIT 1 THE JOB MARKET

Discovering Your Values, Interests, and Abilities 3
Discovering the Types of Jobs and Careers Available 8
Benefiting from Part-time Jobs and Vocational Classes 12
Finding and Applying for a Job 14
Interviewing for the Job 23
Understanding Income Taxes 28
Further Discoveries 31

UNIT 2 CHECKING ACCOUNTS

Knowing the Differences Among Financial Institutions 35
Opening a Checking Account 37
Writing a Check and Keeping Accurate Check Records 41
Depositing Money in a Checking Account 44
Interpreting and Reconciling a Bank Statement 48
Further Discoveries 54

UNIT 3 SAVINGS ACCOUNTS AND BANK SERVICES

Figuring Simple Interest 57
Calculating Compound Interest 60
Understanding Savings Plans 63
Handling Routine Financial Transactions Electronically 67
Utilizing Special Checks, Money Orders, and Safe-Deposit Boxes 71
Further Discoveries 73

UNIT 4 CREDIT

Recognizing the Requirements for Buying on Credit 76
Obtaining a Loan 81
Understanding Installment Contracts 88
Understanding Charge Accounts 92
Further Discoveries 96

UNIT 5 BUDGETING

How to Determine Budget Goals, Total Income, and Expenditures 99
How to Keep Records: Making a Budget Work 107
How to Prepare a Yearly Budget 115
Further Discoveries 116

UNIT 6 INVESTMENT OPPORTUNITIES

Investing in Stocks 120
Investing in Bonds 124
Investing in Mutual Funds 126
Understanding Other Investment Alternatives 127
Investing in an IRA 128
Making Investment Decisions 129
Further Discoveries 131

UNIT 7 INSURANCE: HEALTH/LIFE/SOCIAL

Buying Health Insurance 134
Buying Life Insurance 141
Knowing About Protection Through Social Security 145
Further Discovery 151

UNIT 8 INSURANCE: AUTO AND HOME

Buying Auto Insurance 153
Buying Home and Property Insurance 161
Further Discoveries 168

UNIT 9 OWNING AND OPERATING A CAR

Estimating Expenses 171
Shopping for a Used Car 174
Shopping for a New Car 180
Applying for a Car Loan 185
Further Discoveries 188

UNIT 10 HOUSING

Determining Choices Available 191
Understanding a Lease 196
Buying a Home 203
Further Discoveries 208

UNIT 11 CONSUMER PROTECTION

What You Should Know About Your Rights as a Consumer 213
How to Use Consumer Publications 215
How to Handle Complaints as a Consumer 219
How to Interpret Legal Agreements and Warranties as a Consumer 227
Further Discoveries 232

UNIT 1

THE JOB MARKET

SKILL 1   **Discovering Your Values, Interests, and Abilities**

SKILL 2   **Discovering the Types of Jobs and Careers Available**

SKILL 3   **Benefiting from Part-time Jobs and Vocational Classes**

SKILL 4   **Finding and Applying for a Job**

SKILL 5   **Interviewing for the Job**

SKILL 6   **Understanding Income Taxes**

Further Discoveries

When Susan Thompson was a senior at Towne High, she didn't know much about surviving in a world outside school. During her senior year, Susan's one dream had been to leave home and be on her own. After graduation she planned to get a job, rent an apartment, buy a car, and just have fun. She daydreamed through many a class about parties in her new apartment and trips to the beach in her car. Had it not been for Mr. Fernandez, the school counselor, Susan might have left Towne High without the least notion of what she was getting into.

"What are you doing next year?" Mr. Fernandez casually asked Susan one day.

For the first time Susan realized "next year" was not mapped out for her. Before her senior year, one school year had blended into the next. Now she had to make a decision about next year. The thought terrified her.

Well, Susan Thompson survived just fine. Thanks to Mr. Fernandez and others, she eventually became a successful consumer. But she often thought about her senior year—and more important—the years afterwards when she was on her own. Susan suspected that she wasn't the only senior at Towne High who had little or no knowledge about life as a consumer in the real world.

Illustration 1-1

Skills for Consumer Success

So she compiled this book. It is a book about skills one needs to become a successful consumer. It is not the kind of book you are used to. This is not a book that you read just to learn facts for a test. Instead, you will practice the skills as you read about them. You will fill out a job application, a loan application, and a credit card application. You will write checks and balance a checkbook, shop for a car, and interpret a lease agreement for an apartment. You will discover many things that you need to know to be a successful consumer.

Susan has arranged *Skills for Consumer Success* into eleven units. Each unit is divided into closely related skills and contains *Student Activities* which should help you develop these skills. After mastering the skills, you may wish to do some of the activities in Susan's *Further Discoveries*. Also, when you have finished the *Student Activities*, you will complete a checklist of the skills you have learned. Finally, Susan has developed a special test (*Susan Thompson Test*) for each unit. You must get this test from your teacher. If you pass the test, you may go on to the next unit.

DISCOVERING YOUR VALUES, INTERESTS, AND ABILITIES

When Susan finally worked up the courage to go to Mr. Fernandez's office, the first thing she announced was, "I know one thing I don't want—more school."

"Hey, let's not put the cart before the horse," Mr. Fernandez said, pointing to a chair for Susan. "I'm not here to talk you into going to college. You may not need to go to college for the career you want to pursue. Your job choice may require another type of schooling, on-the-job training, or no schooling at all.

"First of all, let's look at your interests and values; then we'll evaluate your abilities and what kind of schooling you may or may not need. Have you ever had a job, Susan?"

"At fast food places," she said. "But I don't want to flip hamburgers for the rest of my life," she quickly added.

Mr. Fernandez smiled. He had heard that comment hundreds of times during his many years as a school counselor.

"What would you *like* to do?" Mr. Fernandez asked.

"Oh, I don't know," Susan said. "Maybe work in a bank. I'm good with numbers. Sometimes I think I'd like to be a nurse. My mom says I'm pretty patient with sick people. I take care of my grandmother a lot."

"You said a mouthful just now," Mr. Fernandez said. "In that one statement you revealed a great deal about your interests and abilities."

"But it's all so confusing to me," Susan insisted. "I still have no idea what I want to do."

Mr. Fernandez began by explaining the difference between a job and a career. He said that a *career* involves progressive achievement in a particular occupational area; whereas, a *job* is a specific task or stint of work.

"You had a job at the fast food restaurant," he explained. "Unless you choose to pursue the job of managing the restaurant yourself, there is little chance that you will progress beyond cooking hamburgers or serving customers.

"The same is true in almost every occupation. You say you might like to be a nurse. You may choose to become a nurse's aide, with only on-the-job training required. A job as a nurse's aide may prove satisfactory for you. A career in nursing, however, requires schooling beyond high school and offers advancement in the nursing profession. If you have any hope of becoming head nurse, you will need more education and training."

Mr. Fernandez explained that a career choice is not necessarily permanent. Many people, especially today, change careers three or four times in a lifetime. Sometimes their second and third choices are vastly different from their original choices. Teachers may become insurance representatives, start businesses of their own, or work as plumbers.

"So career choices, like job choices, are flexible," said Mr. Fernandez. "For a seventeen- or eighteen-year-old to view a career choice as a final decision is unrealistic. How many eighteen-year-olds, or perhaps even thirty-year-olds, know what they want to do for the rest of their lives?

"That is not to say career choices are unimportant," Mr. Fernandez added, "because frequently these choices cannot be changed easily, especially if years of education and experience have gone into them."

Mr. Fernandez suggested that before making a career choice, a person should give consideration to three areas in particular: *personal interests*, *personal values*, and *personal abilities*.

He said that an examination of one's interests, values, and abilities is the first step in choosing a career and, unfortunately, is the step often omitted. He told of a young man who came into his office years ago and said he wanted to make a lot of money. The young man had been successful in his science and math courses, so he decided on dentistry. Well into graduate courses at dental school, he quit. Mr. Fernandez heard later that the young man had become a pilot.

Mr. Fernandez said that a lot of heartache can be prevented with some investigation of one's interests, values, and abilities *before* a career choice is made. Consideration of different careers, however, as well as reevaluation of one's personal criteria for choosing a career usually continue even after a choice is made. Thus, the cycle of career or job choice goes on throughout an individual's life.

Mr. Fernandez told Susan that when a career matches one's interests and values, work can be fun. On the other hand, if one's values and interests are in conflict with one's work, each day can be torture. This is why it is so important to understand oneself in relation to a career. It is difficult to judge what type of career you will enjoy when you have so little experience, but with a little reflection, you can discover more about yourself than perhaps you realize.

STUDENT ACTIVITY A

Mr. Fernandez gave Susan a worksheet on values and interests to complete. Fill out the worksheet for yourself.

VALUES-INTERESTS WORKSHEET

Work vs. Play

1. Work and play are an important part of our lives. Next to the word *Work*, write any words that you associate with work. Next to the word *Play*, write any words that you associate with play.

   Work: _____

   Play: _____

2. Here are four descriptions of jobs, each providing different sources of satisfaction. *Rank* these in order of their appeal to you (4 = high appeal, 3 = some appeal, 2 = little appeal, 1 = no appeal). Which job would you take first? Be honest with yourself. For example, would you really reject the secure, dull job if it paid well?

Rank

_____ a. *Secure* but rather dull job. You will always be sure of having your job and getting salary raises. It is possible that you can build some excitement into this job if you are imaginative enough, but that will take a lot of effort.

_____ b. *Exciting* but very risky job. You're never sure from one month to the next whether you will have a job. You learn a great deal in this job and are always being challenged, but the uncertainties worry you day and night.

_____ c. *Prosperous.* This is a job where you can learn a lot, attain prestige, and have a great deal of power and responsibility for decisions. You are so busy earning money, however, that you really do not have time to learn new ideas or move the company in the direction you'd like to see it go.

_____ d. *Free Time and Fringe Benefits.* This job is the least demanding of all the jobs. The pay is low, and you do not learn very much that is new to you. You can travel to many places, however, and arrange your working hours to suit yourself. You have a company car, work only 30 hours a week if you like, and you don't have to produce much to satisfy your boss.

3. Would you work if you didn't have to? Why or why not?

   _____

   _____

4. Name three people whose work you really admire. Tell exactly why you admire the kinds of work they do.

   _____

   _____

   _____

   _____

   _____

   _____

5. In what kinds of work situations would you be willing to work for less than the normal pay? What rewards from work are more important than money?

_____

_____

_____

_____

6. People who work with me think that I am _____

_____

_____

_____

_____

(complete this sentence)

7. *Rank* these sources of satisfaction from work from 1 to 5 according to their importance to you (5 = very important; 1 = not important).

_____ Money

_____ Prestige

_____ Security

_____ Recognition

_____ Independence

After completing the Values-Interests Worksheet, Susan said that even though the worksheet helped her to determine her values and interests, she was still not sure what she was capable of doing.

Mr. Fernandez assured her she was not alone. "Few high school students are aware of their abilities because they have had so little work experience. There are methods, however, of getting some idea of what your abilities are. Many careers are related to subject areas that you study in school.

"You may have an interest in becoming a lawyer (perhaps, because of prestige or money). But if you have always hated to study and you barely made it through English classes, pursuing a career as a lawyer may be unrealistic.

"Years of hard study are necessary to become a lawyer. Maybe you always wanted to be a doctor or a nurse, but you hated biology and nearly flunked chemistry. Because those subjects are necessary to become a doctor or a registered nurse, you may have to make another career choice. As you can see, ability is as important in selecting a career as interests and values. One way to determine your abilities when in high school is to recall your interest in and success with certain subjects."

Mr. Fernandez gave Susan a worksheet on abilities to complete.

SELF-EVALUATION OF ABILITIES

Complete the worksheet below.

1. Answer the following questions on your subjects:

   a. List the subject you like best.   Why?

   _____   _____

   _____   _____

   _____   _____

   _____   _____

   b. List the subjects you dislike.   Why?

   _____   _____

   _____   _____

   _____   _____

   c. List the subjects in which you make
      the best grades.   Why?

   _____   _____

   _____   _____

   _____   _____

   _____   _____

   d. List the subjects in which you make
      the worst grades.   Why?

   _____   _____

   _____   _____

   _____   _____

   _____   _____

2. What are the things that you do best? You may consider them talents or skills. They
   need not be related to a particular job or career. Name and define them as specifically as possible.

   a. _____

   b. _____

   c. _____

   d. _____

   e. _____

   f. _____

Susan discovered several things about herself after completing Mr. Fernandez's worksheets. She discovered that she liked working with numbers and doing routine work. Her friend, Carlos, who also filled out the worksheets, was just the opposite. He liked writing poetry and making his own work schedule.

Mr. Fernandez said that knowing one's interests, values, and abilities is the first step in making a satisfactory career choice. The second step is equally important: familiarizing oneself with what is available in the job market, and matching one's traits and talents with particular jobs.

Illustration 1-2

DISCOVERING THE TYPES OF JOBS AND CAREERS AVAILABLE

Mr. Fernandez realized that Susan had a very limited view of the job market. When he asked her to name the kinds of occupations she knew about, she mentioned only those which she had been exposed to during her school years: teachers, counselors, principals, cafeteria workers, cooks, doctors, nurses, and secretaries. Mr. Fernandez suggested that she observe workers in her community for a day or so and report what she discovered. The list she came up with follows:

mail carrier   x-ray technician
building contractor   police officer
bank teller   dietician
gardener   telephone installer
computer operator   insurance salesperson
librarian   laboratory technician
electrician

Susan was amazed at the different types of jobs available. Before Mr. Fernandez had suggested it, she had not thought to look at what people do around her.

STUDENT ACTIVITY C

Make a list of the jobs you have observed in your community. In the second column, indicate whether the job will satisfy your interests, values, and abilities (as best as you can judge at this point).

	Jobs	Yes/No
1.	_____	_____
2.	_____	_____
3.	_____	_____
4.	_____	_____
5.	_____	_____
6.	_____	_____
7.	_____	_____
8.	_____	_____
9.	_____	_____
10.	_____	_____

Mr. Fernandez told Susan there are many ways to learn about a variety of jobs. Some sources of information can be located in the school. *School counselors* usually have job information. Many school libraries have copies of the *Dictionary of Occupational Titles*, a publication in which many jobs are classified and coded. School libraries usually keep a copy of the *Occupational Outlook Handbook*, which includes job descriptions. Some schools have *Career Centers*, which provide information and services. There are *work-study programs* around the country that allow a student to get on-the-job training and receive high school credit for the work experience.

In addition to sources of information in the school, there are numerous other means of learning about jobs in your community. Looking through the Yellow Pages of a local telephone directory can give you an idea of places and types of employment in a community. The want ads in the *classified section of the local newspaper* list jobs available in the community, often including the job requirements too. Many communities have a *state employment office*, which provides information and services related to the job market, including free pre-employment testing.

Private employment agencies—sometimes called *placement firms*—are another source for finding a job. Their function is to match people with jobs. Employers hire placement firms to find needed employees. There is always a fee, which is paid by either the employer or the person seeking the job. Ask about the fee before you engage the firm. Sometimes the job may be worth the price of the fee, sometimes not. There are hundreds of placement firms around the country. Some are small; others are members of franchised chains, such as Snelling & Snelling and the Dunhill Personnel System.

Finally, one of the best ways to learn about jobs is to ask people what they do for a living. People usually love to talk about their jobs. Some valuable information can be gathered through conversation with other people in the job market. You can find out what the job entails, the education and/or skills needed for the job, personal and professional benefits, disadvantages of the job, expected income, and so forth.

Mr. Fernandez concluded his conversation with Susan by showing her fifteen clusters of occupations. He explained that these categories are general, but people are usually employed in one of these fifteen specific areas. Figure 1-1 displays the career clusters that Mr. Fernandez showed Susan.

Figure 1-1:
Career Clusters

Agri-business and Natural Resources

Hospitality and Recreation

Transportation

Public Service

Marine Science

Business and Office

Manufacturing

Consumer and Homemaking Education

Environment

Personal Services

Health

Marketing and Distribution

Fine Arts and Humanities

Communications and Media

Construction

Source: United States Office of Education

STUDENT ACTIVITY D

1. Check the want ads in the classified section of the newspaper and list specific jobs in which you are interested. Note the education, skills, or previous work experience required.

Job	Education Required	Skills Needed	Experience Required
Example: teacher	college degree	teaching ability	student teaching
a. _____	_____	_____	_____
b. _____	_____	_____	_____
c. _____	_____	_____	_____
d. _____	_____	_____	_____
e. _____	_____	_____	_____
f. _____	_____	_____	_____
g. _____	_____	_____	_____

2. Check the Yellow Pages of the local telephone directory for jobs available in your community. List jobs in which you are interested. Indicate the education and skills needed, if you know them.

Place of Business	Job	Education/Skills Required
Example: New Life Hair Stylers	beautician	beauty school certificate
a. _____	_____	_____
b. _____	_____	_____
c. _____	_____	_____
d. _____	_____	_____
e. _____	_____	_____
f. _____	_____	_____
g. _____	_____	_____

3. From the fifteen career clusters in Figure 1-1, list the three clusters in which you are most interested.

   a. _____

   b. _____

   c. _____

BENEFITING FROM PART-TIME JOBS AND VOCATIONAL CLASSES

The next time Susan saw her friend Carlos, she was full of ideas about choosing a career. She suggested that her friend consider a part-time job to help determine what he wants to do with his life. Carlos laughed.

"How did working at Connie's Cafe help you to know any more about your career?" he asked.

"As a matter of fact," Susan said, a little irritated, "I learned a lot at Connie's Cafe. I know I don't want to cook hamburgers the rest of my life. I liked working the cash register and realized I like to do most anything with numbers. I learned that I enjoy working with people. I might even start my own business one day."

Carlos admitted that a part-time job can be a helpful way to discover one's interests and abilities. But part-time jobs are not easy to find, especially if you are looking for a particular kind of job. There are ways to find one though.

1. Check federal- and state-funded jobs offered for young people in your community. The state employment office usually has job information for young people.

2. Locate companies that offer summer jobs for students. Friends or relatives may know about such jobs.

3. Read the want ads in the classified section of your local newspaper.

4. Check for "Help Wanted" signs in store windows.

5. Ask friends and relatives to keep you in mind if they hear about job openings.

6. Ask for assistance from your school counselor.

7. Check with temporary-help employment agencies listed in the phone book, such as Kelly or Olsten.

STUDENT ACTIVITY E

1. Give two reasons why part-time jobs can be helpful.

   a. _____

   _____

   b. _____

   _____

2. Have you ever had a part-time job?

   _____

   If yes, what type of job?

   _____

   _____

What did you learn about your likes and dislikes? List your likes and dislikes in the space below.

Likes   Dislikes

a. _____   _____
   _____   _____
   _____   _____

b. _____   _____
   _____   _____
   _____   _____

c. _____   _____
   _____   _____
   _____   _____

Vocational training programs can be another helpful means of understanding one's interests and abilities. Because he likes mechanical work, Carlos's older brother attends a community college that offers vocational training. In the future, if he wants to complete a four-year college degree, he will be able to transfer with full college credit for his current courses.

Sometimes vocational classes are offered in high school. If you have an interest in a particular vocational area, high school is a good time to find out about your abilities.

There are some free or inexpensive vocational training courses offered through public education after high school. Some are government sponsored. Some are offered as adult education programs, and many are offered at community colleges. Your school counselor probably knows about the public vocational programs in your community.

There are private vocational schools as well. One of the major advantages of a private vocational school or college is that the training can usually be completed in less time than in a publicly supported school. Remember, however, that you will pay a great deal more money for a private school program than you will for the publicly supported program.

Before enrolling in a private vocational school, you should be well informed about the accreditation and benefits of the school. Obtain information from several schools that offer the training you desire, then compare the cost and benefits. It's a good idea to visit the schools you are seriously considering. Make sure the facilities and programs being advertised are actually offered. Try to talk with some of the students and get their reactions to the training they are receiving. Obtain a list of recent graduates with their addresses and phone numbers. The school should be willing to furnish such a list. Contact some of the graduates and ask about the percentage of students being placed in jobs for which they were trained. Did the training help them to get a better job or could they have obtained a similar job with similar pay without a certificate from the vocational school? Check with the Better Business Bureau about the reputation of the school. If you do decide to enroll in a particular school, make sure you read the school contract carefully. You might have your parents or your school counselor look over the contract with you to make sure that you thoroughly understand it.

STUDENT ACTIVITY F

1. Name some ways to determine your interest in and ability to do a specific job.

   _____

   _____

   _____

2. List at least four steps to take before enrolling at a private vocational school.

   a. _____

   b. _____

   c. _____

   d. _____

3. Look under "Schools or Colleges" in the Yellow Pages of a local telephone directory. Under the subheadings of "Business, Secretarial, Industrial, Technical, Trade, or Vocational," check for and list several vocational schools in your community.

   _____

   _____

   _____

   _____

4. Look under "Vocational Guidance or Consultants" in the Yellow Pages of a local telephone directory. List several, if any, vocational guidance agencies in your community.

   _____

   _____

   _____

   _____

FINDING AND APPLYING FOR A JOB

As the date for high school graduation grew nearer, Susan seemed to become more indefinite than ever. She told Carlos that she had nightmares about suddenly finding herself outside the security of the halls of her school with a diploma in her hand and no place to go for a job but Connie's Cafe. Carlos's brother had been lucky. He had found a job in one afternoon. It was in a field he enjoyed, and he could still attend classes in mechanics at the community college nearby. Susan knew that everybody wasn't so lucky.

Susan had a right to be frightened. Looking for a job, especially a job that you will like, can be a trying experience. Some people, whether high school or college graduates, have little idea where to begin. Some common sources for finding a job are listed below.

1. *Work experience office of your high school.* Many schools have work experience programs that provide job information and placement for students.

2. *Former employers.* You may be able to find a full-time job through a former boss if you have done part-time or volunteer work.

3. *Friends and relatives.* Inform friends and relatives of your interest in a job.

4. *Classified want ads in newspapers.* Want ads in newspapers can be a helpful source of information for jobs available in a community. The job skills needed for employment and the salary are often listed.

5. *Personnel office of a company or organization.* If you are interested in the work of a particular company, contact the personnel office about job openings.

6. *State employment department.* Offices are located in most larger communities and the services are free.

7. *Private employment agencies.* If a private placement firm finds you a job and you take it, you may have to pay a percentage of your first year's earnings to the agency. Many employers, however, pay the fee for jobs listed with private agencies.

Mr. Fernandez told Susan about his first experience applying for a job, long before he decided to become a school counselor. He said he walked into the office and said he would do anything. He meant to sound like a willing worker. The boss interpreted his statement as an admission that he had no particular skills. He was not hired.

"Even though you may be willing to do most anything," Mr. Fernandez told Susan, "you should specify skills you have that relate to the job you are applying for."

Mr. Fernandez explained the procedures of applying for a job. Most of the time the applicant is asked to fill out an application form. Frequently the applicant is asked for a *data sheet.* A data sheet, sometimes called a *vita* or *resume*, includes a history of the person's education and job experience.

Mr. Fernandez told Susan that when applying for a job, she should have all the information needed to complete a job application. A good way to anticipate the questions asked on a job application is through the preparation of a data sheet. Many businesses, especially smaller ones without any formal application procedures, will request one. At other times, a person might like to present a data sheet, even though one is not required.

When you compile a data sheet, you should emphasize the experience that relates to the job for which you are applying. If you are applying for a job as a typist, you should mention any past experience as a typist, even if it was volunteer work. If the job applied for is your first, you might mention high school classes and any special honors related to the job. As you gain work experience, you will need to update your data sheet.

Illustration 1-3

The appearance of a personal data sheet is important. One that is sloppy and contains misspelled words and errors in typing is a poor reflection on you. Your data sheet should be typed on good quality typing paper. If you are not sure of yourself, you should have someone check it for misspelled words and typographical errors. Arrange the contents so that the categories are clear and the general appearance is neat. You do not want your data sheet to appear cluttered. The person hiring should be able to get an idea of your educational and professional background at a glance.

Some data sheets include *references*, that is, names of people who will testify to your character, scholarship, or school and community service. Before listing someone as a reference, you should ask the person's permission. A negative response from someone whom you have given as a reference could certainly hurt your chances of getting a job.

You should list personal information only when it is to your benefit. It is not necessary to give your age, sex, marital status, weight, or height.

Figure 1-2 is a sample data sheet for Joseph Thompson, Susan's older brother. Notice how the categories are divided. The jobs are listed from the *most* recent to the *least* recent. The style Joseph used represents only one approach to preparing a data sheet. There are entire books that include instructions for writing data sheets as well as examples of styles. Study Joseph's carefully. Many employers require a data sheet instead of a formal job application, especially small companies.

Joseph Thompson's data sheet is very short. Most data sheets should be limited to one page. Do not try to impress an employer by adding information that is unimportant or unrelated to the job for which you are applying. Information may be added or dropped as you apply for different types of jobs.

Figure 1-2:
Joseph's
Personal Data
Sheet

```
                          DATA SHEET


        Joseph Thompson
        109 Wilshire Avenue
        New Orleans, LA 70117-5432
        Telephone:  (504) 555-6611


        Educational Background

        Long High School                      1964-1968
        New Orleans, LA                       Graduated
                                              June, 1968


        Loyola University                     1971-1975
        New Orleans, LA
        Bachelor of Science,                  May, 1975
        Business Management


        Military Service

        United States Navy                    1968-1970


        Work Experience

        Accountant                            1975-
        Adams and Adams, Inc.                 present
        3794 Seventh Street
        New Orleans, LA 71201-7829

        Cashier in campus bookstore           1974-1975
        Loyola University
        Saint Charles Avenue
        New Orleans, LA 70118-1217

        U.S. Navy keypunch operator           1969-1970
        Petty Officer William W. Stevens,
           Supervisor
        United States Naval Station
        Norfolk, VA 23514-3109


        References will be provided upon request.
```

Notice that Joseph did not list references. By not listing references, a person may use the same data sheet for several jobs and choose different references.

Joseph's data sheet was easy to write because he had a college education and work experience. Let us suppose that Susan is applying for a job in a clothing store. Her data sheet might look something like the one in Figure 1-3.

Figure 1-3:
Susan's
Personal Data
Sheet

```
                         DATA SHEET

     Susan Thompson
     4839 Jasmine Boulevard
     Our Towne, CA 95551-1445
     Telephone:  (415) 555-7070


     Education

     Seton Elementary, New Orleans, LA, 1975-83
     Kennedy High School, New Orleans, LA, 1983-85
     Our Towne High, Our Towne, CA, 1985-87

     Honors, Achievements, and Outside Interests

     Honors Certificates in Math (11th, 12th Grades)
        Our Towne High, Our Towne, CA
     Basketball Team, Captain (12th Grade)

     Work Experience

     Volunteer work for Washington Hospital, Our Towne, CA, 1986
     Cashier at Connie's Cafe, Our Towne, CA, 1986 to present

     Skills

     Typing
     Cashiering
     Solving basic mathematics problems
     Dealing with customers

     References

     Mrs. Connie Cane, Manager        Mrs. Margaret Fuller
     Connie's Cafe                    Math Department
     4168 Dove Road                   Our Towne High School
     Our Towne, CA 95551-1445         7442 Wrigley Avenue
     (415) 555-7810                   Our Towne, CA 95550-2224
                                      (415) 555-3222, Ext. 25


     Mr. J. T. Fernandez
     Counseling Department
     Our Towne High School
     7442 Wrigley Avenue
     Our Towne, CA 95550-2224
     (415) 555-3222, Ext. 73
```

Skills for Consumer Success

Prepare a data sheet for yourself. Make it realistic by giving the name of your school and the anticipated date of your graduation. If you have no information for a particular data sheet category, do not list the category. Some suggested categories in addition to education and employment are as follows: special skills, club memberships, academic honors, community and school service, and volunteer work. First, prepare the data sheet on a plain sheet of paper. If you type or know someone who does, you may wish to submit a typed final copy. If you do not type, print neatly in pen.

There are times when you will mail your data sheet. If so, you should send a letter of *application*, or *cover letter*, which basically explains why you are interested in the job and why you think you are particularly well-qualified for it. Do not repeat everything you said on your data sheet. Keep the letter short and to the point. Emphasize information that you would like the employer to remember about you. Include the letter of application with your data sheet.

Figure 1-4 is a copy of the letter of application that Joseph Thompson sent with his data sheet.

Figure 1-4:
Joseph's Letter of Application

```
                                        109 Wilshire Avenue
                                        New Orleans, LA 70117-5432
                                        September 10, 19--



Ms. Denise Smith, Vice President
Accounting Department
Acme Imports, Inc.
117 Laurel Avenue
New Orleans, LA 70129-3533

Dear Ms. Smith:

I am interested in applying for the accounting manager position
that you advertised in the Times Picayune.  As is evident from
my data sheet, I have had accounting experience and feel I would
be qualified for the opening advertised.

You can reach me at 555-6611 from 9:00 a.m. to 4:30 p.m., Monday
through Friday, or at 555-2414 after 6:00 p.m.  I will be available
for an interview at your convenience.

I look forward to hearing from you.

                              Sincerely,

                              Joseph Thompson
                              Joseph Thompson
```

Every letter of application will vary according to the nature of the job for which you are applying and the circumstances of your educational background and job experience. Susan's letter of application for a position as a salesperson would have to be more detailed. She needs to convince the employer that she is capable of handling the job despite her limited job experience and education. Figure 1-5 is a sample of Susan's letter.

Figure 1-5:
Susan's Letter of Application

```
                                      4839 Jasmine Boulevard
                                      Our Towne, CA 95551-1445
                                      September 15, 19--


    Mr. Harold P. Lee
    Uptown Apparel
    3838 Park Avenue
    Our Towne, CA 95551-1449

    Dear Mr. Lee:

    Please consider me as an applicant for a position as salesperson
    at Uptown Apparel, which you advertised in Our Towne Herald,
    September 14, 19--.

    I have always liked working with people and have excelled in
    math courses in elementary school and high school.  My background
    at Connie's Cafe in dealing with people and cashiering should
    help me in learning the duties of a salesperson.

    I will be available for an interview at your convenience.  You
    can reach me at 555-7070.

                                      Sincerely,

                                      Susan Thompson

                                      Susan Thompson
```

A letter of application should always contain the following information:

1. Position for which you are applying.

2. Reasons why you are qualified for the job.

3. Request for an interview.

If you wish to write to a company or an organization to ask about job openings, you should write a *letter of inquiry*, which is simply a letter asking about possible openings. Enclose your data sheet with the letter.

Make sure you have all the needed information with you when applying for a job in person. Your data sheet should contain most of the information asked for on an application form, so remember to take it with you.

When filling out an application form, you should heed the following reminders:

- follow directions carefully
- complete the form in blue or black ink
- print answers neatly
- answer *all* questions
- give complete answers

Remember, the job application form is often the first impression an employer has of you, and first impressions are lasting. If there is a question you do not understand on the form, ask for an explanation. Take a pocket dictionary with you to check for misspelled words.

Sometimes an employer will allow you to take an application form home. In such a case, make a copy of the application first and complete the copy. Then, type or print the original form in ink.

STUDENT ACTIVITY H

1. You are applying for your first full-time job after graduation. Complete the job application form on page 22 as if it were the real thing.

2. Rate yourself on your ability to fill out an application by answering *yes* or *no* to the following questions.

   _____ Did you read the application through before you filled it out, so you knew what was coming? (If you filled in your first name where they wanted your last, the employer might assume that you cannot follow directions on the job.)

   _____ Did you fill it out in ink?

   _____ Did you fill in every space, even if you had to put "no," "none," or "not applicable." (The person reviewing the application may assume you overlooked the questions or just didn't care to answer.)

   _____ Were you neat? (Some firms use forms merely to test how exact you are.)

   _____ Did you give exact dates of education and experience, and not vague answers? (Don't pretend to have knowledge or experience that you lack.)

   _____ Where it said "Date" did you put today's date, and not when you want the job? Did you spell out the month and include the year?

   _____ Did you give your name in full, as you would like it on the permanent record of the company?

   _____ Did you give the complete company name and address of previous employment? Did you list the most recent job first?

GENERAL INFORMATION

Name	Date	Work Desired
Street Address	Phone Number	Full-time _____ Part-time _____
City State ZIP	Social Security Number	Seasonal _____ Temporary _____

RECORD OF EDUCATION

High School	_____ _____ _____	Coll. Prep. ☐ Business ☐ Other Voc. ☐	9 10 11 12	Yes ☐* No ☐ *Year ____	
Business College	_____ _____ _____		1 2 3 4	Yes ☐* No ☐ *Year ____	
College	_____ _____ _____		1 2 3 4	Yes ☐* No ☐ *Year ____	Major Area:

WORK EXPERIENCE

List all present and past employment, including part-time or seasonal, beginning with the most recent.

Company	Employment Dates and Salary	Describe the work you did in detail	Reason for leaving
Name _____ Address _____ Phone ____ Supervisor ____	From: _____ To: _____ Salary _____		
Name _____ Address _____ Phone ____ Supervisor ____	From: _____ To: _____ Salary _____		
Name _____ Address _____ Phone ____ Supervisor ____	From: _____ To: _____ Salary _____		

MEDICAL HISTORY

Do you have any impairments, physical, mental, or medical, which would interfere with your ability to perform the job for which you have applied?   Yes _____   No _____

If yes, describe such impairments and specific work limitations.

UNITED STATES MILITARY SERVICE

Veteran   YES _____   NO _____   Service Branch _____
Service Dates: FROM   TO

Please indicate other abilities, experience, skills or special knowledge which you particularly feel would qualify you for the type of work for which you are now applying, such as experience in the Armed Forces, volunteer work, etc.

_____

_____

_____

_____

I authorize investigation of all statements in this application, and I understand that any false statements or deliberate omissions on this application will be cause for my discharge

Signature of Applicant

_____ Did you remember to sign the application? (An un-signed application is not valid.)

_____ Did you say "yes" to all of the above? Or do you need to do some homework before the next job application?

3. Find a job advertised in the want ads of your newspaper (or elsewhere), and write a letter of application for the job. Assume that you have the necessary qualifications. Remember, correct grammar, correct spelling, and neatness are as important as the content of the letter.

INTERVIEWING FOR THE JOB

Usually, you will have an interview for a job. Even at Connie's Cafe the employees had an interview before being hired. Some interviews are more formal than others. The formality of the interview usually depends upon the type of job.

You should wear appropriate clothes for the interview. If you apply at Connie's, you will not need to wear a suit. On the other hand, you should not wear your worst pair of jeans. As a general rule, you should dress modestly and conservatively. Much of an employer's opinion of you will be based on the way you look and the way you act during an interview.

Joseph's Interview Guidelines

Susan Thompson's brother, Joseph, knows how important an interview can be. He knows that it may last only twenty minutes, but within this short period of time, decisions are being made about you that can affect your life in an important way. Joseph's high school counselor had given him a set of interview guidelines to follow; he, in turn, gave copies of the guidelines to Susan.

Before the Interview

1. Make sure you know the time and place of the interview; be certain you know how to get there and about how long it will take, so you won't be late.

2. Know the full name and position of the person who will interview you.

3. Get sufficient rest the night before your interview, so that you will be at your best physically and mentally.

4. Take a pen, pencil, notebook, social security card, and your data sheet with you.

5. Gather as much information as possible about the company's background, products and services; know something about the position you are applying for and be prepared to give reasons for wanting the job. Employers frequently complain about applicants who know little or nothing about the job they are seeking.

6. Show your independence by going to the interview alone.

7. Prepare to go to the interview clean, well-groomed, and appropriately dressed. Be sure to attend to personal hygiene (brush teeth, use deodorant, etc.). Employers notice these important traits in job applicants.

Selling Yourself in the Interview

1. Enter the room confident and poised, but not overconfident. Greet the interviewer and use his or her name. Introduce yourself, giving your name distinctly. For instance: "Good morning, Ms. Morrow. I am Susan Thompson." Remain standing until invited to sit down.

2. Maintain good posture during the interview. Do not touch any articles on the interviewer's desk. Try to avoid any nervous habits such as biting nails. Do not chew gum and do not smoke unless the interviewer invites you to do so. Look directly at the interviewer occasionally.

3. Let the interviewer direct the conversation but do not hesitate to focus attention on your strengths. Answer questions sincerely; do not mislead the interviewer by telling half-truths. Admit any limitations, and explain what you are willing to do to eliminate shortcomings.

4. Listen carefully to the questions and comments of the interviewer, so that you do not miss the point or overlook some valuable information.

5. Do not discuss your personal problems, air your prejudices, or criticize others. You will gain nothing by complaining about a former employer or teacher.

6. Although you do not want to give the impression your only interest is salary, you do want to have an idea of the pay range and potential pay increases. If the interviewer has not offered this information by the end of the interview, ask what the pay will be for a person with your education and experience.

7. If you have not been offered the job at the conclusion of the interview, ask (diplomatically) how long it will be before you know the company's decision.

8. When the interview is over, don't hang around. Thank the interviewer for the consideration, reemphasize your interest in the job, and politely leave.

After the Interview

1. After the interview you might write the interviewer a *short* thank-you letter in which you express your appreciation for his or her time and consideration of you as an applicant. Indicate again your interest in the job.

2. If the job is offered to you, make sure you understand all the requirements for acceptance (completing health examination, having a social security number, etc.), and fulfill them as soon as possible.

3. After accepting a job, inform those who wrote references for you and thank them. They have taken time to write on your behalf, and would be interested to learn about your employment.

4. Don't be discouraged if you do not get the first few jobs for which you apply. Think about the interviews, and try to discover how you could have improved them. If you feel comfortable enough with the person who interviewed you, call and ask his or her opinion of the interview. Ask how you might improve your next interview. Successful job interviews require a lot of skill. Keep trying until you get the job you want.

If you have anticipated some of the questions before the interview, you will probably answer the interviewer's questions better. If possible, take the time the day before to analyze what might be asked. Questions which are commonly asked during a job interview are included in Student Activity I.

STUDENT ACTIVITY I

Choose a job advertised in the want ads of a local newspaper, or choose any job that you might be interested in applying for after graduation.

Answer the questions below honestly, as if you were really being interviewed for the particular jobs you selected.

Questions Commonly Asked in an Interview

Name of job _____

1. Why do you think you would like to work for our company?

   _____

   _____

2. What jobs have you had, and why did you leave them?

   _____

   _____

3. Why do you think you would like this particular type of job?

   _____

   _____

4. Are you looking for a permanent or a temporary job?

   _____

   _____

5. What special abilities do you have that would qualify you for this job?

   _____

   _____

6. Why should we hire *you* for this job rather than anyone else?

   _____

   _____

7. What are your ideas about pay for this job? [Hint: You should find out the general pay range before the interview.]

_____

_____

Article VII of the Civil Rights Act of 1964, as amended by the Equal Employment Opportunity Act of 1972, prohibits job discrimination because of race, color, religion, sex, or national origin. This is enforced by the U.S. Equal Employment Opportunity Commission. Because of these laws, it is illegal for an interviewer to ask certain questions about the birthplace of the applicant, dependents, plans for pregnancy, religious background, history of arrests (history of convictions can be asked). A photograph of the applicant cannot be required. The applicant may *offer* any personal information that he or she wishes but should certainly dwell on information that will increase the chances of getting the job.

Illustration 1-4

Near the end of the interview, you should be asked if *you* have any questions. Do not take this opportunity lightly. First of all, you need to make sure you know the conditions of employment; secondly, interviewers are impressed with an applicant who shows interest in a job by asking questions. The following are questions related to working conditions that you might consider asking if not fully answered during an interview:

1. *Salary*—how much? paid monthly, weekly?

2. *Required deductions*—social security, insurance, retirement, etc.?

3. *Vacation time*—how long? paid or unpaid? what is the holiday schedule?

4. *Fringe benefits*—group health insurance, recreational facilities or programs, discounts on company products, educational benefits, etc.?

5. *Financial benefits*—company stock purchase plan?

6. *Promotions and advancements*—general procedure for promotion? possibilities for advancement and salary increases?

Write the questions in a notebook ahead of time if you wish. An employer or personnel director will probably be impressed.

The type of *follow-up letter* you write after the interview will depend on how things went during the interview. If you feel that you were favorably received and that you have a good chance of getting the job, keep your letter general and friendly. Avoid flowery language. If there were several people interviewing you, kindly mention each of them. You seldom know who has the most influence.

After the interview, if you were left with the impression that you were lacking in some particular ability, you might offer a solution in your follow-up letter. For example, you might offer to enroll in a course in an area in which you were considered particularly weak. However, if nothing was openly said about a weakness (even though you felt it was noticed), it might be best to avoid mentioning it in a follow-up letter. As a general rule, it is best to keep the letter positive and avoid mentioning any weakness that the interviewer may have forgotten or never noticed. Figure 1-6 is a copy of a typical follow-up letter.

Figure 1-6:
Follow-up
Letter

```
                                      601 Tudor Avenue
                                      Our Towne, CA 95551-1445
                                      October 8, 19--




    Mr. Aldous B. Healy
    Manager
    Smart's Shoe Store
    444 Earhart Boulevard
    Our Towne, CA 95551-1440

    Dear Mr. Healy:

    Thank you for giving me the opportunity to meet with you
    Thursday to discuss the position of assistant manager at
    Smart's Shoe Store.  The job is most attractive to me and
    offers the kind of opportunity that I am looking for.  I
    know I would find the position challenging and rewarding.

    Please express my appreciation to Miss Clydesdale as well.

                                      Sincerely,

                                      James Lacey

                                      James Lacey
```

1. List some steps you should follow when preparing for a job interview.

   a. _____

   b. _____

   c. _____

   d. _____

   e. _____

2. May you ask the interviewer questions when applying for a job?_____
   If so, what kinds of questions might you ask?

   a. _____

   b. _____

   c. _____

   d. _____

   e. _____

3. Select a job you might want and can realistically apply for after graduation. You have had a successful interview for the job. Now write a
   follow-up letter to the interviewer.

UNDERSTANDING INCOME TAXES

When Susan got her first job at Connie's Cafe, she took on the citizen-
ship responsibility of paying taxes. Immediately after being employed at
Connie's, she was asked to fill out *Form W-4*, Employee's Withholding
Allowance Certificate. See Figure 1-7 for Susan's Form W-4. In completing

Figure 1-7:
Susan's
Form W-4

Form **W-4** (Rev. January 1985)	Department of the Treasury—Internal Revenue Service **Employee's Withholding Allowance Certificate**		OMB No. 1545-0010 Expires: 11-30-87
1 Type or print your full name Susan A. Thompson	**2** Your social security number 261-70-4520		
Home address (number and street or rural route) 4839 Jasmine Boulevard	**3** Marital Status	☑ Single ☐ Married ☐ Married, but withhold at higher Single rate **Note:** If married, but legally separated, or spouse is a nonresident alien, check the Single box.	
City or town, State, and ZIP code Our Towne, CA 95551-1445			

4 Total number of allowances you are claiming (from line F of the worksheet on page 2) 1

5 Additional amount, if any, you want deducted from each pay . . . . $

6 I claim exemption from withholding because (see instructions and check boxes below that apply):

   a ☐ Last year I did not owe any Federal income tax and had a right to a full refund of **ALL** income tax withheld, **AND**

   b ☐ This year I do not expect to owe any Federal income tax and expect to have a right to a full refund of **ALL** income tax withheld. If both a and b apply, enter the year effective and "EXEMPT" here ▶ Year

   c If you entered "EXEMPT" on line 6b, are you a full-time student? . . . . ☐Yes ☐No

Under penalties of perjury, I certify that I am entitled to the number of withholding allowances claimed on this certificate, or if claiming exemption from withholding, that I am entitled to claim the exempt status.
Employee's signature ▶ Susan A. Thompson   Date ▶ August 4 , 19 - -

7 Employer's name and address (**Employer: Complete 7, 8, and 9 only if sending to IRS**) | **8** Office code | **9** Employer identification number

- - - - - - - - - - - Detach along this line. Give the top part of this form to employer; keep the lower part for your records. - - - - - - - - - - - -

Form W-4, Susan permitted her employer to withhold a certain amount from each paycheck for taxes.

Susan claimed one allowance (for herself) on Form W-4. Generally, each taxpayer may claim an automatic allowance for oneself. Additional allowances may be taken for each person dependent on a taxpayer's income—spouse, children, or elderly parents. Each allowance claimed on Form W-4 will reduce the amount of income taxes withheld. Notice Susan did not check "Exempt" (6b). If after one year's work at Connie's Cafe, Susan did not have to pay income tax, or even received a refund from the federal government, she may want to check "Exempt" the following year; that is, if her wages and circumstances remain the same.

In January, Susan was given *Form W-2*, Wage and Tax Statement, by her employer, Connie's Cafe. Every employer you work for during the calendar year must give you a W-2 form in January. This form provides a record of wages earned and lists the total amount of income tax (and any other taxes) deducted from your pay. Keep your Form W-2 because you must attach it to the income tax return you file. See Figure 1-8 for an example of Form W-2.

Figure 1-8:
Form W-2

1 Control number					
	OMB No. 1545-0008				
2 Employer's name, address, and ZIP code		3 Employer's identification number		4 Employer's state I.D. number	
		5 Statutory employee □ Deceased □ Legal rep. □ 942 emp. □ Subtotal □ Void □			
		6 Allocated tips		7 Advance EIC payment	
8 Employee's social security number	9 Federal income tax withheld	10 Wages, tips, other compensation		11 Social security tax withheld	
12 Employee's name, address, and ZIP code		13 Social security wages		14 Social security tips	
		16		16a Fringe benefits incl. in Box 10	
		17 State income tax	18 State wages, tips, etc.	19 Name of state	
		20 Local income tax	21 Local wages, tips, etc.	22 Name of locality	

Form **W-2 Wage and Tax Statement   1986**

Copy B To be filed with employee's FEDERAL tax return   Department of the Treasury
This information is being furnished to the Internal Revenue Service.   Internal Revenue Service

When Susan had to prepare a federal income tax return for the first time, she was lost. Her mother explained that she would have to use one of the forms provided by the Internal Revenue Service, an agency of the federal government that collects income taxes. Offices are located around the country. Susan's mother told her that students usually get a tax refund; however, unless a return is filed, they will not receive the refund. (A *tax refund* is the amount returned by the government because a taxpayer has paid taxes in excess of what was owed.)

In filing a return, Susan had to decide to fill out either a short form (1040A or 1040EZ) or use the long form (1040). With the help of her mother, Susan learned that she could use Form 1040EZ, a simplified form that can be used only by single taxpayers. The 1040EZ tax return required only twenty minutes for Susan to prepare with the help of her mother.

At the time, paying taxes for Susan was pretty simple. She earned only a small amount of money from babysitting and working at Connie's Cafe. She also had interest income from her savings of less than $200. But, after seeing the tax return prepared by her parents, Susan knew that filing an income tax return can be a complicated process.

In preparing a tax return, line-by-line instructions are given on the tax forms. Your classroom instructor may wish to order free sample income tax forms from the federal government and provide you the opportunity to fill out one of the forms in class.

Those taxpayers who want or need help in filling out their tax forms have four major sources of help: the IRS (Internal Revenue Service), professional tax consultants, certified public accountants (CPAs), and tax lawyers. Service from the IRS is free. You should check with the IRS to determine regulations and procedures you do not understand after reading the booklet that accompanies all tax forms mailed by the IRS. You may have an IRS tax assistance center in your area. The IRS has a toll-free telephone number that you can call for tax information. Professional tax consultants abound between January 1 and April 15. (April 15 is the deadline for filing income tax returns.) For a fee, tax consultants will prepare your forms, but you have to provide all the essential records. Certified public accountants often charge by the hour and are used for complicated tax returns. Tax lawyers are sometimes used as consultants about new or existing tax laws or for help if you are being investigated by the Fraud Section of the IRS. Tax lawyers have special knowledge about the tax rulings of the IRS.

STUDENT ACTIVITY K

1. Examine Figure 1-7 and answer the following questions.

   a. How many allowances did Susan claim?

   _____

   b. Why didn't Susan write "Exempt" after 6b?

   _____

2. Which tax form would you most likely use in filing your federal income tax return?

   _____

3. Define the following:

   a. tax refund _____

   b. IRS _____

4. What sources of help are available for preparing income tax returns?

   _____

FURTHER DISCOVERIES

1. Two members of the class select a job from a want ad in a local news-paper. Have a mock interview with one student playing the role of the interviewer, and the other student playing the role of the applicant. The "interviewer" should have made a list of questions ahead of time, but should not read from the list during the interview. After the interview, students in the class are given time to comment constructively on the conduct of the applicant and the interviewer. Members of the class might rate the applicant on a scale of 1 to 5 (5 = excellent; 4 = pretty good; 3 = fair; 2 = needs improvement; 1 = poor) for grooming, friendliness, experience for the job, confidence, knowledge about job, use of correct grammar, logical expression of ideas, composure, and interest in job. Should the applicant be hired? Why or why not?

2. Check your school or public library for the current edition of *Occupational Outlook Handbook*. Find three jobs that interest you. Investigate these jobs for their employment outlook, earnings and working conditions, training required, and advancement opportunities. Write a report about your findings.

3. Find the meaning to each of the following terms commonly used in regard to taxation:

deduction	earned income	exemption
taxable income	exclusion	unearned income
tax table	credits	adjusted gross income

   Your instructor may want to provide federal tax forms for you to fill out.

CHECKLIST

If you have completed the student activities in this unit, you should have mastered the skills below. Check off the skills you know, and review the ones you are not sure of.

(   ) How to ascertain one's interests, values, and abilities

(   ) How to determine the difference between a job and a career

(   ) How to review the career choice process

(   ) Where to find information about types of jobs available

(   ) How to discover the benefits of vocational training in the types of programs offered

(   ) Where to go and whom to contact when looking for a part-time or full-time job

(   ) How to prepare a data sheet

(   ) How to fill out an application form properly

(   ) How to prepare for a job interview

(   ) What to do during a job interview

(   ) What to do after a job interview

(   ) How to write a follow-up letter

(   ) How to follow the procedures to fulfill one's taxpaying responsibilities

If you have checked all of the above, ask your teacher for the Susan Thompson Test on The Job Market.

For Your Personal Use

A copy of a fact sheet for you to fill out and use for your personal convenience can be found on page 33. Complete the form in pencil so you can change or add to the sheet as you change jobs. Tear out the sheet, keep it in your wallet or personal files, and take it with you whenever you apply for a job.

MY FACT SHEET FOR JOB APPLICATIONS

Name: _____

Social security number: _____

Schools attended, their addresses, dates of attendance:

_____

_____

_____

_____

Names, addresses, and dates of part-time or full-time previous jobs and employers. Include name of immediate employer and present salary. List most recent jobs first.

1. _____

2. _____

3. _____

4. _____

Volunteer work, with names and addresses of employers:

1. _____

2. _____

3. _____

4. _____

Skills or awards received:

_____

_____

Name and address of person to notify in case of emergency:

_____

Names, addresses, occupations, and telephone numbers of three references other than relatives who have granted permission for their names to be used:

1. _____

_____

2. _____

_____

3. _____

_____

(continued next page)

MY FACT SHEET (cont'd)

Checkpoints

1. Did you complete the application form in ink and fill in every blank?
2. Did you double-check addresses and dates?
3. Did you complete the form neatly? If not, ask for another form.
4. Did you list all extracurricular activities and skills that might help you get the job?
5. Did you date and sign the application form?

Additional Information

_____

_____

_____

_____

_____

_____

_____

_____

_____

_____

_____

_____

_____

_____

_____

_____

_____

_____

_____

_____

_____

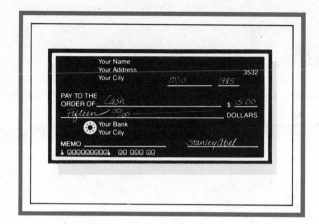

UNIT 2
CHECKING ACCOUNTS

SKILL 1 **Knowing the Differences Among Financial Institutions**

SKILL 2 **Opening a Checking Account**

SKILL 3 **Writing a Check and Keeping Accurate Check Records**

SKILL 4 **Depositing Money in a Checking Account**

SKILL 5 **Interpreting and Reconciling a Bank Statement**

Further Discoveries

KNOWING THE DIFFERENCES AMONG FINANCIAL INSTITUTIONS

At Susan's request, Mr. Fernandez started a weekly seminar after school for students interested in becoming competent consumers. The group agreed to begin with the topic of checking accounts. "The first step toward opening a checking account is to look at the kinds of institutions offering checking accounts," said Mr. Fernandez.

The main types of financial institutions offering checking accounts are commercial banks, savings and loan associations, and credit unions. In the past, *commercial banks* were the most common financial institutions to offer multiple services such as checking accounts, savings accounts, small consumer loans, credit cards, safe-deposit boxes, and other consumer services. *Savings and loan associations* specialized in handling savings deposits and loaning money for the purchase of a home. In 1981 Congress authorized savings and loan associations to offer services that were previously provided by commercial banks for the most part. As a result of the change in the law, many savings and loan associations now offer most of the consumer services traditionally provided by commercial banks, including checking accounts.

Illustration 2-1

"What's happened," said Mr. Fernandez, "is that many savings and loans have become one-stop family financial centers with the granting of home loans still a primary service. It is often difficult to tell the difference between a commercial bank and a savings and loan today. In fact, one survey showed that some people think their savings and loan association is a bank."

The last type of financial institution explained by Mr. Fernandez was the credit union. A *credit union* is different from commercial banks and savings and loan associations in that it is a nonprofit organization whose membership is limited to the members of a particular group. For instance, credit unions are formed by such groups as teachers in a school system, workers in a large factory, store employees, and even members of a church.

Aside from the group membership requirement, there is little difference between a credit union and a commercial bank or a savings and loan. Credit unions offer savings accounts, loan money to members, and offer a type of checking account called share draft accounts. *Share draft accounts* are interest-bearing checking accounts.

"Before opening a checking account," cautioned Mr. Fernandez, "make sure that your account is insured. Insurance is offered by the federal government through agencies called the Federal Deposit Insurance Corporation (FDIC) and the Federal Savings and Loan Insurance Corporation (FSLIC)."

The FDIC insures accounts in most commercial banks; the FSLIC insures accounts in many savings and loan associations. These agencies were established in 1933 to protect consumer deposits. Currently, the maximum amount of insurance per account is $100,000.

In 1970 the National Credit Union Administration (NCUA) was created to protect customers' accounts in federally chartered credit unions. (A *charter* is a document that gives a financial institution legal authority to operate.) Again, insurance protection up to $100,000 per account is offered.

"It's a good idea," Mr. Fernandez advised, "to look for the FDIC, FSLIC, and NCUA symbols on the window or entrance door of the financial institution you intend to deal with. Not all financial institutions protect accounts with customer insurance."

STUDENT ACTIVITY A

1. In the past, what was the main difference between savings and loan associations and commercial banks?

    _____

    _____

2. What financial institution would you go to for a loan to purchase a home?

    _____

3. What is the essential difference between a credit union and other financial institutions?

    _____

4. Identify the following:

    a. FDIC _____

    b. FSLIC _____

    c. NCUA _____

OPENING A CHECKING ACCOUNT

After discussing the types of financial institutions, Mr. Fernandez took his group to visit Mrs. Joyce Washington, manager of Our Towne Bank. He knew that Mrs. Washington would be happy to tell the students everything they needed to know about checking accounts.

"To open a checking account," explained Mrs. Washington, "you need money, not necessarily a lot of money, but some money—usually $50-$100. You will go to a person at the counter, called a *teller*, and ask him or her to open a checking account for you. The teller may then direct you to someone who handles new accounts. You'll be asked to provide some form of identification (your birth certificate, driver's license, or social security card will do) before opening a checking account. You will then be given a signature card to fill out."

Mrs. Washington gave each member of the group a signature card similar to the one in Figure 2-1 that Susan filled out. Examine the signature card very carefully.

ACCOUNT NUMBER	TYPE OF ACCOUNT		
07227679	☐ JOINT ☑ INDIVIDUAL	☐ NOW ☐ SUPER NOW	☑ REGULAR ☐ ECONOMY PLAN

We, the undersigned, hereby open an account with Citizens' Common Street Bank, and do authorize, empower and direct the said Bank to open an account with us in the name set forth below, and we hereby agree and notify said Bank that each or either of us, or the survivor of either of us, the undersigned, may, at any and all times, endorse and deposit to the credit of said account any check, draft or other voucher payable to the order of each or either of us and draw and receive from said Bank the whole or any part of said moneys now deposited, or which may thereafter be deposited to the credit of said account, or any interest of same, and the payment made to either of us or the survivor of either of us, shall operate to discharge said Bank from all obligations in the premises, and any such check, draft or other voucher for the money so drawn, signed by either one of us or the survivor of either of us, (unless the contrary is indicated hereon), shall constitute a full aquittance to said Bank for all moneys drawn. We hereby agree to the rules and regulations governing checking accounts set out on the reverse hereof.

SIGNATURE _Susan Thompson_

SIGNATURE

HOME ADDRESS 4839 Jasmin Blvd. Our Towne, CA 95551-1445	HOME PHONE 555-7070	OFFICE PHONE 555-6070
EMPLOYER Mrs. Connie Lane	OCCUPATION Cashier-Waitress	
EMPLOYER'S ADDRESS 4168 Dove Road Our Towne, CA 95551-1440	SOCIAL SEC. NO. 437-58-7039	DATE 4/2/--

ACCEPTED BY _Paul R. Reken_

Signature Card — Checking Account

Notice the space for the *account number*. When you open an account you receive an account number. Susan's account number is 07227679. The number will be printed on the bottom of the checks in her checkbook and on the bottom of her deposit slip. Checkbooks and deposit slips will be discussed in detail later. Susan's account number is printed after a bank number, so that the numbers at the bottom of her checks look like this: 065000883:07227679. When she is asked for her account number, she gives only the second set of numbers: 07227679.

Also notice that Susan's signature card lists either an individual or a joint account. An *individual account* has one holder. That individual is the only person who can make withdrawals from the account. A *joint account* is held between two or more individuals, and grants each individual all the rights and privileges attached to the account. Susan's parents have a joint account, which means that either of them can make withdrawals independently of the other.

The names on her parents' joint account are recorded as follows:

Arthur H. Thompson or
Martha Rae Thompson

With such a recording, one individual may withdraw money or make payments to the account without the signature of the other holder. Such is not the case if the names are joined by *and.* If the names were recorded Arthur H. Thompson and Martha Rae Thompson, both signatures would be required for any withdrawals.

The signature card also lists the types of accounts: economy, regular, NOW, and Super NOW. Most *economy accounts* include a service charge. A *service charge* is a fee the financial institution charges for checking services rendered to a customer. You might choose an account that allows you to write an unlimited number of checks if you pay a monthly service charge (for example, $4). Or, you might select an account that has no monthly charge but that charges a certain amount for each check you write (for example, fifteen cents per check).

In addition to the economy account, Our Towne Bank offers a *regular account.* The following table shows how the service charge is computed for the regular account. If the balance falls below the minimum any day of the month, a service charge as shown in the table is imposed.

If your *mimimum balance* for the month is:	Your monthly *service charge* is:
$300 or over	Free
$200 to $299.99	$1
$100 to $199.99	$2
$99.99 or below	$3

The *Negotiable Order of Withdrawal (NOW) account* is an interest-bearing checking account. A minimum balance, which varies from institution to institution, is usually required for NOW accounts. As long as the minimum balance does not fall below a certain level—usually $500 to $1,500, your money in a NOW account earns a maximum of 5¼ percent interest. If your balance falls below the minimum, you may lose any interest earned and have to pay a service charge.

Super NOW accounts are checking accounts that offer a higher rate of interest than NOW accounts, but a minimum balance of $2,500 is usually required. Everything below that amount earns 5¼ percent, as with NOW accounts. Everything above $2,500 earns a higher rate of interest, which is determined by the financial institution.

STUDENT ACTIVITY B

1. Explain the difference between an individual account and a joint account.

   _____

   _____

   _____

2. Explain the significance of recording signatures on a joint account as follows:

Arthur H. Thompson *or* Martha Rae Thompson

_____

Arthur H. Thompson *and* Martha Rae Thompson

_____

3. What is meant by a checking account service charge?

_____

4. Why might a service charge be imposed on a checking account?

_____

5. Explain the difference between the NOW account and the Super NOW account.

_____

_____

_____

Before signing a signature card, read the fine print on the back of the card. The following fine print appeared on the back of Susan's card.

We, the undersigned, hereby open an account with Our Towne Bank, and do authorize, empower, and direct the said bank to open an account with us in the name set forth above, and we hereby agree and notify said Bank that each or either of us, or the survivor of either of us, the undersigned, may, at any and all times, endorse and deposit to the credit of said account any check, draft or other voucher payable to the order of each or either of us and draw and receive from said Bank the whole or any part of said money now deposited, or which may hereafter be deposited to the credit of said account. Checks, drafts, and other items drawn on this office of this bank not paid for any reason as of close of business day on which they have been deposited may be charged back to the customer. This bank will act only as the agent of the customer from which it receives such items, and will assume no responsibility or liability except for its own negligence, nor will it assume any responsibility or liability for any items lost in the mail.

Many financial institutions will not permit a minor to sign the card unless it is signed jointly by a parent or guardian. This requirement varies according to state law.

STUDENT ACTIVITY C

The following statements are based on the information on the back of Susan's signature card. Answer *true* or *false* to the following statements.

_____ 1. If you open an account with someone else, your partner can write a check on the account by simply signing his or her name.

2. The bank can charge you for checks you write that exceed the amount you have in the bank.

3. The bank agrees to sue a customer who owes you money.

4. The bank assumes responsibility for checks you put in the mail.

5. The bank accepts responsibility for any errors the bank makes regarding your account.

WRITING CHECKS AND KEEPING ACCURATE CHECK RECORDS

After students had completed and signed their sample signature cards, Mrs. Washington showed them a *checkbook*. The checkbook contains *checks* that are used for making payments in place of cash. Each check is processed and charged against a checking account. Therefore, it is important to always keep an accurate record of how much money is in your account. A checking account is not just a convenience in making payments. When used properly, it's an effective way to keep a record of expenditures.

Some checkbooks have check stubs for keeping records. The *check stub* is located beside or on top of each check and is used for recording checks written, deposits made, and any fees or charges by the bank. Figure 2-2 shows a check stub and the accompanying check. Some checkbooks have a check register instead of check stubs. The *check register* is usually at the front or back of the checkbook. Figure 2-3 shows a check register.

Checkbooks are sometimes given to depositors without charge, but most financial institutions charge for the printing of checks. You have the option of choosing any style check you want. Many customers prefer personalized checks with their name, address, and phone number. Personalized checks are numbered for you. When choosing checks, you need not buy ones with the fanciest design or the most attractive checkbook cover. They usually cost extra.

To demonstrate check writing, Mrs. Washington used Sharon Moore's checkbook. Sharon Moore was a participant in the consumer education

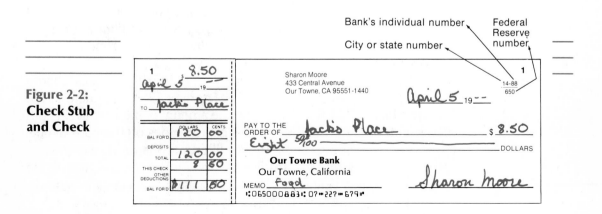

Figure 2-2:
Check Stub and Check

CHECK NO.	DATE	CHECK ISSUED TO	BAL. BR'T. F'R'D	✓	117	27
676	4/22	Jay's Record Shop	AMOUNT OF CHECK OR DEPOSIT		- 7	25
		Records	BALANCE		110	02
677	4/24	Martin's Eat-Out	AMOUNT OF CHECK OR DEPOSIT		- 12	93
		Food	BALANCE		97	09
678	4/28	Sock-It-To-You	AMOUNT OF CHECK OR DEPOSIT		- 5	89
		Socks	BALANCE		91	20
679	4/30	Our Towne Utilities	AMOUNT OF CHECK OR DEPOSIT		- 39	57
		Utility Bill	BALANCE		51	63
			AMOUNT OF CHECK OR DEPOSIT			
			BALANCE			
			AMOUNT OF CHECK OR DEPOSIT			
			BALANCE			

Figure 2-3:
Check Register

seminar at Our Towne High, and volunteered the use of her checkbook as a sample. Sharon uses a checkbook with check stubs. Notice each check is identified by the number of the bank on which it is drawn. The number is assigned to each commercial bank in the country by the American Bankers Association. You can see this number (14-88/650) in Figure 2-2. The numbers above the line indicate the city or state in which the bank is located and the *bank's individual number*. The number below the line is a *Federal Reserve number*, used in routing checks.

Magnetic ink numbers at the lower left can be processed electronically. The first group of numbers identifies the bank. The second group is the customer's account number.

Check Stub. Before giving a person a check, you should fill out your check stub. Sharon's stub is numbered 1, the same as her check. She has a personal record of who received check 1, the amount of the check, and the date of the check. The stub also has a place for *Bal. For'd.*, which is an abbreviation for *Balance Forward*. The balance is the amount of money in the checking account *before* a check is written. In other words, the balance is the difference between money on deposit and the amount for which the check was written. Sharon had $120 in her account before she wrote the check to Jack's Place. *Deposits* refer to any money added to the account. *Total* is derived by adding any *Deposits* to *Bal. For'd. This Check* refers to the amount of the check to Jack's Place. The term *Other Deductions* is money subtracted from your checking account for miscellaneous amounts such as a monthly service charge. The second *Bal. For'd.* is for the amount left in the checking account after *This Check* and *Other Deductions* have been subtracted from the *Total*.

The Check. The check number (1) is printed on the check. Sharon records the date she wrote the check (April 5, 19--), the name of the business she paid (Jack's Place), and the amount of money paid in both figures and words ($8.50). Sharon's signature goes on the bottom line. The space by *memo* may or may not be filled out. Sharon always makes a note of what she purchases (in this case, *food*). The check is given to the business or person being paid, so it is important to record the same information on the check stub, which is your record of a transaction.

1. When writing a check, spell out the amount of the check and draw a line to the word *Dollars*. For instance, if you are writing a check for $105.50, you write: One hundred five 50/100. You always indicate the *cents* by writing that amount over 100. If the check is for an even dollar amount, you write the check as follows: Thirty-five 00/100. It is important that you write the amount properly because the *written amount is considered the correct amount by law*. Write the following amounts:

    a. $ 21.60 _____

    b. $139.72 _____

    c. $ 54.00 _____

    d. $184.90 _____

2. Write your own check to a local grocery store for $23.98. Fill out the check stub. Give yourself a previous balance of $114.67. Use today's date. See Sharon's check in Figure 2-2 as an example.

    VERY IMPORTANT: When writing a check, give the exact date. A financial institution can refuse to cash a check that's dated ahead. Never leave space between the dollar sign and the first digit of the amount in figures. Begin writing the amount at the far left edge of the writing line. Draw a wavy line after writing out the amount (⌇⌇⌇). Use the signature you used on the signature card when signing a check. If it's Sharon Moore, do not sign your checks Shari Moore. *Always write a check in ink.*

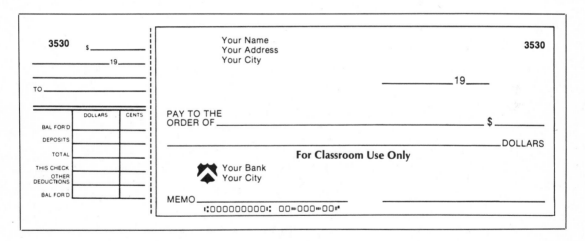

3. You can write a check payable to "Cash." Your bank will give you cash for the amount indicated on the check. Below is an example of a check for $15 payable to "Cash."

Figure 2-4:
Check Payable to Cash

NOTE: A check made payable to "Cash" can be cashed by anyone. If such a check is lost, it can be cashed by whoever finds it. For this reason, a check should usually be made payable to a person or business.

Write a check for $10 to cash.

```
┌─────────────────────────────────────────────────────────────────┐
│  Your Name                                              3532      │
│  Your Address                                                     │
│  Your City                                                        │
│                                                                   │
│                                    _____ 19____          │
│                                                                   │
│  PAY TO THE                                                       │
│  ORDER OF _____  $ _____  │
│                                                                   │
│  _____ DOLLARS │
│                       For Classroom Use Only                      │
│        ◆   Your Bank                                               │
│            Your City                                              │
│                                                                   │
│  MEMO_____      _____    │
│      ⑈000000000⑈ 00⑈000⑈00⑈                                       │
└─────────────────────────────────────────────────────────────────┘
```

NOTE: You should never make a check payable to "Cash" unless you are going to cash it at the time it is written.

Mrs. Washington said there may be times when you want to stop payment on a check. For instance, if a check is lost or stolen or you are not satisfied with some merchandise that you purchased, you can request the bank to stop payment. The request can be made by telephoning the financial institution. Financial institutions usually charge a fee for a stop payment request. The individual or place of business to whom the check is made out should also be informed of the *stop payment order*.

DEPOSITING MONEY IN A CHECKING ACCOUNT

Sharon Moore was paid $218.50 every two weeks. She went to the bank every two weeks and deposited the check in her checking account except for $20. When depositing money, you must fill out a *deposit slip*. Deposit slips are in the back of checkbooks, or they may have to be ordered separately. The bank always has extra slips if you do not have any. Simply ask the teller for one. Deposit slips differ slightly in form. Figure 2-5 is a copy of the deposit slip from Our Towne Bank. Notice how Sharon filled it out. As you will recall, each check has an ABA (American Bankers Association) number. Record the two top numbers for each check you deposit.

Figure 2-5: Sharon's Completed Deposit Slip

CHECKING ACCOUNT DEPOSIT TICKET

Sharon Moore
433 Central Avenue
Our Towne, CA 95551-1440

DATE April 10 19 – –

Our Towne Bank
Our Towne, California

14-88
650

		DOLLARS	CENTS
CASH →			
CHECKS	14-101	218	50
TOTAL FROM OTHER SIDE			
TOTAL		218	50
LESS CASH RECEIVED		20	00
NET DEPOSIT		198	50

USE OTHER SIDE FOR ADDITIONAL LISTING

BE SURE EACH ITEM IS PROPERLY ENDORSED

⑆065000883⑆ 07‴227‴679⑈

CHECKS AND OTHER ITEMS ARE RECEIVED FOR DEPOSIT SUBJECT TO THE TERMS AND CONDITIONS OF THIS BANK'S COLLECTION AGREEMENT.

STUDENT ACTIVITY E

A neighbor wrote Sharon a check for $15 for some cassette tapes, and she paid her $10 in cash for babysitting her young son. Sharon wants to deposit the check and the cash. The number to record for the check is 14-88. Make out her deposit slip for her. Use today's date.

CHECKING ACCOUNT DEPOSIT TICKET

Sharon Moore
433 Central Avenue
Our Towne, CA 95551-1440

DATE ______________ 19____

Our Towne Bank
Our Towne, California

14-88
650

		DOLLARS	CENTS
CASH →			
CHECKS			
TOTAL FROM OTHER SIDE			
TOTAL			
LESS CASH RECEIVED			
NET DEPOSIT			

USE OTHER SIDE FOR ADDITIONAL LISTING

BE SURE EACH ITEM IS PROPERLY ENDORSED

⑆065000883⑆ 07‴227‴679⑈

CHECKS AND OTHER ITEMS ARE RECEIVED FOR DEPOSIT SUBJECT TO THE TERMS AND CONDITIONS OF THIS BANK'S COLLECTION AGREEMENT.

When you cash or deposit a check made out to you, endorse the check (sign your name). This endorsement is called a *blank endorsement.* If the check was made payable to you, but your name was spelled incorrectly, endorse the check on the back just as your name is written on the front. Then endorse the check again with your name as it appears on the signature card.

You should never endorse a check until you are ready to cash or deposit it. A blank endorsement makes a check payable to anyone who has the check. If you lose a check with a blank endorsement, anyone can cash it simply by endorsing one's name to the back of the check. See Figure 2-6 for an example of a blank endorsement.

Figure 2-6:
Blank
Endorsement

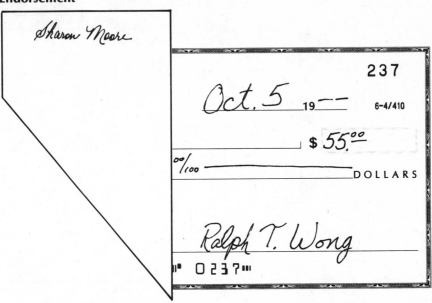

To deposit a check and receive no cash, you should indicate *for deposit only* on the back of the check. Such an endorsement is called a *restrictive endorsement*. See Figure 2-7 for an example of a restrictive endorsement.

Figure 2-7:
Restrictive
Endorsement

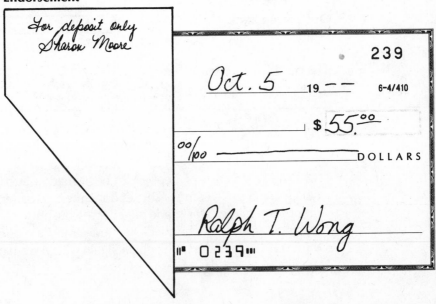

There are times when you might wish to pay someone else by giving the person a check that was paid to you. In such a case, you should prepare an *endorsement in full*. See Figure 2-8 for an example of an endorsement in full.

Figure 2-8:
Endorsement
in Full

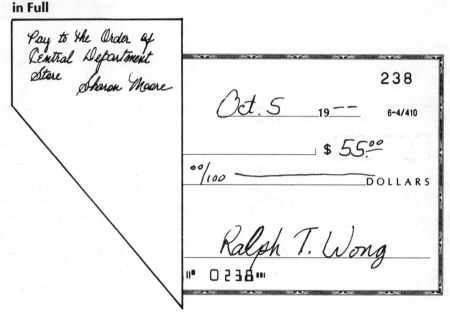

In Figure 2-8, Sharon Moore paid a bill due at Central Department Store with a check someone had written her. She merely indicated on the back of the check that the check should "Pay to the order of Central Department Store," and signed her name. Before cashing the check, Central Department Store will need to endorse it.

You should cash checks made out to you as soon as possible. If you keep a check longer than six months, it is called a *stale check*, and the check usually has to be written again.

STUDENT ACTIVITY F

1. For each of the situations identified below, name the endorsement that should be used, and write the endorsement.

   a. Sharon Moore is in the bank and wants to cash her payroll check.

   _____

   _____

   b. Sharon uses a check she received from her employer to pay for a new winter coat at Jason's Department Store.

   _____

   _____

c. Sharon Moore gets a check from her aunt and she wants to deposit the check directly in her account.

_____

_____

2. Using the following information, fill out the deposit slip for Sharon on April 21, 19--.

Cash: $41.82; $10.00

Checks: $\frac{14\text{-}1044}{650}$ $120.00; $\frac{92\text{-}403}{1241}$ $9.00; $\frac{7\text{-}28}{520}$ $7.50

CHECKING ACCOUNT DEPOSIT TICKET

Sharon Moore
433 Central Avenue
Our Towne, CA 95551-1440

DATE _____ 19_____

Our Towne Bank
Our Towne, California

	DOLLARS	CENTS	14-88
CASH ⟶			650
C H E C K S			
			USE OTHER SIDE FOR ADDITIONAL LISTING
TOTAL FROM OTHER SIDE			
TOTAL			
LESS CASH RECEIVED			BE SURE EACH ITEM IS PROPERLY ENDORSED
NET DEPOSIT			

⑈065000883⑈ 07⊷227⊷679⑈⊷

CHECKS AND OTHER ITEMS ARE RECEIVED FOR DEPOSIT SUBJECT TO THE TERMS AND CONDITIONS OF THIS BANK'S COLLECTION AGREEMENT.

INTERPRETING AND RECONCILING A BANK STATEMENT

At various intervals, usually monthly, a bank mails a depositor a *bank statement*. The bank statement is a list of all the checks the bank processed for you since the last statement. It is also a record of your balance (cash on deposit in your account) at the time the statement is prepared. At the end of May 19--, Sharon's bank statement appeared as shown in Figure 2-9.

Notice that on Sharon's bank statement the checks are listed by amounts only. A bank statement also shows the deposits made and the service charge for the month. The date column on the bank statement indicates when the bank paid the checks and recorded the deposits and any service charge.

Sharon must examine her *canceled checks* (checks that have been paid by the bank) to determine if all the checks written have been returned. Canceled checks are usually returned with the bank statement.

Skills for Consumer Success

**Figure 2-9:
Sharon's Bank
Statement**

STATEMENT OF ACCOUNT						ACCOUNT NUMBER	07227683

Statement of Account

SHARON MOORE
433 Central Avenue
Our Towne, CA 95551-1440

Our Towne Bank
Our Towne, California

ACCOUNT NUMBER 07227683

STATEMENT DATE MAY 29, 19--

BALANCE LAST STATEMENT	TOTAL AMOUNT CHECKS	NO. OF CHECKS	NO. OF DEPOSITS	TOTAL AMOUNT DEPOSITS	SERVICE CHARGE	BALANCE THIS STATEMENT
208 50	309 07	9	2	397 00	90	94 93

CHECKS		DEPOSITS	DATE	BALANCE
45.00		198.50	MAY 5	163.50
19.62	15.20		MAY 8	128.68
36.56			MAY 10	92.12
22.00			MAY 15	70.12
		198.50	MAY 18	268.62
12.78	84.90		MAY 19	170.94
13.66			MAY 26	157.28
59.35	3.00 SC		MAY 28	94.93

SC - SERVICE CHARGE   MC - MISCELLANEOUS CHARGE
CC - CHECK CHARGE   RT - RETURN CHECK

STUDENT ACTIVITY G

Study Sharon's bank statement in Figure 2-9 and answer the following questions.

1. What is the balance on May 28?

_____

2. What was the balance on May 10?

_____

3. Why had the balance increased to $268.62 by May 18?

_____

4. Why are two amounts listed in the checks column for May 19?

_____

5. How many checks did Sharon write in May?

_____

6. What is her account number?

_____

7. How many deposits did she make in May?

_____

As you will recall, the first checkbook Sharon used contained check stubs. After a while, however, Sharon thought that she might prefer a checkbook with a register.

Figure 2-10 shows Sharon's check register. When she compared her check register with the bank statement, the two did not agree. Can you tell why Sharon's check register in Figure 2-10 did not agree with her bank statement in Figure 2-9?

CHECK NO.	DATE	CHECK ISSUED TO	BAL. BR'T. F'R'D.	✔	10	00
	5/5	Deposit	AMOUNT OF CHECK OR DEPOSIT		+ 198	50
			BALANCE		208	50
56	5/5	The Corner Boutique Clothes	AMOUNT OF CHECK OR DEPOSIT		- 45	00
			BALANCE		163	50
57	5/7	Carry-ALL food	AMOUNT OF CHECK OR DEPOSIT		- 19	62
			BALANCE		143	88
59	5/9	Ellie's Book Store books	AMOUNT OF CHECK OR DEPOSIT		- 36	56
			BALANCE		107	32
60	5/14	Carry-ALL food	AMOUNT OF CHECK OR DEPOSIT		- 22	00
			BALANCE		85	32
	5/18	Deposit	AMOUNT OF CHECK OR DEPOSIT		+198	50
			BALANCE		283	82

CHECK NO.	DATE	CHECK ISSUED TO	BAL. BR'T. F'R'D.	✔	283	82
61	5/18	The Corner Boutique Clothes	AMOUNT OF CHECK OR DEPOSIT		- 12	78
			BALANCE		271	04
62	5/18	Mr. Bentley stereo radio	AMOUNT OF CHECK OR DEPOSIT		- 84	90
			BALANCE		186	14
64	5/27	Big Foot shoes	AMOUNT OF CHECK OR DEPOSIT		- 59	35
			BALANCE		126	79
			AMOUNT OF CHECK OR DEPOSIT			
			BALANCE			
			AMOUNT OF CHECK OR DEPOSIT			
			BALANCE			
			AMOUNT OF CHECK OR DEPOSIT			
			BALANCE			

Figure 2-10:
Sharon's Check Register

STUDENT ACTIVITY H

After studying Figure 2-10, answer the following questions.

1. Which two checks are not recorded in Sharon's check register?

   No. _____ for $_____

   No. _____ for $_____

2. Also, Sharon had made no record of the bank service charge, which was

   _____.

Checks written but not received by a bank are called *outstanding checks*. Sometimes a checkbook does not balance with a bank statement because some checks have not yet been deducted by the bank. Sharon had no outstanding checks for the month of May, but she had failed to keep an accurate record of the checks that she had written.

After receiving her bank statement in the mail, Sharon promptly prepared a *reconciliation statement*. This is a statement that balances your check stub record or register with the bank's statement. Sharon did the following:

First, she put canceled checks in order

56 ✓
57 ✓

Next, she checked off each check recorded on the check register.

(58)
59 ✓
60 ✓
61 ✓
62 ✓
(63)
64 ✓

Sharon noticed she had not recorded No. 58 for $15.20 and No. 63 for $13.66 on her check register.

She computed the total of her un-recorded checks; then subtracted total from her checkbook balance. She subtracted the service charge from her checkbook balance.

No. 58: $ 15.20
No. 63: + 13.66
Total: $ 28.86
Checkbook balance: $126.79
– 28.86
$ 97.93
Service Charge: – 3.00
Adjusted checkbook balance: $ 94.93

Once Sharon discovered the reason for the difference in her checkbook balance and the balance on the bank statement, she used the reconciliation statement form on the back of her bank statement. Figure 2-11 is a copy of Sharon's completed reconciliation statement.

Figure 2-11: Sharon's Reconciliation Statement

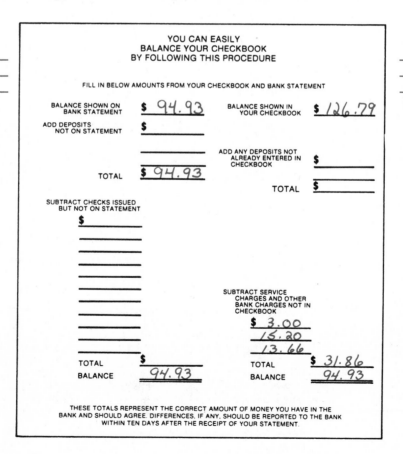

YOU CAN EASILY
BALANCE YOUR CHECKBOOK
BY FOLLOWING THIS PROCEDURE

FILL IN BELOW AMOUNTS FROM YOUR CHECKBOOK AND BANK STATEMENT

BALANCE SHOWN ON BANK STATEMENT $ 94.93   BALANCE SHOWN IN YOUR CHECKBOOK $ 126.79

ADD DEPOSITS NOT ON STATEMENT $

TOTAL $ 94.93

ADD ANY DEPOSITS NOT ALREADY ENTERED IN CHECKBOOK $

TOTAL $

SUBTRACT CHECKS ISSUED BUT NOT ON STATEMENT
$

SUBTRACT SERVICE CHARGES AND OTHER BANK CHARGES NOT IN CHECKBOOK
$ 3.00
15.20
13.66

TOTAL BALANCE $ 94.93

TOTAL $ 31.86
BALANCE 94.93

THESE TOTALS REPRESENT THE CORRECT AMOUNT OF MONEY YOU HAVE IN THE BANK AND SHOULD AGREE. DIFFERENCES, IF ANY, SHOULD BE REPORTED TO THE BANK WITHIN TEN DAYS AFTER THE RECEIPT OF YOUR STATEMENT.

1. Study Sharon's reconciliation statement (Figure 2-11) and answer the following questions about it.

   a. What was the balance shown on the bank statement?

   _____

   b. What was the balance shown in Sharon's checkbook?

   _____

   c. Which three amounts caused the discrepancy between Sharon's checkbook balance and her bank balance?

   _____

   _____

   _____

   d. Had Sharon made any deposits in the bank that had not been recorded in her checkbook?

   _____

   _____

   _____

2. Some of Sharon's friends had trouble with their bank balances. See if you can solve their problems.

   Chay Wong found that her bank statement balance in June was $80. She was extremely happy because her checkbook balance showed $52. However, Chay was not happy for long, because she discovered the following checks were outstanding (had not been received by the bank): No. 182, $10; No. 179, $5; and No. 190, $13.

   a. Add the amounts of the outstanding checks and record the total amount of the three checks:

   _____

   _____

   _____

   b. What is Chay's adjusted bank statement balance?

   _____

   _____

   _____

3. Another friend of Sharon's, Leon, was confused. His checkbook showed a balance of $179. His bank statement indicated a balance of $219. He discovered his outstanding checks were as follows: No. 92, $20; No. 101, $15; No. 103, $8. The bank deducted a service charge of $3. Prepare a reconciliation statement for Leon.

```
YOU CAN EASILY
BALANCE YOUR CHECKBOOK
BY FOLLOWING THIS PROCEDURE


FILL IN BELOW AMOUNTS FROM YOUR CHECKBOOK AND BANK STATEMENT

BALANCE SHOWN ON        $ _____          BALANCE SHOWN IN        $ _____
   BANK STATEMENT                                  YOUR CHECKBOOK

ADD DEPOSITS            $ _____
  NOT ON STATEMENT

                         _____          ADD ANY DEPOSITS NOT
                                                 ALREADY ENTERED IN    $ _____
                         _____              CHECKBOOK

        TOTAL          $ _____
                                                        TOTAL         $ _____

SUBTRACT CHECKS ISSUED
  BUT NOT ON STATEMENT
    $ _____

      _____

      _____

      _____

      _____

      _____                             SUBTRACT SERVICE
                                                CHARGES AND OTHER
      _____                               BANK CHARGES NOT IN
                                                CHECKBOOK
      _____
                                                  $ _____
      _____

                                                  _____

    TOTAL    $ _____                       TOTAL    $ _____

    BALANCE  ═══════════                         BALANCE  ═══════════


      THESE TOTALS REPRESENT THE CORRECT AMOUNT OF MONEY YOU HAVE IN THE
    BANK AND SHOULD AGREE  DIFFERENCES, IF ANY, SHOULD BE REPORTED TO THE BANK
           WITHIN TEN DAYS AFTER THE RECEIPT OF YOUR STATEMENT.
```

When Sharon first opened a checking account, she felt quite grown up taking out her checkbook and writing her first check. In fact, it felt so good that the very next day she wrote several more checks for a variety of reasons.

It wasn't long before Sharon received an overdraft notice from Our Towne Bank. She was $70 overdrawn on her account, which meant that she had written checks for $70 more than she had in her account. The bank was charging $10 for each check that "bounced."

Writing checks for more money than you have on deposit is called *overdrafting*, or *overdrawing*. If you do not keep an accurate record of *each* check you write and a record of service charges, you may overdraw your account. Both the financial institution and the business to which you write the check will probably charge a hefty fee for a check not covered by sufficient funds.

Many financial institutions have a "no-bounce" plan, but you have to *arrange* for the plan either when you open your account or at a later date. "No-bounce" plans are not automatic services of financial institutions. Essentially, the plan involves the financial institution's depositing money in your checking account when your balance nears zero, that is, when you have insufficient funds in your account.

1. You have studied several financial terms in completing the previous student activities, and you have observed these terms on various forms. Match each term below with the appropriate definition.

    _____ 1. reconciliation statement

    _____ 2. check stubs

    _____ 3. service charge

    _____ 4. signature card

    _____ 5. bank statement

    _____ 6. deposit slip

    _____ 7. overdraft

    _____ 8. joint account

    _____ 9. endorsement

a. the amount withdrawn from an account exceeds the amount deposited
b. to sign your name on the back of a check
c. held by two people
d. fee for checking services
e. record of checks written
f. the record of checks paid, deposits made, and services rendered to an account
g. used for depositing money in checking accounts
h. filled out and signed when opening a checking account
i. balances checkbook record with the bank statement

2. Define the following:

a. Canceled check _____

_____

_____

b. Outstanding check _____

_____

_____

c. Stop payment order _____

_____

_____

FURTHER DISCOVERIES

1. Call three different financial institutions in your community to find out about the types of checking services offered and the cost of these services to a customer. Write a short report comparing the services offered by the three financial institutions.

2. Go to a financial institution by yourself or with a group of students and obtain the following: (a) all forms needed to open a checking account, (b) a list of the regulations governing a checking account, and (c) samples of the items used by checking account customers such as a deposit slip, a counter check (if available), signature card, checkbook, etc. Next, prepare a bulletin board display showing the steps (with actual forms) a depositor goes through in opening a checking account.

CHECKLIST

If you have completed the student activities in this unit, you should have mastered the skills below. Check off the skills you know, and review the ones you are not sure of.

( ) How to open a checking account

( ) How to write a check and keep accurate check records

( ) How to fill out a deposit slip

( ) How to endorse a check properly

( ) How to interpret a bank statement

( ) How to reconcile a bank statement balance with a checkbook balance

( ) How to recognize terms used by financial institutions

If you have checked all of the above, ask your teacher for the Susan Thompson Test on Checking Accounts.

UNIT 3
SAVINGS ACCOUNTS AND BANK SERVICES

SKILL 1 Figuring Simple Interest

SKILL 2 Calculating Compound Interest

SKILL 3 Understanding Savings Plans

SKILL 4 Handling Routine Financial Transactions Electronically

SKILL 5 Utilizing Special Checks, Money Orders, and Safe-Deposit Boxes

Further Discoveries

FIGURING SIMPLE INTEREST

The next meeting of the consumer education seminar at Our Towne High was held again at Our Towne Bank. Mrs. Washington was responsible for this session, which focused on savings accounts.

"Before we go on to savings accounts and other services offered by financial institutions, you need to understand how interest works," Mrs. Washington explained. "If you deposit money in a savings account, the financial institution pays you interest. If you borrow money from the institution, you pay interest. Essentially, the bank is borrowing from you when you deposit your money in a savings account.

Illustration 3-1

Photo location courtesy Eagle Savings Association

"For example, let's suppose you put $100 in savings at 6 percent interest and left the money in savings for one year." Mrs. Washington showed the interest calculations while defining terms on the chalkboard.

Principal — the amount of money deposited

Time — the number of years or months the money is deposited

Rate of Interest — the amount paid on each dollar saved during a time period

Interest — what you earn by letting the bank use your money

This is how you figure the interest paid on $100 at 6 percent interest for one year.

Principal	×	Rate	×	Time	=	Interest
$100	×	.06	×	1	=	$6

The class basically understood how to figure interest, but they were not sure how Mrs. Washington got .06 out of 6 percent. "Don't you remember how to convert percentages to decimals?" asked Mrs. Washington. "Let me explain the concept once again.

"When converting percent to decimal," Mrs. Washington said, "move the decimal point two places to the left and drop the percent sign."

Example: 6 percent = ?

.06 (add zero to show place value)

6 percent = .06

If you have a fraction as part of your percent, convert the fraction to a decimal first.

Example: 6½ percent = ?

½ = .50 (fraction converted to a decimal)

6½ = 6.50 or simply 6.5

Then 06.5 = .065

Most fractions related to interest are expressed in fourths or halves, so you might just remember the following fraction conversions for convenience.

¼ = .25

½ = .50

¾ = .75

If you do have to convert a fraction to a decimal, divide the denominator of the fraction into the numerator.

Example: ⅕ = ?

$$\begin{array}{r} .20 \\ 5\overline{)1.00} \\ \underline{10} \\ 0 \\ 0 \end{array}$$

Therefore:

⅕ = .20

According to Mrs. Washington, the following procedure should be followed when converting a mixed number (a whole number and a fraction) to a decimal number.

Example: 5¼ = ?

Whole number 5 = 5.0

$$\text{Fraction } ¼ = 4\overline{)1.00} \begin{array}{r} .25 \\ 8 \\ 20 \\ 20 \end{array}$$

Mixed number 5¼ = 5.25

To find the decimal number, move the decimal point two places to the left:

05.25 = .0525

STUDENT ACTIVITY A

Convert the following percentages into decimals:

1. 5½ percent = _____

2. 5¼ percent = _____

3. 8¼ percent = _____

4. 6 percent = _____

5. 1½ percent = _____

"So you see," explained Mrs. Washington, "if you leave $100 in savings at 6 percent interest for one year, you will earn $6. That is not much money, for sure. But you are talking about money making money for you by simply being invested in a savings account. When money is put into an account to earn interest, it has been invested.

"Now," asked Mrs. Washington, "if you leave $200 in savings at 6 percent interest for one year, what is the amount saved at the end of one year?"

Remember:

Principal	+	Interest	=	Amount Saved
$200	+	$12	=	$212

The group could easily see that putting money in a savings account is far better than leaving it in a shoe box for a year. Most people try to add to their savings on a regular basis to increase the principal because the greater the principal, the more interest earned.

STUDENT ACTIVITY B

In each case below, find the simple interest and amount saved.

	Interest	Amount Saved
1. $300 for 1 year at 7¼ percent	_____	_____
2. $2,000 for 1 year at 5½ percent	_____	_____
3. $400 for 1 year at 6 percent	_____	_____

CALCULATING COMPOUND INTEREST

A person who receives interest on interest is receiving *compound interest*. For example, if Susan invests $100 in a savings account at the rate of 6 percent, by the end of one year her money will have earned $6. She can take the $6 out of savings and spend it if she wants, or she can leave it in her account. If she leaves it in her account, the principal will be increased to $106, and she will receive interest on her total of $106.

Interest is calculated in one of the following ways:

annually (every year)

seminannually (every six months)

quarterly (every three months)

monthly

daily

Whenever interest is compounded, the interest is added to the principal, thus increasing the amount of the principal. Remember, the larger your principal and the more frequently interest is compounded, the greater the amount of interest you will earn. Interest compounded daily is preferred over interest compounded monthly, quarterly, or semiannually. Notice the difference in interest between interest compounded annually and interest compounded semiannually in the following examples.

Example: Interest Compounded Annually for Two Years at 5 percent

$100	=	original principal
×.05	=	interest rate annually
$ 5	=	interest, first year
+$100	=	original principal
$105	=	principal at end of first year

$105	=	principal at end of first year
×.05	=	interest rate annually
$5.25	=	interest, second year
+$105.00	=	principal, second year
$110.25	=	principal at end of second year

Example: Interest Compounded Seminannually for Two Years at 5 percent. When interest is compounded semiannually, the percentage rate is divided by 2 (5 percent divided by 2 = 2½ percent or .025).

$100.00	=	original principal
×.025	=	interest rate for one-half year
$2.50	=	interest, one-half year
+$100.00	=	original principal
$102.50	=	principal at end of first half of year

$102.50	=	principal at end of first half of year
×.025	=	interest rate for one-half year
$2.56	=	interest, one-half year
+$102.50	=	principal at end of first half of year
$105.06	=	principal at end of first year

$105.06 = $ principal at end of second half of year
$\times.025 = $ interest rate for one-half year

$\underline{\hspace{2cm}}$

$\$2.63 = $ interest, one-half year
$+\$105.06 = $ principal at end of first year

$\underline{\hspace{2cm}}$

$\$107.69 = $ principal at end of a year and one-half

$\$107.69 = $ principal at end of a year and one-half
$\times.025 = $ interest rate for one-half year

$\underline{\hspace{2cm}}$

$\$2.69 = $ interest, one-half year
$+\$107.69 = $ principal at end of a year and one-half

$\underline{\hspace{2cm}}$

$\$110.38 = $ principal at end of second year

STUDENT ACTIVITY C

1. Figure out the compound interest and the amount on deposit at the end of each time period. Remember: When interest is compounded semi-annually, you divide the percentage rate by 2 (6 percent interest divided by 2 = 3 percent or .03). If interest is compounded quarterly, you divide the percentage rate by 4 (6 percent interest divided by 4 = 1½ percent or .015).

	Interest	Amount on Deposit
a. $500 for 3 years at 6 percent compounded annually	_____	_____
b. $1,000 for 1 year at 5 percent compounded quarterly	_____	_____
c. $600 for 2 years at 5 percent compounded annually	_____	_____
d. $2,000 for 1 year at 6 percent compounded quarterly	_____	_____

2. Mr. Fernandez's savings account pays 5¼ percent interest, compounded semiannually. If his balance on January 1, 19––, is $800, and he made no additional deposits or withdrawals, what would be his balance on January 1, 19--, of the following year?

$\underline{\hspace{12cm}}$

Mrs. Washington explained that compound interest can be calculated with compound interest tables. There is no figuring on your part; you simply check a chart. You should always check the *interest rate* and *how often interest is compounded,* however, before deciding on a financial institution in which to deposit money.

Mrs. Washington asked the students to study the interest chart in Figure 3-1. Can you interpret it? If you leave $50 in savings for two years, how much will you have saved at the end of two years? ($55.54).

Figure 3-1:
Example of
a Compound
Interest Chart*

How Savings Grow	$50	$100	$500	$1,000	$5,000	$10,000
6 mos	51.34	102.69	513.47	1026.95	5134.75	10289.50
1 year	52.70	105.39	526.95	1053.90	5269.50	10538.00
2 years	55.54	111.07	555.35	1110.71	5553.53	11107.06
3 years	58.53	117.06	585.29	1170.57	5852.86	11705.72
4 years	61.68	123.37	616.83	1233.67	6168.33	12336.66
5 years	65.01	130.02	650.08	1300.16	6500.80	13001.81
10 years	84.52	169.04	845.21	1690.42	8452.09	16904.18
20 years	142.88	285.75	1428.76	2857.51	14287.56	28575.12

* This chart shows how given amounts grow when left in your savings account for various periods of time. Figures are projected at 5¼ percent a year, compounded daily. The chart is based on a fixed amount in savings. If you added to your principal on a regular basis, your savings would be increased considerably each year.

STUDENT ACTIVITY D

Answer the following questions according to Figure 3-1.

1. According to Figure 3-1, how much will you have saved if you leave $500 in savings for three years?

_____

2. How much will you have saved if you leave $1,000 in for one year?

_____

3. How much will you have earned on $10,000 in savings for one year as opposed to having $10,000 hidden in a shoe box for one year?

_____

4. What is the rate of interest on the chart?

_____

5. How often is the interest compounded?

_____

UNDERSTANDING SAVINGS PLANS

"An important factor in choosing the right savings plan is *yield*—the amount your money will earn in the form of interest," said Mrs. Washington. "As you will recall from our discussion of interest when you put your money in a savings account, you are loaning that money to the financial institution. The institution agrees to pay you for the privilege of using your money."

Mrs. Washington said that many people choose a *passbook savings account*, which is an account that usually offers the lowest interest rate, but with few risks and restrictions. A passbook savings account has the following features:

1. *Liquidity (sometimes called flexibility).* The money deposited in passbook savings can be easily and quickly turned into cash. If you own property and need money, for example, you have to wait for that property to sell before you can get your hands on the needed cash. Property is not very liquid.

2. *Low minimum balance.* A small deposit is required to open a passbook savings account. However, a minimum balance may be required in the account to keep it open.

3. *Safety of amount deposited.* Passbook savings are safe because most commercial banks, savings and loans, and credit unions have insurance to cover deposits up to $100,000 per account. Their yield is low compared to other types of savings plans, however.

When you open a passbook savings account, you receive a passbook, or a savings account register, which is to be used for recording deposits, withdrawals, and interest earned on your account. When you deposit or

Illustration 3-2

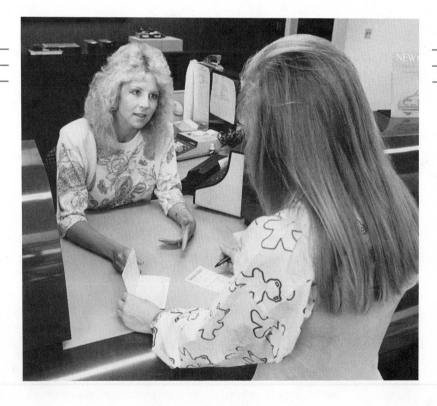

Photo location courtesy Eagle Savings Association

Skills for Consumer Success

withdraw money from your account, you should have your passbook with you unless the financial institution indicates otherwise. Your deposit or withdrawal may be recorded in your passbook by a teller, or sometimes you may have to make the entry. As with checking accounts, you receive an account number when you open a savings account. In case your passbook is stolen or lost, you should have a record of this number.

The form used when opening a passbook savings account is similar to the one used when opening a checking account. There are separate forms used for depositing and for withdrawing money from the account. When depositing money, you fill out a deposit form; when withdrawing cash from the account, you fill out a withdrawal slip for the amount you wish to withdraw. Most financial institutions offer the convenience of depositing and withdrawing money by mail.

A *certificate of deposit (CD)* is a special type of savings plan. The interest rate is higher than the rate offered on a passbook savings account, but there are certain restrictions that make a CD not as liquid as a passbook account. You may not withdraw money from a CD without a hefty penalty—usually some lost interest. There is a minimum deposit required—often $500 or more. CDs run for a specific length of time. Therefore, when you make a deposit, you commit yourself to keeping your money on deposit for a certain period of time. Certainly, the longer you keep your money on deposit, the higher the *fixed rate of interest* earned on the account. When purchasing a CD, it is advisable to shop around for the highest interest rate given on the amount of money you wish to keep on deposit for a certain period of time. Many financial institutions advertise the rates offered on CDs in the newspaper. Look for CDs that are backed by federal insurance and offer daily compounding of interest.

Money market deposit accounts (MMDA) provide *variable interest rates*; that is, rates may go up or down. Financial institutions are allowed to guarantee the rate paid for one month. The interest rate on money market accounts is not usually as high as that on many CDs because you may withdraw your money at any time from money market accounts. MMDAs generally pay a higher interest rate than most passbook accounts, however. Most accounts allow you to write a limited number of checks on the account (usually three per month). There is an initial minimum deposit required, which varies among institutions. If your balance goes below the required minimum deposit, you may earn as little as 5¼ percent. These accounts are usually backed by federal insurance.

STUDENT ACTIVITY E

1. Savings deposit forms vary, but most are similar to the one illustrated below. Fill out the savings deposit form as if it were your own. Deposit a $500 check. Your passbook number is 445189; the branch number is 3. The bank usually fills out the space for *passbook balance*.

Savings Deposit

DATE _____

This deposit subject to conditions printed
in the passbook

DEPOSIT TO THE ACCOUNT OF:

NAME _____

ADDRESS _____

CITY _____ STATE _____

$ _____
PASSBOOK BALANCE

BRANCH	PASSBOOK NUMBER

ENDORSE CHECKS PROPERLY	DOLLARS	CENTS
CURRENCY		
COIN		
CHECKS		
TOTAL DEPOSIT		

2. Fill out the following savings withdrawal form by withdrawing $250 from your account.

Savings Withdrawal

DATE _____

BRANCH	PASSBOOK NUMBER

RECEIVED FROM OUR TOWNE BANK $ _____

_____ DOLLARS

$ _____
PASSBOOK BALANCE

_____
SIGNED

3. Define the following terms:

a. yield _____

b. liquidity _____

c. fixed interest rate _____

d. variable interest rate _____

e. money market deposit account _____

_____

f. passbook savings account _____

_____

g. certificate of deposit _____

_____

HANDLING ROUTINE FINANCIAL TRANSACTIONS ELECTRONICALLY

One of Mrs. Washington's favorite topics is computerized banking. "Computer technology, known as *electronic fund transfer systems (EFTS)*, is gradually replacing paper-based banking procedures," Mrs. Washington said.

Electronic fund transfers (EFT) eliminate the costly and time-consuming procedures involved in handling and processing checks, deposit slips, and related pieces of paper. It also cuts down on the time consumers spend writing checks, paying monthly bills through the mail, and waiting in line at the bank to deposit a paycheck or to obtain cash.

One of Our Towne Bank's first applications of EFT was the *automatic transfer of funds*, whereby one preauthorizes the bank to periodically pay certain bills on a regular basis. Instead of writing a check to make a payment (such as for a home mortgage or a car loan), the bank automatically transfers money directly to the payees' account. (The *payee* is the one to whom money is paid.) An agreement between the person paying the bill and the payee is signed to preauthorize such transactions. An accurate record of the amount of money deducted each month by the bank for *preauthorized transactions* should be kept by the individual paying the bill. The monthly bank statement lists all preauthorized transactions.

Another popular EFT feature is *direct deposit* of payroll and social security checks. Some employers offer employees the option of receiving a paycheck that must be personally deposited in a bank, or having the pay deposited directly in the employee's bank. Direct deposit prevents the check from being lost or misplaced before being deposited. It also eliminates the interval between the time a check is issued and the time a check is deposited in person. When a paycheck is directly deposited, the bank or your employer is required to give you a *nonnegotiable copy* (cannot be cashed) of the paycheck.

According to Mrs. Washington, the most common form of EFT is the *automated teller machine (ATM)* where customers of a bank perform financial transactions themselves. Mrs. Washington took the students outside the bank to show them the automated teller.

"The ATM may be located on the site of the financial institution or at another location, such as a shopping center," she said. "Our Towne Bank has an ATM at the airport."

Automated tellers are a convenience for the consumer. They can provide financial services 24 hours a day, seven days a week, and every day of the year. You can perform any financial transaction at an ATM that you can with a human teller. The ATM can accept deposits, provide cash, transfer funds between checking and savings accounts, make payments, loan money, and give a statement of your current checking account balance. Automated tellers are activated by inserting a plastic (EFT) card that resembles a credit card, and by punching in your *personal identification number or code* (your PIN or PIC). Your PIN should be known only to you. You should choose a PIN that you can readily remember without writing it down. (Never write your PIN on your EFT card.) When you complete a transaction using an automated teller, the machine should issue a receipt verifying the transaction.

Illustration 3-3

Photo courtesy The First National Bank of Cincinnati. "Tellerific" is a trademark of The First National Bank of Cincinnati

Point-of-sale transfers (POS) are another type of EFT. A customer can pay a retailer (seller) by using a debit card instead of a check or currency. A *debit card* activates a financial transaction in a store at the point of sale (usually the check-out counter). A debit card is similar to a credit card with one major difference. The credit card allows you to buy today and pay at the end of the month or even later. The debit card immediately transfers the money from the customer's checking account to the retailer's account.

Mrs. Washington explained how a debit card is used. In a completely automated system, the customer passes a debit card through a reader and punches a secret code into a computer terminal. The computer (or point-of-sale) terminal functions like a cash register. The amount of the purchase is electronically withdrawn from the customer's checking account and transferred to the seller's checking account at the time of sale.

Mrs. Washington believes that eventually all self-service gas stations will be completely automated with POS terminals. Terminals will be used to handle transactions that now involve cash or an oil company credit card. Today some grocery stores accept debit cards in place of checks or cash. Retailers, in general, like the POS system because no currency or checks change hands.

"*At-home banking* is popular in some communities today," said Mrs. Washington. "By using a Touch-Tone telephone service, customers can pay their bills and transfer funds to another account without ever writing a check. The most advanced electronic financial services use either a phone line or cable-TV line to link up a bank's computer with a home computer or television set. Customers can summon information about their personal accounts to the screen. Futurists envision at-home banking providing immediate account information, bill paying services, checkbook reconciliation, and a reduction in the need for paper checks. It is one more step toward a 'paperless society.' "

As Mrs. Washington brought the students back to the conference room, she said, "Electronic banking is not a rose garden, by any means. There are problems associated with this advanced technology. Therefore, there are certain precautions customers should take regarding EFT and rules that everyone should follow." Mrs. Washington gave each student a handout of the rules shown below.

Joyce Washington's Do's and Don'ts Regarding EFT

1. Know where your EFT card is at all times.

2. Memorize your PIN (personal identification number). Do not write it on your EFT card or carry it in your wallet.

3. Immediately examine all EFT receipts.

4. Promptly report all errors.

5. Immediately report a lost or stolen EFT card.

6. Keep your check stubs or register accurate. Enter all EFT transactions in your check register or on the stubs as you would each check written or deposit made.

7. When you receive the bank statement, reconcile your EFT transactions as well as your check transactions with the bank statement.

In 1979 Congress passed the Electronic Fund Transfers Act (Regulation E) which provided some protection for consumers using EFT. Mrs. Washington said that anyone engaging in EFT transactions should be familiar with the act. Special features of the act are explained as follows.

When you initiate an EFT at a terminal (automated teller machines or point-of-sale transfers), you are entitled to get a written receipt. Each transaction must be recorded and appear on your periodic account statement. You have *60 days* from the date a problem or error appears on your statement or terminal receipt to notify your financial institution.

After being notified, the financial institution has *ten business days* to investigate and tell you the results. If the financial institution needs more time, it may take up to 45 days to complete the investigation—but only if the money in dispute is returned to your account. At the end of this investigation, if no error is found, the financial institution may take the money back, as long as it sends you a written explanation.

If you fail to notify the financial institution of the error within 60 days, you may be out of luck. The financial institution has no obligation under the federal law to conduct an investigation if you have missed the 60-day deadline.

You cannot lose more than $50 if your *credit card* is lost or stolen. But if someone uses your *EFT* card without your permission, you can lose much more. If your EFT card is lost or stolen, notify your financial institution within *two business* days after discovering the card is missing. You will then lose no more than $50 if someone else has used your card. If you do not notify the financial institution within two business days and your card is used, you can lose as much as $500.

After reporting the loss or theft of your EFT card, you cannot lose any more money if further unauthorized transactions are made. The best way to protect yourself is to notify your financial institution by telephone and follow up with a letter, keeping a copy for yourself.

It is also important to check your periodic statement. If it shows unauthorized transactions, tell the financial institution within 60 days after the statement was mailed. If you do not, the financial institution may not have to return any of the missing money. You could lose all the money that was taken from your account.

You have no stop payment rights on point-of-sale transactions—as is the case with check transactions. If your purchase is defective or if your order is not delivered, it is up to you to resolve the problem directly with the seller and get your money back—just as if you had paid with cash.

STUDENT ACTIVITY F

1. Define the following:

   a. EFT _____

   _____

   b. ATM _____

   _____

   c. POS _____

   _____

   d. debit card _____

   _____

   e. preauthorized transfers _____

   _____

   f. PIN _____

   _____

   g. Electronic Fund Transfers Act_____

   _____

2. Answer true or *false* to the following statements.

   _____ a. Keep your PIN in a safe place where you can find it at all times.

   _____ b. One of the advantages of EFT is that you do not have to keep records of transactions.

_____ c. You are entitled to a written receipt when using EFT.

_____ d. You have 60 days from the date an error appears on your statement to notify your financial institution.

_____ e. If your EFT card is lost or stolen, you can still lose up to $500 if you notify the financial institution within two business days.

UTILIZING SPECIAL CHECKS, MONEY ORDERS, AND SAFE-DEPOSIT BOXES

To conclude the seminar on bank services, Mrs. Washington wanted to take some time to explain special checks and ways to safeguard valuable documents and other possessions. "Although financial institutions offer many kinds of services to its customers, the following are the most commonly asked about," she said.

A *certified check* is a personal check (written by a depositor) on which the financial institution stamps a certification that guarantees its payment. The amount of the check is deducted immediately from the depositor's checking account. The payee is assured of a valid check. A certified check is used when you do not want to carry large amounts of cash while traveling.

Certified checks are not returned with the monthly bank statement. If for some reason, the payee does not cash the check and it is returned to you, do not tear it up. Take it back to the financial institution so that the amount can be added to your checking account. Remember, the money has already been deducted. A fee is charged by the financial institution to certify one's personal check.

A *cashier's check* is frequently used by financial institutions to pay their own bills. Individuals can also purchase cashier's checks and often do so when paying large amounts of money. A cashier's check is signed by the cashier of the financial institution, not by you. Figure 3-2 shows an example of a cashier's check.

Figure 3-2: Cashier's Check

```
                              ✴                        53524
                        Our Towne Bank
                    Our Towne, California              14-88/650
    REMITTER
    _____    _____ 19 _____


    PAY TO THE
    ORDER OF _____ $ _____
                        For Classroom Use Only

    _____ DOLLAR

    CASHIER'S CHECK
                                           _____
    |: 0650008831:07"' 53524               AUTHORIZED SIGNATURE
```

Traveler's checks can be purchased in amounts of $10, $20, $50, $100, or more. Each check is signed at the time of purchase in front of an agent of the company or financial institution issuing the checks. After the checks are issued, they can be cashed wherever traveler's checks are accepted, which is most anywhere in the world. When cashing a traveler's check, it must be signed again *in the presence of the person receiving the check*. Do not sign traveler's checks ahead of time.

Always keep the slip of paper identifying the serial numbers of your traveler's checks separate from your checks in case they are lost or stolen while you are traveling. Report lost or stolen checks to the issuing organization immediately. If checks are lost or stolen, the issuing organization will replace them right away. See Figure 3-3 for an example of a traveler's check.

Figure 3-3:
Traveler's Check

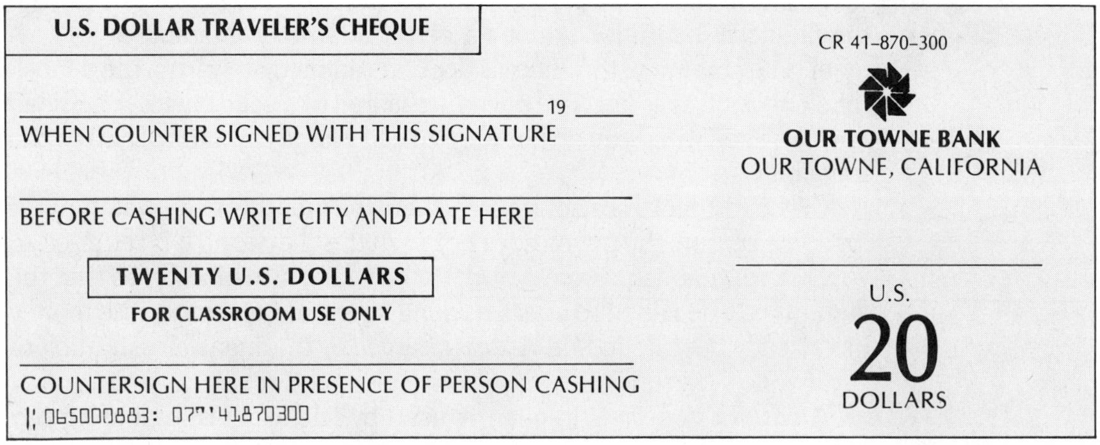

A *money order* is also called a register check or personal money order. Essentially, the money order serves the same purpose as a cashier's check with one difference. The name of the sender is on the money order; whereas, the name of the cashier is on the cashier's check. See Figure 3-4 for an example of a money order.

Figure 3-4:
Money Order

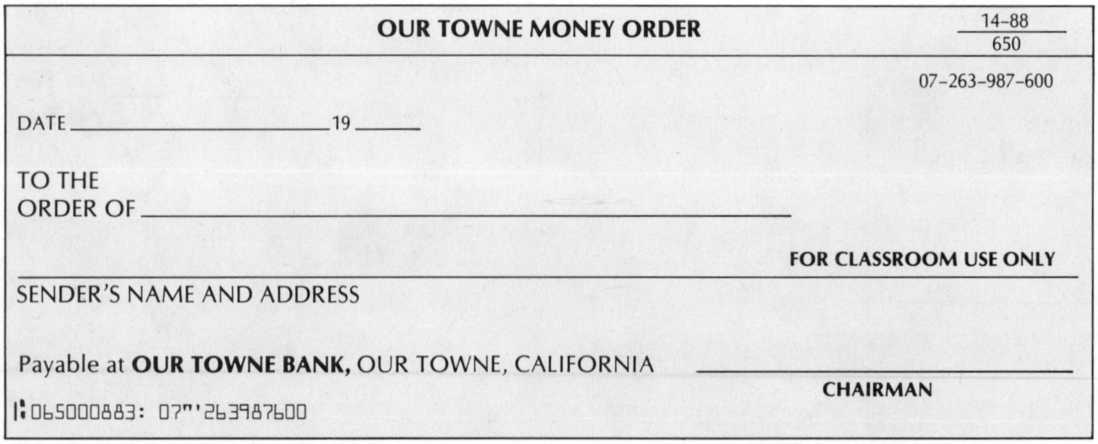

Safe-deposit boxes are containers inside the vaults of financial institutions that are rented to customers. They provide protection for valuables such as jewelry or important documents that might be destroyed by fire. Both businesses and individuals use safe-deposit boxes.

When renting a safe-deposit box, the customer is given a key. The financial institution has a master key. Both keys are necessary to unlock the box. The financial institution cannot open a private safe-deposit box without an order from the court. If a customer loses the key, the bank may, in the presence of witnesses and legal representatives of the renter, have a locksmith open the lock.

Mrs. Washington explained that financial institutions are constantly coming up with new services because they are in competition to attract customers. *Customers should always check available services before using any financial institution.*

STUDENT ACTIVITY G

Answer *true* or *false* to the following statements.

_____ 1. A financial institution guarantees the payment of a certified check.

_____ 2. A cashier's check is frequently signed by the purchaser.

_____ 3. When a traveler's check is lost or stolen, no one can cash it.

_____ 4. The name of the sender appears on a money order.

_____ 5. Always keep a record of the serial numbers on traveler's checks.

_____ 6. The only person who has a key to a safe-deposit box is the renter.

FURTHER DISCOVERIES

1. Tour a few financial institutions in your community. Obtain information on the following questions:

   a. What are the banking hours?

   b. How convenient are the locations of the institutions?

   c. What are the types of services offered by the financial institutions?

   d. How do the institutions compare regarding types of services offered?

   e. How helpful does the financial institutions' personnel seem?

   f. Are there any special services offered to the customer, such as safe-deposit boxes, 24-hour and drive-up banking? Write a report on your findings.

2. Check out a few financial institutions in your community using the Yellow Pages of the telephone directory. Either phone or visit the institutions. Ask the rates being offered on CDs of various lengths; money

market deposit accounts; and passbook savings accounts. Use the form below to record the information that you find.

Name of Institution	Type of Account	Interest Rate	Interest Compounded Daily, Quarterly, Yearly
_____	_____	_____	_____
_____	_____	_____	_____
_____	_____	_____	_____
_____	_____	_____	_____
_____	_____	_____	_____
_____	_____	_____	_____
_____	_____	_____	_____

a. In which account would you earn the most interest?

_____

b. Are there certain restrictions (minimum balance, withdrawal penalties) if you put your money into the account that earns the most interest?

_____

c. If so, what are the specific restrictions?

_____

_____

d. If you had $500, in which account would you put your money?

_____

Why? _____

_____

CHECKLIST

If you have completed the student activities in this unit, you should have mastered the skills below. Check off the skills you know, and review the ones you are not sure of.

(   ) How to figure simple and compound interest

(   ) How to interpret an interest chart

(   ) The types of savings plans available

(   ) How to fill out the forms necessary to deposit and withdraw money from a passbook savings account

(   ) The types of electronic banking services typically offered in many communities

(   ) The reasons for special checks, money orders, and safe-deposit boxes

If you checked all of the above, ask your instructor for the Susan Thompson Test on Savings Accounts and Bank Services.

UNIT 4
CREDIT

SKILL 1 **Recognizing the Requirements for Buying on Credit**

SKILL 2 **Obtaining a Loan**

SKILL 3 **Understanding Installment Contracts**

SKILL 4 **Understanding Charge Accounts**

Further Discoveries

One day, while Susan Thompson was walking to school, an old friend stopped by in the best-looking used car Susan had ever seen.

"Where did you get the money for this car?" Susan asked.

"Bought it on credit, the easy way," said her friend. "Come on. Try it out."

After driving the car, Susan dreamed for weeks about owning her own car. She decided to talk to Mr. Fernandez about credit at the next seminar.

Mr. Fernandez explained that people often buy goods or services on credit because they cannot pay cash at the time of purchase, or they do not want to withdraw money from savings. He said *buying on credit* means buying goods or services with a promise to pay at a future date. Essentially, to buy on credit is to borrow money.

"Buying on credit is particularly convenient for major purchases, such as a car or furniture," said Mr. Fernandez. "Most people cannot afford to pay large amounts of cash at one time. Therefore, they make an agreement to pay a portion of the total cost each month."

Illustration 4-1

He said that buying on credit is convenient for smaller items as well. If someone wants a stereo or new clothes but cannot afford to pay the entire amount at once, the person has the option of paying for the items over a period of time.

"But there is a catch," warned Mr. Fernandez. *"Credit is not free.* You must pay for the convenience of paying later. You are charged for credit services.

"Some people abuse credit," he pointed out, "because buying on credit seems so much easier than paying cash. They forget that they must eventually pay cash—and *more* than they would pay if they had paid the full amount at the time of the purchase."

Mr. Fernandez told Susan that there are several ways to buy on credit; but before credit can be obtained, a person must prove to be credit worthy.

RECOGNIZING THE REQUIREMENTS FOR BUYING ON CREDIT

Credit worthiness must be determined before a person is given the right to buy on credit. The criteria used to determine a person's credit worthiness are character, capacity, and capital (the three C's of credit).

Character is established according to one's conduct and living habits. Has a person lived at the same address for any length of time, or are there indications of frequent changes of residence? How long has a person worked for an employer? What kind of reputation does a person have in general?

Capacity is one's ability to earn enough income to repay a loan. To determine capacity, questions may be asked concerning (1) a person's salary or wages and present debts; (2) time with present and past employers (indicates job stability and the chances of a person maintaining a level of income while paying off a debt); and (3) previous debts satisfactorily paid (indicates an individual's ability to fulfill promises to pay).

Capital is what a person owns. It includes savings, investments, and property. Obviously, one's ability to pay a debt is increased with the more one owns. What sources do you have for repaying a debt other than regular salary or wages?

Susan could see the importance of credit worthiness. She asked Mr. Fernandez how an 18-year-old should go about establishing credit.

"First of all," Mr. Fernandez explained, "in most states parents are responsible for the debts of their children who are under 18 and not married. Young people under 18 who are using charge accounts are probably using their parents' accounts, and their parents are legally responsible for any unpaid debts. As soon as they are legally responsible, young men and women should establish credit worthiness. Married women should establish credit in their own name rather than depend on their husband's credit.

Mr. Fernandez suggested the following ways for a young person to establish credit worthiness.

1. Find a job that earns a steady income, either part-time or full-time.

2. Establish checking and savings accounts at a local financial institution. The way you handle your account tells the institution something about your capacity to manage your personal finances.

3. Apply for a credit card through a local department store, bank, or gas station. Try a store or bank where your parents have an account. Some institutions offer special teenage accounts with low credit limits. (The *credit limit* refers to the maximum amount that can be bought on credit.)

4. Apply for a short-term loan for something you need or want. Your parents may have to *co-sign*, which means they promise to pay for the loan if you fail to do so. If you successfully pay off the loan, the financial institution is more likely to lend you money without a cosigner the next time.

Susan soon realized, with the help of Mr. Fernandez, that individuals cannot simply buy on credit whenever they wish. A person must establish credit standing. *Credit standing* is an indication of a person's ability to pay for goods or services. A good credit standing has to be established over a period of time. Frequently, it is established by borrowing money and fulfilling one's promises to pay a debt. Every time a person satisfactorily completes the payments for money owed, credit standing is strengthened; each time that money is not paid on time, credit standing is weakened.

Credit standing is determined either by a personal judgment based on the three C's of credit or by a scoring system. Sometimes both methods are used. The scoring system was developed as a more objective tool for determining an applicant's credit standing. A *scoring system* consists of a list of factors that frequently determine how risky an applicant is as a potential debtor (borrower). The applicant's answers to respective questions on the scoring sheet are worth a prescribed number of points. The points are added. The total determines whether or not an applicant receives credit. See the scoring sheet in Figure 4-1 used by Our Towne Bank.

Figure 4-1:
Credit Scoring
Worksheet

Credit Scoring Worksheet ———————————————— Office ————

Date ————

NAME			LOAN CLASS LOAN NO.		
	Value	Score		Value	Score
PURPOSE OF LOAN			RESIDENCE		
1. Automobile Purchase	8		1. Home Owner	3	
2. Boat Purchase	5		2. Renter, Other	0	
3. Home Improvement Loan	5				
4. Household Furnishings	5		GROSS MONTHLY INCOME (Exclude Income from Commissions)		
5. Medical or Dental Expense	5				
6. Payment of Taxes	5		Applicant's monthly salary $_____		
7. Vacation Expense	3		Spouse's monthly salary $_____		
8. Auto Repairs	2		Total monthly salary $_____		
9. Consolidation	0		1. Over $1,500 monthly	3	
10. Other	0		2. $1,000 to $1,499 monthly	2	
			3. Less than $1,000 monthly	0	
AGE OF APPLICANT					
1. Over 37 years	3		TIME WITH PRESENT EMPLOYER		
2. 26 to 36 years	2				
3. Under 26 years	0		1. Over two years	6	
			2. One to two years	3	
MARITAL STATUS			3. Less than one year	0	
1. Married	2		BANK ACCOUNTS		
2. Single, Divorced, Other	0				
			1. With Our Towne Bank	3	
IS HOME PHONE SHOWN ON APPLICATION			2. Other Bank or No Acct.	0	
1. Yes	10		RATIO INCOME TO EXPENSE		
2. No	0		*Fixed Monthly Expense*		
			Rent or Mortgage Payment $_____		
TIME AT PRESENT ADDRESS			Auto Loan Mo. Payment _____		
			All Other Mo. Payments _____		
1. Over five years	10		Proposed Loan Payment _____		
2. One to five years	8		Total Fixed Payments _____		
3. Less than one year	0		Gross Monthly Income _____		
			Percentage _____%		
TIME AT PREVIOUS ADDRESS					
(If less than one year at present address)			1. 0% to 25%	10	
1. Over two years	5		2. 26% to 40%	6	
2. Less than two years	0		3. 41% to 50%	2	
			4. Over 50%	0	
NUMBER OF DEPENDENTS (Including Spouse)					
1. Four or under dependents	4		TOTAL CREDIT SCORE		
2. Over four dependents	0				

APPROVED ☐   DECLINED ☐   Reason _____

_____

Signed _____   Signed _____

Loan Officer Number _____   Loan Officer Number _____

Mr. Fernandez told Susan that *credit bureaus* provide credit information about you. If you have ever borrowed money, had a check bounce, or been taken to court, chances are that you have a file in a credit bureau. The contents of that file indicate how you pay your bills, your credit history, and whether you have been sued. The bureaus may get their information about you from banks, local newspapers, court records, and even the local stores at which you shop. You are protected by federal law from having inaccurate or outdated information given about your credit standing.

If you are denied a loan because of your credit standing, you have a right to request the reason for the denial. The financial institution must furnish the name and address of the credit bureau that released the report.

Federal law, however, requires only that the credit bureau disclose the "nature and substance" of the file. In some states you have the right to see your file or obtain a copy of the file for a fee. In order to obtain information in your file, you must either go directly to the credit bureau and provide suitable identification or contact the bureau by phone. When contacted by phone, the bureau will send you disclosure forms and then will call to give you the information about your file.

Since 1969, several important consumer credit laws have been passed by the federal government. Among the most important are the Truth-in-Lending Act, the Fair Credit Reporting Act, the Fair Credit Billing Act, and the Equal Credit Opportunity Act.

The *Truth-in-Lending Act* of 1969 requires that all contracts for credit clearly disclose the *finance charge*, which must be expressed as the *annual percentage rate (APR)*. More will be said about finance charges later in the unit. The purpose of the Truth-in-Lending Act is to let consumers know exactly what they must pay for the use of credit.

Since the passage of the *Fair Credit Reporting Act* of 1971, credit bureaus cannot circulate inaccurate credit information about an individual. Anyone denied credit, insurance, or employment because of an unfavorable report by a credit bureau has the right to know why credit was not granted.

The *Equal Credit Opportunity Act* of 1975 banned sex discrimination and discrimination because of marital status in the granting of credit. In other words, credit cannot be refused to credit-worthy individuals because of sex or marital status. An addition to the act in 1977 prevents discrimination against older people who apply for credit.

The *Fair Credit Billing Act* of 1975 guarantees the right of consumers to settle disputes with retail stores and credit card companies before any information about the dispute is reported to a credit bureau. If a consumer thinks that a billing error has been made, the consumer must notify the credit grantor in writing within 60 days after receiving the bill. A credit grantor must respond within 30 days and resolve the issue within 90 days.

The *Fair Debt Collections Practices Act* of 1977 stops abusive practices engaged in by some debt collectors. The law applies primarily to anyone in the business of collecting debts for others. It does not apply to banks, other lenders, or businesses that collect their own accounts using their own names. The law strictly prohibits harassing or abusive conduct in connection with the collection of a debt, such as threatening phone calls, using false or deceptive means to obtain information, or suggesting that failure to pay will result in arrest or imprisonment.

STUDENT ACTIVITY A

1. Frank Feldman wrote a check that was not covered by sufficient funds in his checking account. The billing department of the store contacted him about the $250. Frank said that he would pay, but he never did. The store's bill collector sent Frank many notices about his check. Six months after the check bounced, the store manager wrote to tell Frank that the matter would be taken to small claims court. Frank still did not pay. The store won a judgment against Frank for $250 when he failed to appear in court.

    a. Do you think Frank could get a credit card from a local retail store if he applied after the court judgment against him?

    _____

    Explain. _____

    _____

    _____

    b. Which of the "three C's" has Frank violated?

    _____

    Explain. _____

    _____

2. Use the scoring sheet in Figure 4-1 to determine your credit standing.

    a. What is your total score?

    _____

    At this point, do you think you can get a loan?

    _____

    In what areas did you lose major points?

    _____

    b. What can you do to improve your scores in those areas?

    _____

    _____

    _____

    c. Why is it difficult for young people to get a loan?

    _____

    _____

    _____

Skills for Consumer Success

3. What is meant by credit standing?

_____

_____

4. How can teenagers establish a good credit standing?

a. _____

b. _____

c. _____

5. What is the function of a credit bureau?

_____

_____

6. Cornelia Random applied for a loan at Our Towne Bank. She received a notice two weeks later saying that she had not been approved for the loan. Cornelia could not understand why, since she was making a good salary. She had apparently taken much longer than expected to pay off her college loan.

a. Should Cornelia have questioned why her loan was rejected?

_____

Explain. _____

_____

_____

b. Does Cornelia have a right to know the reason Our Towne Bank refused to grant her a loan?

_____

What laws apply?

_____

OBTAINING A LOAN

After talking to Mr. Fernandez, Susan began to investigate the different sources of credit. She wanted to buy a used car on credit someday. First, she checked with some institutions that grant loans.

She learned that *personal loans* are loans that are relatively small in amount; they are also referred to as *short-term* or *intermediate-term* loans. Personal loans are generally requested for financial emergencies, household appliances or furniture, and educational expenses. Loans for larger purchases, such as a home, are usually classified as *long-term* loans.

Susan discovered that there are several institutions that lend money. Among them are banks, savings and loan associations, life insurance companies, consumer finance companies, and credit unions.

Illustration 4-2

Photo location courtesy Eagle Savings Association

Banks handle a large portion of loans. Many people borrow from a bank where they have a checking account or a savings account. By holding accounts at the bank, they have already established a credit standing with the bank. Banks are regulated by federal and state lending laws which protect the consumer.

Savings and loan associations specialize in loans for the purchase of real estate (land or home), but they can make personal loans.

Life insurance companies may allow a policyholder to borrow against some types of insurance policies. Usually, life insurance companies charge lower interest rates than banks or other lending institutions, and the loan is fairly easy to get. If the loan has not been repaid by the time the policyholder dies, however, the amount owed is deducted from the proceeds of the policy.

Consumer finance companies often lend to consumers who do not have an established credit standing. Finance companies generally charge a higher rate of interest than other lending institutions for two main reasons: (1) loans are granted to people who are greater credit risks; and (2) small loans, which consumer finance companies deal in mostly, are costly to make. Loans at finance companies are processed more quickly and are usually easier to get.

Credit unions are organizations that grant small loans to their members. Loans from credit unions usually carry a lower interest rate than loans from banks, savings and loan associations, and consumer finance companies.

The rates of interest charged on loans from *pawnbrokers* is extremely high. To get a loan from a pawnbroker, one must turn over personal property, such as a ring or watch, as security or *pawn*. Loans from pawnbrokers must be paid in full before the personal property is returned. Therefore, consumers run the risk of losing valuable property as well as paying high interest rates.

Licensed lending institutions should not be confused with unlicensed lenders, commonly known as *loan sharks*. Loan sharks operate openly in states without usury laws. *Usury laws* limit the rate of interest a lender may charge. Loan sharks frequently swindle consumers who cannot get a loan from any other source by charging them extremely high interest rates. In addition to outrageous interest rates, loan sharks are known for underhanded practices, such as manipulating circumstances to keep the borrower in constant debt, illegal reclaiming of property, and so forth.

Loan sharks even operate in states where there are strict usury laws. They usually function under the cover of some legal business. Unfortunately, they are easily discovered by those who should avoid them most—people with a poor credit standing.

STUDENT ACTIVITY B

Answer *true* or *false* to the following statements.

_____ 1. Savings and loan associations specialize in making real estate loans.

_____ 2. Anyone can borrow from a credit union.

_____ 3. Loan sharks abide by state usury laws.

_____ 4. Personal loans are often referred to as short-term loans.

_____ 5. Anyone can borrow from a life insurance company.

_____ 6. Consumer finance companies frequently grant loans more easily than banks or savings and loans, but they may charge higher interest rates.

Since Susan was acquainted with the personnel at Our Towne Bank, she decided to go there to find out more about obtaining a loan. While at the bank, she recognized John Tanaka, who usually handles loan applications. She asked Mr. Tanaka about applying for a loan.

John Tanaka liked helping young people with financial matters. He had some extra time, so he explained a few basic points about borrowing money. He showed Susan a typical loan application that is filled out by applicants as a first step when applying for a loan. Then he proceeded to explain the types of loans available.

A *single payment loan* is a lump sum at the end of a certain period of time. For example, with a six-month single payment loan of $300, you repay $300 plus interest at the end of the six-month period.

An *installment loan* is repaid with interest in a series of payments. For example, if you have a six-month installment loan, you might pay monthly installments of $55 for six months ($55 × 6 = $330). Your monthly payment includes interest.

An *unsecured loan* is granted to borrowers with a good credit standing. The loan is strictly a written promise to pay a specific amount of money.

You may be asked to sign a *promissory note*, which is a written promise to repay borrowed money at a definite time. Loans made on the basis of a promissory note are often called *signature loans*. Mr. Tanaka showed Susan how to fill out a promissory note. The promissory note in Figure 4-2 is a copy of the note Mr. Tanaka filled out as an illustration.

Figure 4-2:
Promissory Note — Unsecured Loan

PROMISSORY NOTE

Our Towne, California
(City)   (State)
April 1, 19--

For value received, undersigned maker (s), jointly and severally, promise to pay to the order of _Our Towne Bank_ at the above place _One Hundred sixty-eight_ dollars ($168) in _12_ consecutive monthly payments of $14, each beginning one month from the date hereof and thereafter on the same date of each subsequent month until paid in full. Any unpaid balance may be paid at any time without penalty, and any unearned finance charge will be refunded based on the "Rule of 78's." In the event that maker(s) default(s) on any payment, a charge of $3.00 may be assessed.

1. Proceeds .... $ 150.00
2. _____ $ ____
   (Other charges, itemized)
3. Amount financed (1+2) ...... $ 150.00
4. FINANCE CHARGE .... $ 18.00
5. Total of payments .... $ 168.00
   ANNUAL PERCENTAGE RATE .... 12 %

Signed ____John Tanaka____

A *secured loan* is backed by something of value pledged to insure payment of the loan. If you own a house or other property of value, you may be able to offer it as security for a loan. The property pledged as security for a loan is called *collateral*.

Cost of the loan. When you borrow money from a lending institution, you must pay the lender for the use of the money. The amount paid for the use of borrowed money is called *interest*. Interest rates vary, and laws governing interest rates differ in various states. It is important to know the *interest rate* when borrowing money because the interest rate is one of the factors that will determine how much your loan costs.

Finance charge is another term used in lending money. Some people think of a finance charge and interest as the same thing. A finance charge can include more than interest. The finance charge is the total dollar amount you pay to use credit. It includes interest costs and sometimes other costs, such as loan fees, investigation or credit report fees, or the premium for credit life insurance.

Under the Truth-in-Lending Act, lenders must provide the borrower with a written statement clearly explaining the cost of borrowing. The statement must describe the following items:

- Dollar amount of the finance charge

- Annual percentage rate (APR)

- Date on which the finance charge begins

- Number, amount, and due date of payments, and the total amount of the payments

- Penalty for failure to meet the repayment terms of the loan agreement

- Penalty for early payments of the amount due (If the borrower pays off the loan ahead of the repayment schedule, there may be a "penalty" written into the loan agreement. See Rule of 78's on page 86.)

- Collateral held by the lender, if any

Terms Often Used When Borrowing Money

John Tanaka showed Susan a list of terms often used when borrowing money. He explained that she should be familiar with these terms before applying for any type of credit because they are often used in credit applications and contracts.

assets — properties owned

debt — money owed

real estate — land and anything attached to it

securities — another name for stocks and bonds

cash value — the amount of an insurance policy that an insurance company will lend to a policyholder

mortgage — legal contract giving the lender permission to acquire ownership of real estate in case the borrower does not repay a loan

mortgage holder — person or institution that holds a mortgage contract

debt balance — amount still owed on a debt

credit references — people who will recommend the credit applicant as a good credit risk

co-applicant, joint applicant, cosigner — someone who signs a loan with the borrower and promises to assume the responsibility of repaying the debt in the event that the borrower does not repay it

unsatisfied judgment — delinquent debt; payment that is overdue

bankrupt — financial situation in which one's debts are greater than the total value of one's assets

liabilities — financial obligations

alimony — an allowance made to one's former spouse for support after a legal separation or divorce

co-owners — joint ownership; two or more people share ownership rights

creditor — one to whom money is owed

dependents — those who rely on another for support

repossess, reclaim — to take back what was sold on an installment plan if payments are not made as agreed

default — failure to fulfill the terms of the loan agreement

proceeds — the amount of money a borrower receives

Rule of 78's — A method of calculating interest by which the borrower pays more interest during the early months of a loan and less near the end of the loan period. The Rule of 78's works like this. The first month of a one-year loan you pay 12/78 of the interest; the second month, 11/78; the third, 10/78, and so on until the last month when you pay 1/78 of the interest. Obviously, you are paying more interest the first month (12/78) than the last month (1/78). If you pay off the loan at the end of six months, you will save about 27 percent in interest, not 50 percent. In other words, you have paid 12/78, 11/78, 10/78, 9/78, 8/78 and 7/78 in interest which equals 57 when you add the numerators. Subtract 57 from 78. You have saved yourself only 21/78 (27 percent) in interest, which is the total amount of interest owed after six months if the one-year payment schedule had been continued as planned. Early payment, however, always saves the borrower some money, since the amount of time that the loan is outstanding is reduced.

STUDENT ACTIVITY C

1. The following terms should be part of your vocabulary before applying for a loan. Match each term below with the appropriate definition.

_____ 1. single-payment loan

_____ 2. debt

_____ 3. secured loan

_____ 4. consumer finance

_____ 5. APR

_____ 6. installment loan

_____ 7. finance charge

_____ 8. endorser

a. a company which specializes in granting small loans to borrowers with little or no credit standing

b. a loan in which something of value has been pledged to insure repayment of the loan

c. legal contract giving a lender permission to acquire ownership of real estate if the loan is not repaid

_____ 9. mortgage

_____ 10. creditor

_____ 11. garnishment

_____ 12. interest

d. person who promises to re-pay the debt if the person who obtained the loan fails to do so

e. a loan repaid with interest in one payment at the end of a definite period of time

f. a loan repaid with interest in a series of payments

g. amount owed

h. a portion of the debtor's wages paid by an employer to the creditor until the loan is repaid

i. cost of using borrowed money, which may include loan fees, credit insurance, interest, etc.

j. one to whom money is owed

k. an amount paid for the use of money

l. the yearly rate paid for the use of money

2. Read the promissory note in Figure 4-2 carefully, and answer the following questions.

a. How much was borrowed?

_____

b. What is the APR?

_____

c. When is the first payment to be made?

_____

d. What is meant by proceeds?

_____

e. What is the penalty for failing to meet any of the payments as scheduled?

_____

3. Alex Blum was interested in obtaining a loan for $300 to buy a used automobile. He decided to check out a consumer finance company and a local bank for a personal loan. At the finance company, he could borrow the money and pay it back by making twelve equal monthly payments of $29.50. At the bank, he could have the loan by signing a promissory note for $330.

a. The dollar cost of the loan from the finance company would be

_____

Show calculations:

_____

_____

_____

b. The dollar cost of the loan from the bank would be:

_____

c. Are lending institutions required to tell a borrower the total dollar cost of the loan?

_____

Why? _____

_____

4. Why do you think consumer finance companies can charge a higher rate of interest than a bank?

_____

5. On page 89, you will find a loan application that is similar to most application forms. Read the directions carefully; then provide all the information requested. You may make up answers for those questions that you should answer but are unable to because you are unemployed or too young. If you object to any information asked, circle those questions and explain the reason for your objections in the margin of the application.

UNDERSTANDING INSTALLMENT CONTRACTS

Susan decided to ask Bob Wheeler, a local used car dealer, about using the installment plan for the purchase of a used car.

"Basically," Mr. Wheeler said, "installment buying involves making regular payments." Mr. Wheeler explained that installment buying usually includes a *down payment*, which is part of the price of merchandise paid at the time of purchase, and a *finance charge*, sometimes called a carrying charge.

Illustration 4-3

PERSONAL

NAME-LAST, FIRST, MIDDLE		DATE OF BIRTH	SOCIAL SECURITY NO.	DEPENDENTS

MAIL ADDRESS - STREET OR BOX	CITY, STATE, ZIP CODE

HOW LONG	PARISH	HOME PHONE	MARITAL STATUS: DO NOT COMPLETE UNLESS YOU RESIDE IN A COMMUNITY PROPERTY STATE. ☐ MARRIED ☐ UNMARRIED ☐ SEPARATED

RESIDENCE ADDRESS (IF DIFFERENT FROM MAILING)		PARISH

PREVIOUS ADDRESS (WITHIN 2 YEARS)	HOW LONG

NAME OF RELATIVE NOT LIVING WITH YOU	ADDRESS	RELATIONSHIP	HOME PHONE

NAME OF RELATIVE NOT LIVING WITH YOU	ADDRESS	RELATIONSHIP	HOME PHONE

EMPLOYMENT

EMPLOYER'S NAME	ADDRESS	HOW LONG

POSITION OR DEPARTMENT	BADGE OR I.D.	SUPERVISOR'S NAME	SALARY $	☐ MONTH ☐ SEMI-MONTH ☐ ANNUAL	BUSINESS PHONE

PREVIOUS EMPLOYER (WITHIN 3 YEARS)	ADDRESS	HOW LONG

Alimony, child support or separate maintenance income need not be revealed if you do not wish to have it considered as a basis for repaying your obligation.

Alimony, child support, separate maintenance received under: ☐ court order ☐ written agreement ☐ oral understanding

SOURCE OF OTHER INCOME	AMOUNT $	☐ MONTH ☐ SEMI-MONTH ☐ ANNUAL	HOW LONG

CREDIT

NAME OF BANK	ADDRESS	ACCOUNT NO.	SERVICES ☐ CHK. ☐ SAV. ☐ C.D.	☐ COML. LN. ☐ CONS. LN.

MORTGAGE HOLDER OR LANDLORD ☐ BUYING ☐ RENTING	ADDRESS	ACCOUNT NO.	COST	MO. PAY	BALANCE

CREDIT: LIST ALL LOANS, CREDIT CARDS AND REVOLVING CHARGE ACCOUNTS WHICH ARE IN YOUR NAME OR THE NAME OF YOUR SPOUSE WHICH MAY BE SATISFIED OUT OF YOUR INCOME.

CREDITOR'S NAME AND ADDRESS	ACCOUNT IN NAME OF	COLLATERAL	MO. PAY	BALANCE

CO-APPLICANT

(ADDITIONAL CO-APPLICANTS MUST COMPLETE SEPARATE APPLICATION FORMS)

IF ☐ SPOUSE OR ☐ OTHER WILL BE CONTRACTUALLY LIABLE, COMPLETE THIS SECTION. IF APPLICANT RELIES ON COMMUNITY PROPERTY, SPOUSES INCOME, ALIMONY, CHILD SUPPORT OR MAINTENANCE PAYMENTS FROM A SPOUSE OR FORMER SPOUSE, FOR REPAYMENT OF THIS LOAN, FILL IN THIS SECTION ABOUT YOUR SPOUSE OR FORMER SPOUSE.

NAME-LAST, FIRST, MIDDLE		DATE OF BIRTH	SOCIAL SECURITY NO.	DEPENDENTS

RESIDENCE ADDRESS - STREET OR BOX	CITY, STATE, ZIP CODE

HOW LONG	PARISH	HOME PHONE	MARITAL STATUS: DO NOT COMPLETE UNLESS YOU RESIDE IN A COMMUNITY PROPERTY STATE. ☐ MARRIED ☐ UNMARRIED ☐ SEPARATED

PREVIOUS ADDRESS (WITHIN 2 YEARS)	HOW LONG

NAME OF RELATIVE NOT LIVING WITH YOU	ADDRESS	RELATIONSHIP	HOME PHONE

EMPLOYER'S NAME	ADDRESS	HOW LONG

POSITION AND DEPARTMENT	BADGE OR I.D.	SUPERVISOR'S NAME	SALARY $	☐ MONTH ☐ SEMI-MONTH ☐ ANNUAL	BUSINESS PHONE

PREVIOUS EMPLOYER (WITHIN 3 YEARS)	ADDRESS	HOW LONG

Alimony, child support, or separate maintenance income need not be revealed if you do not wish to have it considered as a basis for repaying your obligation.

Alimony, child support, separate maintenance received under: ☐ court order ☐ written agreement ☐ oral understanding

SOURCE OF OTHER INCOME	AMOUNT $	☐ MONTH ☐ SEMI-MONTH ☐ ANNUAL	HOW LONG

NAME OF BANK	ADDRESS	ACCOUNT NO.	SERVICES ☐ CHK. ☐ SAV. ☐ C.D.	☐ COML. LN. ☐ CONS. LN.

MORTGAGE HOLDER OR LANDLORD ☐ BUYING ☐ RENTING	ADDRESS	ACCOUNT NO.	COST	MO. PAY	BALANCE

CREDIT: LIST ALL LOANS, CREDIT CARDS AND REVOLVING CHARGE ACCOUNTS WHICH ARE IN YOUR NAME OR THE NAME OF YOUR SPOUSE WHICH MAY BE SATISFIED OUT OF YOUR INCOME.

CREDITOR'S NAME AND ADDRESS	ACCOUNT IN NAME OF	COLLATERAL	MO. PAY	BALANCE

WARRANTY OF APPLICANT(S)

THE UNDERSIGNED APPLICANT(S) WARRANTS AND REPRESENTS THAT ALL STATEMENTS MADE HEREON ARE TRUE AND CORRECT AND ARE GIVEN TO INDUCE THIS BANK TO APPROVE THIS CREDIT APPLICATION. THE UNDERSIGNED APPLICANT(S) AUTHORIZES OUR TOWNE BANK TO MAKE WHATEVER CREDIT INQUIRIES IT DEEMS NECESSARY IN CONNECTION WITH THIS APPLICATION AND AGREE THAT THIS APPLICATION SHALL REMAIN THE PROPERTY OF THE BANK WHETHER OR NOT THE LOAN IS EXTENDED.

APPLICANT'S SIGNATURE	DATE	CO-APPLICANT'S SIGNATURE	DATE

According to Mr. Wheeler, when a person purchases merchandise from a business on the installment plan, the buyer often makes payments to a *sales finance company*. For instance, Wheels, Inc. (the used car business run by Bob Wheeler) turns over all installment sales contracts to the Ace Sales Finance Company. If Susan should buy a used car on an installment plan from Wheels, Inc., she would make payments to Ace Finance Company. Sales finance companies differ from consumer finance companies; *consumer finance companies* make loans directly to customers.

Susan thanked Mr. Wheeler for all the information on installment buying. That night she told her parents about the finance plan at Wheeler's. Mrs. Thompson was amazed that her daughter knew so much about installment buying. She showed Susan the installment contract that *she* had just signed with Henning's Department Store (see Figure 4-3).

Figure 4-3:
Mrs. Thompson's Installment Contract

Seller's Name: Henning's Dept. Store, Our Towne, CA

Contract # 1506

RETAIL INSTALLMENT CONTRACT AND SECURITY AGREEMENT

The undersigned (herein called Purchaser, whether one or more) purchases from Henning's Dept. Store (seller) and grants to her a security interest in, subject to the terms and conditions hereof, the following described property.

PURCHASER'S NAME Mrs. Martha Thompson

PURCHASER'S ADDRESS 4839 Jasmine Blvd.

CITY Our Towne STATE CA ZIP 95551-1445

QUANTITY	DESCRIPTION	AMOUNT
1	Sofa	295.00
	Sales Tax	5.90
	Total	300.90

1. CASH PRICE $ 295.00
2. LESS: CASH DOWN PAYMENT $ 30.00
3.   TRADE-IN
4.   TOTAL DOWN PAYMENT 30.00   30.00
5. UNPAID BALANCE OF CASH PRICE $ 265.00
6. OTHER CHARGES:

    Sales Tax $ 5.90
       $
7. AMOUNT FINANCED $ 270.90
8. FINANCE CHARGE $ 48.76
9. TOTAL OF PAYMENTS $ 319.66
10. DEFERRED PAYMENT PRICE (1+6+8) $ 349.66
11. ANNUAL PERCENTAGE RATE $ 18 %

Purchaser hereby agrees to pay to Henning's Dept. Store at their offices shown above the "TOTAL OF PAYMENTS" shown above in 12 monthly installments of $ 26.63 (final payment to be $ 26.73), the first installment being payable April 2, 19--, and all subsequent installments on the same day of each consecutive month until paid in full. The finance charge applies from 3/2/--

Signed Mrs. Martha Thompson

Insurance Agreement

The purchase of insurance coverage is voluntary and not required for credit. _____ (Type of Ins.) insurance coverage is available at a cost of $_____ for the term of credit.

I desire insurance coverage

Signed _____ Date _____

I do not desire insurance coverage

Signed Mrs. Martha Thompson Date 3/2/--

NOTICE TO BUYER: YOU ARE ENTITLED TO A COPY OF THE CONTRACT YOU SIGN. YOU HAVE THE RIGHT TO PAY IN ADVANCE THE UNPAID BALANCE OF THIS CONTRACT AND OBTAIN A PARTIAL REFUND OF THE FINANCE CHARGE BASED ON THE "ACTUARIAL METHOD." [Any other method of computation may be so identified, for example, "Rule of 78's," "Sum of the Digits," etc.]

Read Mrs. Thompson's installment contract (Figure 4-3) carefully, and answer the following questions.

1. What is the cash price of the sofa?

   _____

2. How much of the purchase price is financed?

   _____

3. What is the finance charge?

   _____

4. Are there any charges other than the finance charge and purchase price?

   _____

5. Do you understand all the concepts or terms on the contract?

   _____

   If not, which ones are confusing?

   _____

   _____

6. Are all figures on the contract correct?

   _____

Credit agreements frequently include fine print that you should read carefully before you sign them. Notice the insurance agreement at the bottom left hand corner of Mrs. Thompson's installment contract. *Credit insurance* is purchased through the institution financing the loan, and it pays off the debt if the borrower dies. Credit insurance is seldom necessary, especially if the borrower is young and healthy or has adequate life insurance. It is expensive when compared to regular life insurance. By law, the borrower must be told that credit insurance is voluntary.

Always notice and ask about *penalties for early payment* of a debt. The Rule of 78's is mentioned at the bottom of Mrs. Thompson's contract. A *default payment clause* explains a late payment charge or penalty.

A *deficiency clause* is one in which a creditor can repossess and resell goods and, in addition, force the borrower to pay any amount still owed on the installment contract if not recovered through the sale of the goods. *Security interest* is an agreement whereby the creditor keeps the title (ownership) of goods until the borrower completes all the payments. If the borrower (debtor) fails to make payments, the product can be repossessed by the creditor.

Wage assignment, or *garnishment*, involves a clause whereby a lender can collect a portion of the borrower's wages if the borrower has defaulted on a loan. A court order is not necessary to garnish wages with this clause.

A *disclaimer* is an agreement between creditor and borrower (debtor) that unwritten promises will not be recognized by the court in the case of a disagreement. This is another reason the borrower should pay close attention to what is written or not written in the contract.

In general, you should always read a credit agreement thoroughly and carefully. Ask questions about any fine print or legal language you do not understand. Ask to take the form home overnight, if necessary, to study the terms of the agreement.

STUDENT ACTIVITY E

The following terms should be part of your vocabulary before signing a credit agreement. Match each term below with the appropriate definition.

_____ 1. credit insurance

_____ 2. default payment clause

_____ 3. deficiency clause

_____ 4. disclaimer

_____ 5. Rule of 78's

_____ 6. security interest

_____ 7. wage assignment

a. an agreement whereby the creditor keeps the title to goods

b. a deduction from an employee's paycheck to cover payments in default

c. gives the creditor the right to repossess and resell goods

d. pays off a debt if the borrower dies

e. identifies a late payment penalty

f. a method of calculating interest by which the borrower pays more interest during the early months of a loan and less toward the end of the loan period

g. an agreement between creditor and borrower that unwritten promises will not be recognized by the court in case of a disagreement

UNDERSTANDING CHARGE ACCOUNTS

Mr. Tanaka advised Susan to apply for a few credit cards to establish a credit standing. He told her that if she were to apply for a loan at Our Towne Bank for the purchase of a used car, she would need to have a good credit record.

She asked Mr. Tanaka where she could get applications for credit cards. He said that banks usually have application forms for bank cards; gas stations have forms for their gas credit cards; retail stores have application forms for cards which they accept. Mr. Tanaka showed Susan an application for a bank card. See Figure 4-4 for a copy of the application.

**Figure 4-4:
Application for
a Bank Card**

APPLICATION FOR CREDIT

This Application is for: (Check one or both)

☐ MASTER CARD ☐ VISA

Number of sets of above cards requested ____

FILL OUT COMPLETELY, FOLD, SEAL WITH TAPE OR STAPLE BEFORE MAILING

Last Name	First	Initial	Age	Spouse		No. of Dependents

Home Address	City	State	Zip Code	Rent ☐ Own ☐ Live with Parents ☐

How Long	Phone	Previous address if at above less than three years	How Long Yrs. Mos.

Employer	Occupation	Salary MO.	How Long Yrs. Mos.

Business Address	Business Phone	Social Security Number

Previous Employer	Business Address	Occupation	Salary Mo.	How Long Yrs. Mos.

Applicant is not required to provide the information requested in this section unless in applying for this account applicant is relying upon the additional credit worthiness (income and property) of co-applicant.

Full Name Co-Applicant	Age	Social Security No.

Home Address	City	State	Zip

Employer	Occupation	Salary Mo.	How Long Yrs. Mos.

Business Address	Business Phone

Name and Address of nearest relative not living with you	Phone	Relationship

Income from alimony, child support or maintenance payment need not be revealed if the applicant does not wish to rely on such income to qualify for credit.

OTHER SOURCES OF INCOME	Monthly Amount $	Source

CREDIT REFERENCES

COMPANY	ADDRESS	ACCOUNT NO.	BALANCE
1)			
2)			
3)			

Checking Account No. and Bank	Savings Account No. and Bank

THE ABOVE APPLICATION IS TRUE AND CORRECT AND APPLICANT ACKNOWLEDGES RECEIPT OF AND AGREES TO THE CONTRACT AND DISCLOSURES SET FORTH AND FURTHER AGREES TO PAY ALL INDEBTEDNESS INCURRED IN ACCORDANCE WITH SUCH CONTRACT.

Signature of Applicant ____ Date

Signature of Co-Applicant ____ Date

Reprinted with permission of Southern Bankcard, New Orleans, Louisiana.

STUDENT ACTIVITY F

The bank credit card application form is shown in Figure 4-4. Complete the form for yourself. Make up any information that you cannot answer at present, such as occupation, salary, and so forth. Circle any part of the application that you do not understand.

Mr. Tanaka said that the credit card holders establish a line of credit based on their credit standing. *Line of credit* refers to the maximum amount a person can charge at any one time. A credit card company may put a $500 limit on one card holder, whereas another person because of a better credit standing may have a higher limit.

If a credit card is lost or stolen, you should inform the issuer of the credit card immediately by telephone and later by mail. Federal law protects a card holder from paying for any unauthorized charges over $50 for each reported lost or stolen card. (If a person immediately reports a card lost or stolen, the $50 liability does not apply.) A card holder should keep a record of the account number of each credit card owned so a stolen or lost card can be reported quickly.

Credit card issuers must send regular statements to card users. You may challenge either the purchase or the price of an item that appears on your billing statement. The Fair Credit Billing Act of 1975 requires prompt corrections of billing mistakes. Note Mr. Tanaka's bank card statement presented in Figure 4-5.

Figure 4-5:
Mr. Tanaka's Bank Card Statement

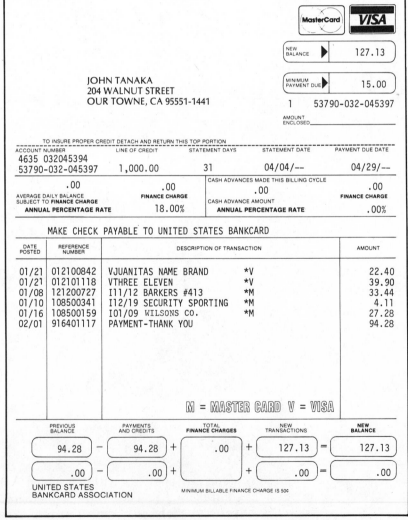

Reprinted with permission of Southern Bankcard, New Orleans, Louisiana

Study Mr. Tanaka's statement carefully, and see if you can interpret it. Answer the questions below.

1. How much does Mr. Tanaka owe?

   _____

2. What is the minimum amount he can pay on the statement?

   _____

3. By what date must he pay it?

   _____

4. Does he have any finance charge on this statement?

   _____

5. What was the balance last month?

   _____

6. Did he pay the full amount last month?

   _____

7. How much can he charge at any one time?

   _____

8. What is the APR charged by the credit card company?

   _____

"Many issuers of credit cards charge a monthly finance fee of 1½ percent on the unpaid balance of an account, which amounts to 18 percent annually," Mr. Tanaka said. "For example, if you charge $100 worth of clothes and pay only $20, you will have a finance charge of $1.20 on your next month's statement ($80 × .015 = $1.20)." Mr. Tanaka stressed that whenever the full balance due is not paid on a credit card statement, interest is charged.

While they were on the subject of credit, Mr. Tanaka used the opportunity to give Susan some guidelines for using credit wisely.

"Credit is a wonderful opportunity to get what we want or need before we're able to pay for it," he said, "but credit has resulted in some people's financial ruin. If we use a few common sense rules, credit can be a helpful tool in financial management."

Mr. Tanaka's guidelines are listed below.

1. Pay for small purchases (under $25) with cash. Cash is *always* cheaper than credit. When you buy on credit, you have to pay for the borrowed money. You are spending future income. Avoid buying something just because you can use credit. Credit is not free.

2. Buy those things on credit that will outlast the payment period. For example, it is difficult to continue payments on a used car that won't run.

3. Limit installment debts to 15-20 percent of take-home pay. Any amount over 20 percent is dangerous. Most borrowers have to use 80 percent of their income for food, shelter, transportation, clothing, and emergencies.

4. Keep accurate up-to-date records of merchandise bought on credit.

5. Shop for the least expensive form of credit as carefully as you shop for the least costly merchandise.

FURTHER DISCOVERIES

1. Contact two banks in your community and ask for a credit rating sheet or chart used to determine the eligibility of a customer for a personal loan. Use the chart to determine your own credit rating. Write a short report about your findings.

2. Find out the cost of credit in your own community. Decide on a personal loan for yourself; for example, to buy a used car. Give the specific amount to be borrowed. Then check with dealers, banks, credit unions, and finance companies to determine the different rates and requirements. Find out how much each place would charge you for the same loan. Prepare a chart to show (1) the dollar amount of the finance charge, (2) the annual percentage rate, (3) the total number of payments, (4) the amount of each monthly payment, and (5) the amount of the total payments. When you finish, rank the loans from the lowest to the highest cost for a consumer.

3. Businesses often give special names to their credit plans. Visit at least three large stores in your community to determine what charge plans are available to a customer. What names do these businesses give to their charge plans? How do the plans differ?

CHECKLIST

If you have completed the student activities in this unit, you should have mastered the skills below. Check off the skills you know, and review the ones you are not sure of.

(   ) The requirements for buying on credit

(   ) How to establish credit standing

(   ) Some of the laws pertaining to credit

(   ) The sources of loans

(   ) The types of loans

(   ) The cost of borrowing money

(   ) The nature of a promissory note

(   ) The terminology related to loans

(   ) How to fill out a loan application

(　) What is meant by an installment contract

(　) How to interpret an installment contract

(　) Where and how to apply for a credit card

(　) How to interpret a statement from a credit card company

(　) How to use credit wisely

If you have checked all of the above skills, ask your teacher for the Susan Thompson Test on Credit.

UNIT 5
BUDGETING

SKILL 1 How to Determine Budget Goals, Total Income, and Expenditures

SKILL 2 How to Keep Records: Making a Budget Work

SKILL 3 How to Prepare a Yearly Budget

Further Discoveries

When Susan was offered a part-time job at Uptown Apparel, she couldn't have been more excited. She had enjoyed her job at Connie's Cafe, but the apparel shop provided more opportunities. She could test her selling skills and her ability to work closely with the public. If she did well, she had a possibility for advancement and managerial training. Not of least importance, she could buy her clothes at Uptown Apparel and receive a 20-percent discount.

As soon as the job was definite, she asked Mr. Fernandez to explain the basics of preparing a budget—a plan for spending and saving money.

HOW TO DETERMINE BUDGET GOALS, TOTAL INCOME, AND EXPENDITURES

"What are your goals?" Mr. Fernandez asked.

"Eventually, I want to buy a used car," Susan explained, "and I may want to go to college next year. My parents can afford to pay tuition, but I'll have to provide spending money."

"Well, you're on the right track, Susan," Mr. Fernandez said. "The first thing you should do when preparing a budget is to write down your goals. Goals will help you determine what you want to achieve.

"Eventually buying a car and going to college next year are future goals that necessitate establishing a savings account. But there are other goals for keeping a budget or, to put it another way, for managing your finances," said Mr. Fernandez.

Mr. Fernandez listed some typical goals of a budget for Susan's age group (those 17 to 25 years old):

1. Plan for financial independence (supporting yourself financially).

2. Train or study for a career.

3. Purchase insurance to cover risks (for example, health or car insurance).

4. Establish credit worthiness.

5. Establish a savings plan.

6. Establish a spending plan that fits your life-style and financial needs.

7. Establish an effective financial record-keeping system.

"So the first step is to write down your goals," Mr. Fernandez said. "The goals may be general, as the ones mentioned, or they may be as specific as saving $1,000 by next September for a down payment on a car. Let's say you listed saving $1,000 as a goal, and you have twenty weeks to accomplish that goal. Budget goals are more easily reached when broken down into weekly or monthly dollar amounts; for example, $1,000 divided by twenty weeks equals $50. To save $1,000 by next September, you will have to save $50 every week. Maybe your weekly salary does not allow $50 a week for savings. You may have to adjust your budget. You may decide to try to save only $500 by next September, or you may want to wait another six months to buy a car.

"The main purpose of a budget," said Mr. Fernandez, "is to help you live as you want without getting yourself into too much debt. The budget should fit your personality. If budgeting makes your life miserable, you have defeated the purpose of budgeting."

"There are different types of budgets for different kinds of people. But whatever your style of budgeting," he continued, "you must first determine two things: *total income* and *expenditures.*"

First, Mr. Fernandez figured out Susan's income on a monthly basis:

Monthly Income	
Net Pay	$200.00
Interest on Savings	2.08
Total Income	$202.08

Mr. Fernandez explained to Susan that she should record her net pay rather than her gross income. *Net pay* is the amount of money that you take home after taxes and other deductions have been subtracted from your earnings. *Gross pay* is the salary or wages received before taxes and other deductions have been withheld.

Mr. Fernandez said that net pay, or take-home pay, is usually about 20 to 30 percent less than gross pay, which is why you should always base your budget on net pay. He showed Susan a paycheck stub and explained the different deductions.

"Your paycheck usually comes in two parts: the *paycheck*, which you will cash or deposit in an account, and the *paycheck stub*, which is a record of your earnings and deductions.

Figure 5-1:
A Paycheck
Stub

						Pay Statement			
Co. Code	Department	File No.	Clock No.Id.	Name			Pay Period		Pay Date
01	012	261	R420	Beth Yoshino			Ending 02/15/--		02/15/--

Hours/Units	Rate	Earnings	Type	Deduction	Type	Deduction	Type
	659.90	659.90	REG				

This Pay	Gross	Fed. With. Tax	Social Security	State With.	City With. Tax	Sui/Dis	Net Pay
	659.90	72.30	40.45	10.01			537.14
YTD	1979.70	216.90	121.35	30.03			

On the paycheck stub in Figure 5-1, the employee received $659.90 in gross, or total pay. Among the deductions are $72.30 for federal income tax (withholding tax), $40.45 for social security (FICA tax—Federal Insurance Contributions Act), and $10.01 for state income tax. All these deductions are required by law. Deductions for health insurance, pension plans, and automatic savings—a service whereby the employee designates part of the gross pay to a savings account and the employer automatically deposits the money—are often optional. This employee chose not to have any of the optional deductions made. When all the required deductions are subtracted from the gross pay, the person receives $537.14 as net pay, or take-home pay.

Mr. Fernandez also said that all income, not just salary or wages, should be included in one's total income unless a person wants the extra income set aside for some other purpose. Susan had $500 in savings at 5 percent interest compounded daily. Because calculating interest compounded daily would be too difficult, Susan merely figured simple interest at 5 percent to get an estimate of how much she earns in interest in one month.

$$\$500 \times 5\% \times 1 \text{ year} = \$25 \text{ interest per year}$$
$$\$25 \text{ divided by } 12 = \$2.08 \text{ interest per month}$$

Susan said she preferred to leave the interest earned on her savings out of her budget. She also received money for occasional babysitting. Mr. Fernandez suggested that Susan leave all wages not earned on a regular basis out of the budget as well.

STUDENT ACTIVITY A

1. What is the first step when preparing a budget?

_____

2. Define the following terms:

   a. net pay _____

   _____

   b. gross pay _____

   _____

   c. FICA _____

   _____

   d. optional deductions _____

   _____

   e. paycheck stub _____

   _____

3. What amount did Susan finally list as total monthly income for her budget?

_____

4. Wanda Fritz, who lives near Susan, takes home $10,000 a year, and she has $10,000 in savings at 9 percent compounded annually. What is her total income per month if she includes interest? (Figure simple interest.)

_____

5. Mr. Fernandez says he has a gross pay of $25,000 a year with 20 percent taken out for deductions, and he earns 5 percent interest compounded daily on $6,000 savings. What is his total income per month if he counts his interest? (Figure simple interest.)

_____

"Once you figure your total income," said Mr. Fernandez, "you should list your fixed expenses. *Fixed expenses* are those predetermined amounts that you must pay every month or during certain months throughout the year."

Mr. Fernandez told Susan that fixed expenses are an important factor when planning a budget. What may appear to be small monthly payments can quickly add up to a sizable sum. He said that the budget-minded person considers fixed payments before buying anything on credit for which he or she must make monthly payments.

"Paying $25 a month on a stereo may not seem like much by itself, but when added to the other monthly payments that must be made, buying a stereo may be unrealistic or even impossible," said Mr. Fernandez.

Mr. Fernandez, who is buying a home and has a family of four, listed his fixed expenses as an example. See Figure 5-2.

Figure 5-2:
Mr. Fernandez's
Fixed Expenses

Expenses	Due Date	Amount
House payment	1st of every month	$440
Property taxes	(included in house payments)	---
Health insurance	15th of every month	50
Car license	January 15	25
Car insurance	15th of July and January	172
Home insurance	(included in house payments)	---
Life insurane	1st of every month	25

STUDENT ACTIVITY B

1. In which months will Mr. Fernandez have extra payments?

_____

2. Omitting the months for extra payments, what is the sum of fixed monthly expenses for Mr. Fernandez?

_____

3. According to Mr. Fernandez's extra expenses, in which month will the most money be paid?

_____

Mr. Fernandez told Susan that in order to meet an extra fixed expense coming up in a particular month, some adjustments in the budget may have to be made the month prior to or the month following the extra expense. If September is going to be a month with many expenses, some financial preparation may be necessary in August, so that the September bills can be paid.

He suggested that Susan may want to delay buying a car in September if she plans to start college in the fall. College would cause some real adjustments in Susan's budget even if her parents do pay the tuition. There will be book bills, school supplies, lunch and snack money, clothes, etc; and a car would mean another monthly fixed expense.

Illustration 5-1

One way to handle months with extra expenses is to save a certain amount each month in a special fund for that purpose, or simply add to a regular savings account with the idea that the extra expenses will be paid from that special fund. Even so, the extra expenses and the month when they are due should be listed within the budget, so that you are prepared for any future expenses.

After determining fixed expenses, the next step is to itemize all regular expenditures that occur each month. People have different spending habits and life-styles, but expenditures for most individuals can be listed in the following categories:

Shelter (house or apartment)	Transportation	Household Needs
	Medical Expenses	Insurance Premiums
Utilities	Education	Savings
Food	Entertainment	Loan Payment
Clothing	Personal Needs	Miscellaneous

Presently, Susan does not have any fixed expenses because she is supported by her parents and living at home. Therefore, her budget for the month of March is relatively simple. It might look something like the one in Figure 5-3.

Figure 5-3:
Susan's Budget*

SUSAN'S BUDGET FOR MARCH*

Net Pay**		$200
Expenses		
	Savings (monthly)	$ 30
	Snacks, Eating Out	30
	Entertainment	30
	Clothes	50
	Personal Needs (hairdresser, etc.)	50
	Miscellaneous (extra)	10
	TOTAL	$200

* Budget if living at home.
** Assume Susan is working part-time (approximately 20 hours a week) while in high school.

However, Susan wants to get her own apartment after graduation and be on her own financially.

"Before making such a decision, you need to put it on paper," Mr. Fernandez recommended. "That goes for major decisions you make during the rest of your life: whether you want to go to college, get married, start a family, go into business for yourself, or make any decision that requires financial adjustments. *Before* making a change, write out an estimated budget for yourself.

"Let's suppose you leave home and get an apartment in June. Do you intend sharing the rent expense with someone else or paying it on your own?" Mr. Fernandez asked.

"Sharing with someone else," Susan said.

So Mr. Fernandez and Susan set up an estimated budget for July, leaving out the idea of college for the present. Mr. Fernandez listed the categories for which Susan would be responsible and Susan estimated the expense. Figure 5-4 is a copy of Susan's tentative budget.

Figure 5-4:
Susan's
Tentative
Budget*

SUSAN'S BUDGET FOR JULY*	
Net Pay	$400
Expenditures	
Shelter (rent)**	$150
Utilities (gas, electricity, water)**	60
Telephone Bill**	15
Furniture (monthly payment on bedroom set)	20
Household Needs	10
Food	50
Eating Out	30
Clothes	30
Laundry	5
Transportation (public)	10
Medical	5
Entertainment (movies, sports, travel)	30
Personal Needs (toothpaste, haircuts, etc.)	15
Savings	10
TOTAL	

*Budget if living away from home.

**These expenses are shared with a roommate.

STUDENT ACTIVITY C

1. Add Susan's expenditures in Figure 5-4. What is the total estimated amount she expects to spend each month?

2. Subtract her estimated expenditures from her monthly net pay (take-home pay). At the outset, what is wrong with Susan's budget?

3. What is Susan's greatest expenditure each month?

4. How much does she estimate to spend on food (at home and eating out)?

5. In your opinion, can Susan support herself on $400 a month?

Explain.

6. If you were Susan, would you decide to stay home or try to adjust your budget?

_____

Explain. _____

_____

7. Make a list of expenditures that you would include in your budget if you were to leave home today and had to support yourself without help from anyone. Give the estimated cost per month for each item. Use Susan's list in Figure 5-4 as a guide.

Expenditures	Estimated Cost per Month
1. _____	_____
2. _____	_____
3. _____	_____
4. _____	_____
5. _____	_____
6. _____	_____
7. _____	_____
8. _____	_____
9. _____	_____
10. _____	_____

a. How much would you have to take home each month in order to support yourself according to your proposed budget?

_____

b. What kind of job can you find now with your education and experience that pays the money you need to support yourself?

_____

HOW TO KEEP RECORDS: MAKING A BUDGET WORK

Mr. Fernandez explained to Susan that a budget can make a person's life pleasant or miserable, depending upon the person's ability to (a) adjust the budget to personal spending habits, and (b) keep accurate records.

Most people stop budgeting for one of three reasons:

1. They try to adopt a budget for a life-style that does not apply to them.

2. They get too particular about recording minor expenditures; therefore, they become discouraged because the budget begins to involve too much time and energy.

3. They are unorganized and have difficulty keeping practical and accurate records.

Mr. Fernandez told Susan that she might have to keep records for two or three months and adjust her estimated expenditures several times before her budget begins to work for her. Mr. Fernandez gave Susan guidelines for record keeping, but he told Susan that she should develop a method of budgeting to suit herself.

Mr. Fernandez's Guidelines for Budgeting

Step One: Write down take-home pay and any other income you wish to include in the budget.

Step Two: Make a list of items, with estimated costs, that are monthly expenditures.

Step Three: Before depositing your paycheck, decide which items will be purchased by check and which will be purchased with cash. It is best not to keep too much cash in your house or in your pocket. If cash is used for an item, write a check every two weeks for "cash," or whenever necessary, and indicate on the bottom of the check what the money is for. The check will be your record of an expenditure. For example, suppose you pay cash for movies. When writing a check for "cash," also write "entertainment" at the bottom of the check. Keep the money for entertainment use in a special place in your wallet or your home.

Step Four: Use some type of filing system for your major expenditures: a file box, shoe box, envelope, or anything that works for you. Label the file with the names of the items on which you spend money regularly. For example, if you write a $25 check for food, put the grocery receipt and/or the canceled check in the envelope marked "food." If you wish to keep records of small purchases, try to record the expenditures after you purchase the items. Keeping records of haircuts, toothpaste, and other small items can become a chore. After determining your spending habits, you may be able to judge that you will need about $25 for personal needs every month. You might write a check for cash, indicating that it is for "personal needs" at the bottom of the check. This eliminates the need to keep a record of each item. Attempting to keep a record of each item purchased is one practice that leads many to abandon budgeting.

Step Five: At the end of the month, find the total amount spent in each category in your budget file. Compare your *actual* expenditures with your *estimated* expenditures. You should be able to see your spending habits at a glance and determine where you need adjustments in your budget categories. Do this for at least three months or until your budget is stabilized.

As you become more aware of your spending habits, you may possibly skip **Step Five** completely and limit the record keeping in **Step Four** to those items needed for income tax purposes and records you cannot keep track of mentally.

Skills for Consumer Success

After talking to Mr. Fernandez, Susan was not so sure about moving out of her parent's home in July. She hadn't realized the expenditures her parents took care of. If she did move out, she certainly couldn't buy a car in September and might not be able to go to college in the fall. She was already $40 over her net pay.

She wasn't ready to give up though. If she shared an apartment with three other people instead of one, her estimated rent would be divided by four: $300 divided by 4 = $75. Utilities divided by four would be less. Her parents might lend her the bedroom set she was now using, or perhaps she and her friends could find a furnished apartment. Mr. Fernandez said that 10 percent of net pay is about all anyone financially independent can save: 10 percent of $400 equals $40. She would have to put off buying the car until later because she wouldn't have the money needed for the down payment (part of the full price required at the time of purchase). Besides, if she bought a car, she would add to her monthly expenditures. She would have to make monthly car payments, buy gas, buy car insurance, and pay for maintenance.

Illustration 5-2

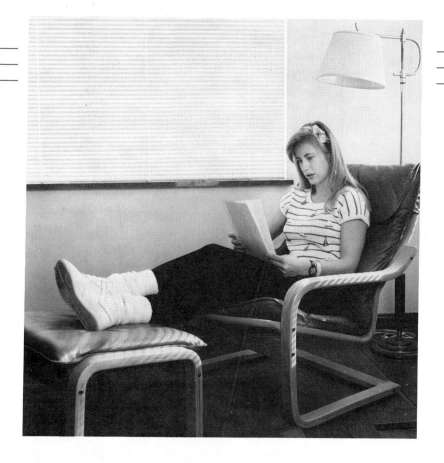

"So adjusting a budget requires some decision making," Mr. Fernandez said when Susan brought in her revised budget. "You have to decide what you want more: a car or living in your own apartment; college or a car; and so forth. One of the wonderful advantages of a budget is that it forces you to face reality. After making out a budget, you may want to change some of your goals. You may want to exchange some short-term goals for some long-term goals. For example, you may want to forfeit the car for a college education if you need a college degree for the career you have chosen.

"The biggest thing to remember is that budgets are not written in stone," said Mr. Fernandez. "You can write as many as you want and adjust them as often as you want, but all of us should set budget guidelines to help us make financially responsible decisions."

Mr. Fernandez helped Susan adjust her budget. She pretended that she was living on her own. Figure 5-5 is a record of Susan's estimated and actual expenditures for the month of July. "Over +" indicates how much she went over her estimated expenditures. "Short –" indicates how much she was under her estimated expenditures.

Figure 5-5:
Susan's Adjusted
Budget

Month: July 19 — —   Net Pay: $400

Item	Method of Payment Cash/Check		Estimated Expenditures	Actual Expenditures	Over + or Short –
Shelter (rent)*		✓	75.00	75.00	
Utilities*		✓	30.00	30.00	
Telephone*		✓	7.50	7.50	
Household Needs	✓		10.00	5.00	
Food	✓		50.00	50.00	
Eating Out	✓		20.00	35.00	
Clothes		✓	30.00	50.00	
Laundry	✓		5.00	—	
Transportation	✓		5.00	3.00	
Medical			5.00	None	
Entertainment	✓		30.00	20.00	
Personal Needs	✓		15.00	10.00	
Savings			10.00	10.00	

TOTAL AMOUNT OF EXPENDITURES: _____ _____ _____

*These items are to be split four ways.

STUDENT ACTIVITY D

1. Fill in the "Over +/ Short –" column in Figure 5–5, showing the extent to which actual expenditures were greater or less than estimated.

2. Are Susan's adjusted budget figures realistic?

   _____

   Explain. _____

   _____

3. In what areas would you make adjustments and by how much? Give reasons.

   _____

   _____

   _____

   _____

   _____

4. Would it be worth it to live in an apartment on Susan's net pay?

   _____

   Explain. _____

   _____

   _____

Susan worked hard at adjusting her budget, and she was finally happy with it. She felt a sense of accomplishment in knowing she was in charge of her own finances; she had plans for the future, and she could enjoy each day without worrying about future and unexpected bills. She even convinced her parents to allow her to prepare a family budget. You may want to help your family with a budget or prepare one for yourself as outlined in Student Activity E.

STUDENT ACTIVITY E

Choose a job in your community that you can possibly get with your education, and plan to support yourself totally on the income earned from the job. If you have a part-time job, you may choose to use the salary or wages you earn as the basis for an estimate of a full-time income. You might check the counseling office, career center, your school library, or newspaper ads for information about jobs, especially salary or wage rates.

You will be preparing a budget based on the income you would receive from the job chosen. Be sure to include the following categories on your budget: shelter, utilities, food, clothes, household and personal needs, and entertainment. Use the worksheets that follow and the budget record that appears on page 114.

a. *Shelter.* Having listed shelter as one of the items in your budget, check the newspaper for apartments, furnished and unfurnished. Choose one which you think you might be able to afford with the income stated for your budget. Write the monthly rental cost next to shelter on your budget record.

b. *Utilities.* If you have to pay utilities for your apartment, write down the cost of utilities. Ask someone to help you with an estimate of the cost of utilities each month for the apartment you select. Write the monthly utilities cost next to utilities on your budget record.

c. *Food.* For food, make a grocery list of items that you will need for one week, then multiply by four. List the items on the chart below, and record the prices. You may have to consult someone who buys groceries regularly or visit a grocery store in order to make an adequate list. Total the prices. Estimate from the list the amount your groceries will cost each month. Write your estimate next to food on your budget.

(**Note**: Do not list pork chops, ham, hamburger, etc., separately. Total the cost of each, and identify the items as meat.)

Food	Costs
_____	_____
_____	_____
_____	_____
_____	_____
_____	_____
_____	_____
_____	_____
_____	_____
_____	_____
Total	_____

d. *Clothes.* Naturally, the clothing category will vary considerably from month to month. You might buy three shirts or blouses one month and none the next. You can prepare an estimate though, by gathering current prices of clothing. List on the chart below the clothing items that you might buy in an average month. Write a monthly estimate of clothing on your budget record.

Clothing	Costs
_____	_____
_____	_____
_____	_____
_____	_____
_____	_____
_____	_____
Total	_____

e. *Household and Personal Needs.* List on the chart below items you will need monthly for your household and personal needs. You might get actual prices from a local business or from the newspaper ads. Write a monthly estimate for household and personal items on your budget record.

Household and Personal Items	Costs
_____	_____
_____	_____
_____	_____
_____	_____
_____	_____
_____	_____
Total	_____

f. *Entertainment.* List on the chart below your recreational activities and the cost of each activity. Write a monthly estimate for entertainment on your budget record.

Entertainment	Costs
_____	_____
_____	_____
_____	_____
_____	_____
_____	_____
_____	_____
Total	_____

g. Determine the cost each month for any other expenses you may have. If you expect any additional expenses, write a monthly estimate for miscellaneous items on your budget record.

Miscellaneous	Costs
_____	_____
_____	_____
_____	_____
_____	_____
_____	_____
_____	_____
Total	_____

h. Total the amount of your estimated expenses, and write the amount on your budget record.

BUDGET RECORD

Name _____

Month of _____ 19_____ Income_____

Items	Method of Payment (Cash/Check)	Estimated Expenditures	Actual Expenditures	Over + or Short −
1. _____	_____	_____	_____	_____
2. _____	_____	_____	_____	_____
3. _____	_____	_____	_____	_____
4. _____	_____	_____	_____	_____
5. _____	_____	_____	_____	_____
6. _____	_____	_____	_____	_____
7. _____	_____	_____	_____	_____
8. _____	_____	_____	_____	_____
9. _____	_____	_____	_____	_____
10. _____	_____	_____	_____	_____
11. _____	_____	_____	_____	_____
12. _____	_____	_____	_____	_____
13. _____	_____	_____	_____	_____
14. _____	_____	_____	_____	_____
15. _____	_____	_____	_____	_____
16. _____	_____	_____	_____	_____
17. _____	_____	_____	_____	_____
18. _____	_____	_____	_____	_____
19. _____	_____	_____	_____	_____
20. _____	_____	_____	_____	_____
Totals:		_____	_____	_____

Note: You may wish to photocopy this record sheet and use it for your personal budget records.

Answer the following questions about your budget.

1. Can you manage your expenditures with the income you recorded on your budget record?

_____

Skills for Consumer Success

2. If your estimated expenditures exceed your income, in which categories can you cut back?

_____

_____

3. Did you consider savings in your budget?

_____

If so, how much?

_____

Are you saving for a specific item or for future security?

_____

HOW TO PREPARE A YEARLY BUDGET

Some people like to prepare a summary budget for the year. They like to know what percentage of their budget goes for food, shelter, entertainment, and so on. This process will be helpful to you only if statistics help you change your spending habits. It bothers some people to know that they are spending 30 percent of their budget on entertainment; others do not care about percentages as long as they are staying within their planned budget. A record collection may be a necessity for some, whereas others may consider it a luxury. The important thing to remember is that you, and those who follow the budget with you, are the only ones who must abide by the budget. It is a helpful tool only if it makes your life easier, not more burdensome.

When figuring out a budget for the next year, follow the steps below.

1. Put down your estimated annual take-home pay. If you receive income by the month or the week, multiply your income by 12 (if paid monthly); by 26 (if paid every two weeks); by 52 (if paid weekly).

   Example: $600 (monthly net pay) x 12 = $7,200 (yearly take home pay).

2. Multiply monthly estimated expenditures on your budget by 12.

Item	Cost per Month	×	12	=	Yearly Budget
Shelter (rent)	300	×	12	=	$3,600

If you have kept a budget for more than one year, you can determine the average amount spent on an item by totaling the actual amount spent the previous year and dividing by 12. Determining the *average* amount spent is especially helpful for items that vary in cost from month to month. Use food as an example.

January	$170	July	$165
February	$150	August	$180
March	$165	September	$172
April	$177	October	$180
May	$180	November	$157
June	$176	December	$180

The total amount spent on food in one year was $2,052. The average amount spent on food per month was $171 ($2,052 ÷ 12 = $171).

STUDENT ACTIVITY F

1. Using Susan's monthly take-home pay recorded on page 106, what is her yearly income?

   _____

2. According to Susan's budget record for shelter, how much should she budget each year for rent?

   _____

3. If the amount she spent on entertainment varied from month to month, how would she estimate a yearly budget for entertainment?

   _____

   _____

FURTHER DISCOVERIES

1. Determine the monthly income of your parents or someone you know well. Ask them to itemize expenditures they might include in a budget. Prepare a budget for them using Mr. Fernandez's guidelines for budgeting on page 108 of this unit.

2. Budgets tend to be accurate only for recurring or regular expenditures. It is helpful for a family to have a financial plan to deal with expensive emergency expenditures. Make a list of unexpected expenditures that a family of four might experience; for example, repairs to a roof for damage caused by a severe storm. In addition, explain how each of the following situations might require a change in a family's budget. Be as specific as possible.

   a. A family that had been renting buys a house.

   b. The oldest child in the family enters college.

   c. A grandparent decides to move in with the family.

   d. The family takes a three-week vacation in Europe.

   e. The family purchases a summer cottage in the mountains.

   f. The family buys a third car because the two teenagers in the family are now driving.

3. From your local public library or other sources, try to find a copy of the current budget for the following units of government within your city or county.

   a. police or sheriff's department

   b. public library

   c. school system

d. park and recreation department

e. welfare or social service department

Find out how much money was budgeted for each of these units of government. What are the similarities and differences among the budget categories used in these budgets? Write a report on your findings.

CHECKLIST

If you have completed the student activities on budgeting, you should have mastered the skills below. Check off the skills you know, and review the ones you are not sure of.

(   ) The meaning of net pay, gross income, and fixed expenses

(   ) How to plan and organize a budget

(   ) How to record actual expenditures and compare them with monthly estimates

(   ) How to revise a budget

(   ) How to prepare a yearly budget

If you have checked all of the above skills, ask your teacher for the Susan Thompson Test on Budgeting.

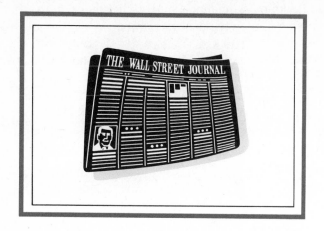

UNIT 6
INVESTMENT OPPORTUNITIES

SKILL 1   **Investing in Stocks**

SKILL 2   **Investing in Bonds**

SKILL 3   **Investing in Mutual Funds**

SKILL 4   **Understanding Other Investment Alternatives**

SKILL 5   **Investing in an IRA**

SKILL 6   **Making Investment Decisions**

Further Discoveries

"What is the difference between saving and investing?" Susan asked, as Mr. Fernandez began the next seminar.

"In my opinion, there is a real distinction," Mr. Fernandez said. Usually we *save*, or put money aside, for either short-term or long-term goals. We might save to buy a car in August or save money for college or save for the day when we might have unexpected large expenses.

"*Investing* is putting your money to work in order to earn money for you. When most people invest money, they think of it primarily as money set aside to earn more money."

Mr. Fernandez reminded the students about the three financial institutions that pay interest for the use of one's money: commercial or full service banks, savings and loan associations, and credit unions. In these institutions, the three most common types of investments are (1) regular savings accounts, (2) certificates of deposit (CDs), and (3) money market deposit accounts. See "Unit 3: Savings Accounts and Bank Services" for descriptions of each of the above.

In addition to regular savings accounts, CDs, and money market deposit accounts, there are other ways of investing. Mr. Fernandez explained some of the common forms of investments such as stocks, bonds, and mutual funds.

INVESTING IN STOCKS

"When you buy *stocks*," Mr. Fernandez said, "you buy a share in the ownership of a corporation. (A *corporation* is a business owned by many people.) In fact, you buy a certain number of *shares* at a designated price per share, depending on the value of the stock at the time you buy. For instance, you may buy 100 shares of stock at $1.00 per share. You will have invested $100. If the corporation is successful, your shares will increase in value. Let's say, the shares increase to $2.00 per share by the end of the year. You will have gained $1.00 per share or a total of $100 (100 shares × $1.00 = $100).

"Suppose, however, that the cost of shares goes down to $ .50 per share. In such a case, you will have lost $50. The important thing to remember about stocks is you never gain or lose until you sell your shares of stock. If stock prices are falling, you may want to wait until shares increase in value before you sell. If the value of your shares increase significantly, you may want to sell and reap the gain. If you sell stock for more than you paid for it, you have made what is known as a *capital gain*."

As you can see, you need some knowledge of the stock market before investing in stocks, and you should invest only money that you can afford to lose. No matter how you look at it, investing in the stock market is a calculated risk. The risk varies according to the type of stock you buy. In fact, some stocks are classified as high-risk stocks. If the corporation is successful, high-risk stocks usually gain in value very quickly. There is also a greater chance the value of the stock will fall quickly if the corporation is not successful. To minimize risk, some investors invest only in blue chip stocks. *Blue chip stocks* are stocks of corporations that have a reputation for financial stability, superior management, and a record of growth and earnings. In general, blue chips are low-risk stocks and cost more per share.

When investing in the stock market, most people go through a broker. A *broker* is a person authorized to buy and sell *securities* (namely, stocks and bonds). The broker gets a *commission*, or fee, for the service. It is possible to buy stocks through a discount brokerage. *Discount brokers* buy and sell stocks for customers for low commissions without giving investment advice. Some large banks and savings and loan associations have a service available called discount brokerage.

A broker should be chosen with great care. Remember, a broker is in the business of selling stocks. Every time the broker sells, he or she earns a fee. So you should not become totally dependent on a broker for information about a stock purchase.

There are two main markets where stocks are bought and sold. The markets are called *exchanges*. There are two national exchanges located in New York City: the *New York Stock Exchange*, the largest, and the *American Stock Exchange*. Regional stock exchanges in various large cities are connected to the national exchanges. Exchanges are sometimes referred to as *security exchanges*.

Illustration 6-1

Courtesy of the New York Stock Exchange

Stocks are bought and sold or traded at security exchanges by the *auction method*. Through brokers, *stockholders* (those who own stock) ask to sell their shares at a certain price; bidders offer to buy shares at a certain price. The sale is made when brokers on the floor of an exchange work out a price that is acceptable to both buyers and sellers. The highest, lowest, and closing prices at which stocks are traded are listed in the newspaper every business day. Official trading hours for stocks listed with an exchange are 9:30 a.m. to 4 p.m., Eastern time, Monday through Friday.

Unlisted securities are those which are not listed on any exchange. The buying and selling of these securities are called over-the-counter (OTC) transactions. OTC trades are made between brokers over the telephone or through the use of computer terminals. Transactions involving over-the-counter securities are listed in the newspaper financial section. The OTC market is the largest security market in terms of the number of stock issues traded. In this market, thousands of smaller, regional, lesser-known companies are traded.

Most investors buy shares of stock in hundreds, which is called a *round lot*. A purchase of less than 100 shares is called an *odd lot*. Small investors pay higher commissions for odd lot purchases because odd lots are harder to sell.

When you buy stocks, you buy one of two main classes: preferred stock or common stock. Investors owning *preferred stock* are promised a rate of return that, when paid, is known as a dividend. *Dividends* are the part of the profits of a corporation that each stockholder receives. Preferred stockholders have rights over holders of common stock; for example, preferred stockholders are entitled to dividends before common stockholders. Investors owning *common stock* do not receive dividends until those owning preferred stock are paid. Common stockholders do get to vote on company-related issues, however, such as the election of the corporation's board of directors and key policies affecting the outcome of the corporation.

"If you invest in stocks, you should know how to interpret the market listings that appear in the financial section of the newspaper," Mr. Fernandez told the class.

He showed them a sample from *Our Towne Daily*. Figure 6-1 shows the closing prices of some of the corporations listed on the New York Stock Exchange (NYSE).

Mr. Fernandez pointed out that there are eight columns to this partial listing of stocks on the NYSE, and he explained what each of them meant. Beginning at the left, the columns represent (1) name of the corporation (*Example*: AAR or Adams-Russell), (2) dividend, (3) price/earnings ratio—PE ratio, (4) sales in hundreds, (5) highest price per share, (6) lowest price per share, (7) price at close of stock market, and (8) change upwards or downwards from the day before.

In other words, the *name of the corporation* (1) in the first listing is AAR. The *dividend* (2) paid annually is 48 cents per share. Dividends are usually distributed quarterly, so if you own AAR stock, you will earn 12 cents per share each quarter. If you own one hundred shares, you earn $12 quarterly (.12 × 100 = $12). The *PE ratio* (3) is 15. So, the current price of a share of AAR stock is 15 times the earnings per share in the last year. Some people use the PE ratio to decide whether or not to buy a particular common stock. It is best to consult a knowledgeable broker if you are not sure what the PE indicates for the future success of the corporation. The *sales* (4) column indicates the hundreds of shares that were sold that day: 10,900 shares of AAR were sold. *High* (5) indicates the highest price per share for the day: 18¾ or $18.75 per share. *Low* (6) indicates the lowest price for the day: 18½ or $18.50 per share. *Close* (7) indicates the closing price for the day: $18.75, and *change* (8) shows the amount of increase or decrease in the price of stock from the day before. AAR stock increased by ¼ or 25 cents from the day before. If you look at yesterday's *Our Towne Daily*, you would see that the closing price of the stock was $18.50 per share.

Figure 6-1:
NYSE

	Div	PE	Sales hds	High	Low	Close	Chg
A							
AAR	.48	15	109	18¾	18½	18¾	+ ¼
AGS		13	596	17⅛	15⅞	16⅞	+1¼
AMCA	1		28	13⅝	d12⅞	13	– ¾
AMF	.50	89	572	16	15⅝	16	+ ⅛
AMR		8	17818	35¼	34	35	+1⅛
AMR	pf 2.18		51	19¾	19⅜	19¾	+ ½
AMR	pf 2.13		1801	35⅛	34¼	34⅞	+1⅜
ANR	pf 2.67		2	24	24	24	
APL		3	2	10⅞	10⅞	10⅞	+ ⅛
ASA	3		1777	50⅞	50¼	50½	+ ⅛
AVX	.32	11	696	18	17¾	18	+ ½
AblLab	1.20	13	3687	45⅜	43¾	44⅞	+1
AccoWd	s.44	18	561	22⅜	22	22¼	– ⅛
AcmeC	.40		239	16⅜	15½	16⅛	– ⅛
AcmeE	.32b	12	13	10	9⅞	9⅞	+ ⅛
AdaEx	2.11e		87	16¼	16	16⅛	+ ¼
AdmMl	.32	8	19	16⅜	16⅛	16⅜	+ ⅜
AdvSys	.811	20	427	13¼	12⅜	12½	– ½
AMD		14	4601	33½	32¼	33⅜	+1¼
Advest	.12		118	9⅞	9⅜	9⅞	+ ½
Aerflex		12	136	13⅜	13	13¼	
AetnLf	2.64	32	5324	38⅝	37¾	38⅜	+ ⅝
AetL	pf 5.87e		16	55¾	55½	55½	+ ¼
Ahmns	1.20	13	1277	30⅛	28¾	30⅛	+1⅛

STUDENT ACTIVITY A

A. Study the listings in Figure 6-1, and answer the following questions.

1. What is the day's change for AVX?

_____

2. What was the closing price of AVX per share?

_____

3. What was the closing cost yesterday?

_____

4. What was the lowest price for AVX per share today?

_____

5. What dividend is AVX paying?

_____

6. If you own 100 shares of AVX, how much would you earn in one quarter?

_____

7. Did AdvSys close up or down?

_____

8. What was the price of AdvSys stock yesterday?

_____

9. How many shares of AGS were traded today?

_____

B. Match each term below with the appropriate definition.

_____ 1. saving

_____ 2. investing

_____ 3. common stock

_____ 4. preferred stock

_____ 5. broker

_____ 6. commission

_____ 7. securities

_____ 8. exchanges

a. markets where stocks and bonds are sold
b. shareholders are promised a certain rate of return
c. fee for buying/selling of stock
d. stocks and bonds
e. putting money aside for specific short-term or long-term goals
f. individual who buys and sells stocks for others
g. putting money to work for the purpose of earning money
h. shareholders vote on company issues

INVESTING IN BONDS

A *bond* is written evidence of an obligation to pay a definite amount of money, with interest, at a specified date in the future. Every bond has printed on its front the face value and the rate of interest to be paid. Bonds, except for savings bonds, are usually sold in denominations having face values of $1,000, $5,000, or $10,000. The issuer usually pays bondholders interest twice a year.

A bond is usually considered a safe investment. Bonds are less risky than either common or preferred stocks. Bonds usually provide investors with a stable return in the form of interest income. The return or interest rate paid on bonds tends to be higher than the return on savings accounts or certificates of deposit.

One of the safest and most popular ways of investing is through U.S. savings bonds, especially Series EE and HH. *Series EE bonds* are available in denominations of $50, $75, $100, $200, $500, $1,000, $5,000, and $10,000. The purchase price is one half of the face value. For example, it takes $25 to buy a $50 EE bond. The present maturity of EE bonds is about ten years. That's how long it takes the purchase price to double at the guaranteed minimum rate of 7.5 percent on a newly issued EE bond. Series EE, however, typically pay more than the guaranteed rate. Interest on Series EE bonds can be deferred for income taxes until the bonds are cashed, which is usually at maturity.

Another type of U.S. savings bond that some investors like is the Series HH bond. *Series HH* bonds can be purchased in denominations of $500, $1,000, $5,000, and $10,000. They have a ten-year term to maturity, pay a fixed 7.5 percent interest rate, and checks for interest earned are issued by the U.S. Treasury twice a year. The interest on Series HH bonds is taxable every year. As you can see, the main difference between the Series HH and Series EE is the method in which interest is paid.

U.S. savings bonds can be purchased at commercial banks, savings and loan institutions, credit unions, and United States post offices. Some companies offer automatic payroll deductions for U.S. savings bonds. A certain amount is deducted each month for the purchase of bonds. You do not have to pay state income tax for interest earned on U.S. savings bonds.

Other securities issued by the federal government are Treasury bills, notes, and bonds. *Treasury bills* are short-term securities issued with maturities of 13 weeks, 26 weeks, and 52 weeks. More will be said about Treasury bills on page 127. *Treasury notes* and *bonds* have longer maturities than Treasury bills. Notes have a fixed maturity of not less than one year and not more than ten years from date of issue. Bonds normally have a fixed maturity of more than ten years.

Besides securities issued by the federal government, there are bonds issued by states, counties, cities, etc. These are called *municipal bonds.* Municipal bonds are generally considered safe but are really only as dependable as the issuer. Municipal bonds are exempt from federal income tax.

Corporate bonds are issued, as the name indicates, by a corporation. They are sold at different face amounts and various dates of maturity. Bondholders do have rights prior to stockholders. In other words, they will be paid interest before the stockholders are paid dividends. Corporate bonds are purchased and sold through brokers.

STUDENT ACTIVITY B

Answer *true* or *false* to the following statements.

_____ 1. When you buy a bond, you are actually borrowing money from the issuer of the bond.

_____ 2. Treasury bonds mature in more than ten years.

_____ 3. Series EE bonds are U.S. savings bonds.

_____ 4. Series HH bonds pay high interest but are very risky.

_____ 5. U.S. savings bonds must be purchased through a broker.

_____ 6. Municipal bonds are exempt from federal income tax.

_____ 7. Series EE bonds are available in any denomination desired.

INVESTING IN MUTUAL FUNDS

A *mutual fund*, also called an open-end investment company, is a corporation that sells its own stock to buy the securities of other companies and organizations. Mr. Fernandez told the seminar that mutual funds are popular because they offer the small investor the opportunity to indirectly own an interest in several different corporations. Essentially, a mutual fund works in the following way. Instead of buying $1,000 worth of shares in one company, you buy $1,000 worth of shares in a mutual fund. The management of that fund pools your money with that of others to invest in a group of securities. The management of the fund determines all investment strategies, such as when to buy and sell securities.

A fund receives dividends and interest from the money it invests. When a fund makes a gain from the sale of stocks owned by the fund, proceeds from dividends and gains on the sale of stock are distributed to shareholders of the fund. A small portion of the earnings of a fund are used to cover its operating expenses.

The advantages of this type of investment are as follows:

1. Your money is managed by investment professionals.

2. Your risk (the chance of a loss) is reduced through ownership of a diversified group of securities.

3. You can hold securities that you could never afford to own as a small investor.

Mutual funds should be investigated before investing. The success of the mutual fund depends upon how well it is managed. Therefore, seek advice from a trusted broker or financial advisor or read about mutual funds in publications such as the *Wall Street Journal, Money, Changing Times, Consumer Reports,* and the like before making a decision. The reputation and success of the mutual fund should be checked out thoroughly.

STUDENT ACTIVITY C

1. What is the essential difference between buying shares of stock in a corporation and buying into a mutual fund?

_____

_____

_____

2. Name two advantages of mutual funds.

    a. _____

    b. _____

3. Name two sources of information about mutual funds.

    a. _____

    b. _____

UNDERSTANDING OTHER INVESTMENT ALTERNATIVES

In addition to stocks, bonds, and mutual funds, there are other investment alternatives. Among these are U.S. Treasury bills, real estate, collectibles, and investment clubs.

A *Treasury bill* is a one-year or less (short-term) federal government obligation. Treasury bills are sold weekly for three- and six-month maturities, and monthly for one-year maturities. Treasury bills may be purchased for a minimum of $10,000 through a commercial bank, directly from a Federal Reserve Bank, or your broker. Treasury bills are considered very safe investments since they are backed by the United States government.

Real estate is another means of investing money. The first type of real estate investment for most people is a home. Buying a home is considered to be an investment because a home can increase in value and, therefore, increase the value of your assets.

Illustration 6-2

In addition to buying a home, some people invest in real estate such as commercial buildings, apartment buildings, or land for the purpose of gaining additional income. A building may produce rental income. Undeveloped land may increase in value.

Buying real estate as an investment is not a simple matter, however. There are risks involved that should be evaluated carefully before a decision is made to purchase real estate.

Collectibles such as jewelry, art, antiques, gold and silver, and the like are considered investments. If bought solely as investments, the risk lies in whether or not the objects will increase in value. It is essential to know something about (1) the worth of the object at the time of purchase, and (2) the probability of the object increasing in value. Most of the time we can only guess about the future value of a collectible, but it should be an educated guess at the very least.

Investment clubs have been set up around the country as another way of investing money. An *investment club* consists of a small group organized to study stocks and invest members' money. Members have regular meetings to study and discuss certain stocks. They pool their money and invest as a group in particular stocks. The members share in the earnings, expenses, and losses of the club. These clubs are a good way for small investors to learn about stocks and the stock market.

STUDENT ACTIVITY D

Complete the statements below by filling in the correct word or phrase.

1. A _____ is sold for a minimum price of $10,000.

2. Buying a home is considered an investment in _____.

3. Before buying collectibles as an investment, it is important to know their _____ at the time of purchase; and the probability of the object _____.

4. Members of _____ pool their money to invest as a group.

INVESTING IN AN IRA

Everyone should make provisions for retirement income. Social security (to be discussed in Unit 7) provides some income for many retired people, but the income provided is often not enough and was never intended to be a sole means of support. Frequently, places of employment offer pension plans that supplement social security income.

In 1981, the Economic Recovery Tax Act allowed individuals, even those covered by employer-sponsored retirement plans, to establish what is known as an IRA (Individual Retirement Account). Anyone earning wages or a salary can invest $2,000 a year in an IRA. An individual can deduct up to $2,000 a year from his or her gross (total) income when filing a federal income tax return.

The earnings on the investment are tax deferred (that is, tax-free until the earnings are withdrawn at age 59½ or later). By retirement age, people have lower incomes; therefore, people pay less income taxes than they would if working. The law requires that withdrawals begin by age 70½.

If you withdraw money from an IRA before age 59½, the amount withdrawn is taxed as ordinary income for the year in which it is withdrawn, and in addition, the Internal Revenue Service assesses a 10 percent penalty tax on the amount. Because of this penalty, it is best to think of money in an IRA as money to invest and reinvest but not to spend.

An IRA must be opened with a custodian—an individual or institution responsible for controlling money invested. An IRA can be moved from custodian to custodian—from a bank to a mutual fund, for example— without incurring the tax penalty as long as you reinvest the money within 60 days before it becomes taxable. That's what's called a rollover. In a *rollover*, you close one account with a custodian and put your money into a new account with another custodian. You are allowed to roll over money deposited in an IRA only once each year.

You can make contributions to your IRA until the deadline for filing income taxes. For example, you'll have until April 15 to deposit IRA money for the previous calendar year. It's wise, however, to make your contribution as early in the year as you can since you will immediately begin to earn tax-deferred income and to compound it.

STUDENT ACTIVITY E

1. Give two advantages of investing in an IRA.

   a. _____

   b. _____

2. How much can an individual earning a salary invest in an IRA per year?

   _____

3. Explain a rollover.

   _____

   _____

   _____

MAKING INVESTMENT DECISIONS

"Before deciding on types of investments to make, you should set goals," Mr. Fernandez said. "Your goals will change as you reach different points in your life. As a young person, you may be able to wait many years for a piece of undeveloped land to increase in value. At 55, you may wish to make investments that will increase in value within a short period of time."

In general, the following guidelines will help you make wise investment decisions at any age.

1. Examine your *personal needs*. Decide how much you are willing and able to invest. Your decision about how and where to invest depends primarily on three factors.

   a. Your willingness to take a risk

   b. Your financial ability to take a risk

   c. Your careful investigation of investment possibilities

   Basically, before investing for the long term, you should have enough money set aside in a savings account to take care of your immediate needs, whether an emergency or otherwise.

2. Assess the *stability of the return* and the *potential for the investment to grow in value*. Many investors want their investments to earn good returns. Such investors are very concerned with receiving interest or dividends regularly. Most investors in stocks, real estate, or collectibles would like to see the value of their investment increase in value over a period of time.

3. Consider *safety of the principal*. In investing, *principal* refers to the amount of money that is invested. The safety of the principal is more important than a satisfactory return. If the principal is lost, there will be no income. At no age level do you want to invest most or all of your savings in high-risk securities.

4. Determine the *liquidity*. Liquidity refers to the ease and speed of converting your investment into cash without losing money. In some cases, invested money can be easily turned into cash without loss of principal. A passbook savings account or money market account is probably the most liquid form of an investment. In other cases, it may take weeks or even months to obtain cash for some investments. Even then, the investment may have to be sold at a loss. Examples of investments that are not very liquid include real estate and collectibles. If you want liquidity, you may have to accept a relatively low rate of return on your investment.

Having seriously considered four major guidelines for investing, you can set investment goals according to your individual situation. You may want to accrue a certain amount of money by age thirty, or invest for a long-term goal, such as retirement. Whatever the case, it is important to set goals, for your personal goals will determine the kinds of investment decisions you make.

In making investment decisions, there are publications available which may help you do a better job of investing. Some of the more popular publications are *Moody's Manuals, Value Line, Standard and Poor's,* the *Wall Street Journal, Barron's,* and *Forbes.* Most can be found in any public library.

Illustration 6-3

Moody's, Value Line, and Standard and Poor's devote at least a page or more to helpful ratings of various corporations. The Wall Street Journal is a financial newspaper published daily. Barron's and Forbes are well-known business magazines. Barron's is published once a week. Forbes is a bimonthly magazine. Both give valuable investment information.

STUDENT ACTIVITY F

A. Name four investment guidelines.

1. _____

2. _____

3. _____

4. _____

B. Name four publications that include information on investing.

1. _____

2. _____

3. _____

4. _____

FURTHER DISCOVERIES

1. Using the financial section of your newspaper or the Wall Street Journal, chart the rise and fall of five stocks you are interested in. Prepare the chart for five consecutive days. Your family may be interested in following the progress of the stocks with you. Use the chart below.

Name of Stock	Date	Closing Price					Change (+, −)				
		1	*2*	*3*	*4*	*5*	*1*	*2*	*3*	*4*	*5*

2. State several investment goals for yourself at age twenty. Identify the types of investments that will most likely help you achieve your goals.

CHECKLIST

If you have completed all the student activities in this unit, you should have mastered the skills below. Check off the skills you know, and review the ones you are not sure of.

(   ) How to determine the differences between saving and investing

(   ) How to choose between stocks and bonds

(   ) How to interpret stock listings

(   ) How to invest in stocks

(   ) How to invest in various types of bonds

(   ) How and when to invest in mutual funds

(   ) How to choose among several investment alternatives

(   ) How to determine the advantages of IRAs

(   ) How to set guidelines for investment goals

If you have checked all of the above skills, ask your teacher for the Susan Thompson Test on Investment Opportunities.

UNIT 7
INSURANCE: HEALTH/LIFE/ SOCIAL

SKILL 1 Buying Health Insurance

SKILL 2 Buying Life Insurance

SKILL 3 Knowing about Protection Through Social Security

Further Discovery

Mr. Fernandez devoted the next two seminars to the topic of insurance. Before explaining the types of insurance in detail, he took time to define some terms that are basic to an understanding of all types of insurance. He began by asking if anyone could tell him the purpose of insurance.

Carlos was the first to raise his hand. He told several horror stories about friends of his who were caught without insurance, but the worst was his uncle who lost everything in a flash flood. "He didn't have a dime of insurance," Carlos said.

"How would you define insurance, then?" Mr. Fernandez asked Carlos.

"I'd say it's a promise you'll get repaid for what you lose," Carlos answered.

"That's a pretty accurate definition," Mr. Fernandez said. "If you have insurance, you have an agreement (or contract) with a company that promises to reimburse you for financial losses—whether that loss is the result of poor health (health insurance), death (life insurance), a car accident (auto insurance), or property damage (homeowners' insurance). These are the four basic areas of our lives for which we generally need insurance."

Mr. Fernandez went to the board and wrote the terms and definitions that apply to all types of insurance.

policy — an insurance contract

premium — amount paid for insurance

insured — person or persons covered by the policy

policyholder — person who purchases the insurance policy

insurance agent or broker — person who sells insurance

insurable interest — financial interest a person has in the life of another or in property

coverage — items or circumstances for which the insured is promised payment

benefits — payments for losses

claims — formal requests for payment of amount due as a result of loss

BUYING HEALTH INSURANCE

Susan and her classmates had given little thought to any kind of insurance, let alone health insurance. Susan was typical of most other young people in her thoughts about illness and hospitals. The worst illness that she had experienced was a week-long battle with the flu. Even then she had not thought of expenses, but only of the day she could get out of bed again. Even young people who have been seriously ill do not always realize the cost of medical care.

Susan was surprised when her father told her that she should consider buying health insurance because she would no longer be covered by the family's insurance policy if she decided to live on her own. Susan had not thought about the risk of getting sick, but as her father explained, few people do until they are actually ill. Her father said that one week in the hospital could wipe her out financially. Susan had no savings to speak of, and she certainly would not be assured of an income if absent from work too long because of illness.

Mr. Fernandez explained that health insurance is based on the concept of sharing risks. Most people plan ahead for the risk of an accident or illness by buying health insurance. No matter how careful we are, there is no way to eliminate the risk of accident or illness entirely. Since we cannot eliminate risks completely, we periodically pay a small amount of money to an insurance company to cover the expenses of an accident or illness.

Susan learned that there are hundreds of health insurance companies and many types of coverage from which to choose. The decision to buy health insurance is a relatively easy one, but deciding which company to buy from and the amount of coverage to buy are different matters. Comparison shopping is as important when buying health insurance as when buying clothes, a car, or any other item. Many people think insurance *premiums* are about the same for every company. This is not true. There are substantial differences in costs of premiums for the same coverage, so the consumer should shop around for cost differences. Many insurance agents are not likely to dwell on the cost of premiums. It is up to the buyer to check for the best premium for the coverage desired. At least two or three health insurance companies should be compared for premium differences before a policy is bought. Most people can't afford *not* to shop around.

Another consideration in shopping for insurance is the reliability of the company. Check in *Best's Insurance Reports*, which can be found in most libraries, for ratings of insurance companies in which you are interested. *Best's Insurance Reports* rates insurance companies on management practices, financial stability (Is the company about to go out of business?), cost of premiums, and so forth.

While investigating the reliability of the company, check the company's *loss ratio*; that is, the percentage of health insurance premiums that the company pays to policyholders as benefits. As a general rule, one should probably avoid companies that do not have a loss ratio of at least 50 percent. The company with less than 50 percent loss ratio may be reluctant to pay claims. The last thing a person needs when ill is an insurance company that is slow in paying claims.

There are exceptions to the rule of 50 percent loss ratio, however. An extremely high loss ratio may mean the company is in financial trouble and may have to raise its premiums to stay in business. A low loss ratio from a new company may simply mean that the policyholders have made few claims.

Finally, when checking the reliability of a company, make sure the company is licensed by your state. If not, your state department of insurance may not be able to help you in settling any unpaid claims.

Shopping for the best buy among health insurance companies involves more than comparing the premiums and the reliability of the company. One of the most important factors of a health insurance policy is coverage. Essentially, health insurance coverage can be listed in three categories.

1. *Basic hospital/surgical/physician* coverage includes payment for a hospital room (usually semiprivate), doctor's visits to your room, surgeon's fees, and operating room costs. Some policies pay almost the full cost of hospitalization; other policies pay only a part of the cost.

2. *Major medical* usually covers services not provided by a basic plan. It is back-up protection for hospital/surgical/physician coverage, usually picking up just about where basic coverage ends. The policy covers serious and costly accidents and prolonged illnesses. Major medical often covers such items as blood, physical therapy, and treatment of mental illness. Since the risk of serious illness is slight, the extra cost for major medical coverage is less than most people think and well worth the additional premium.

Illustration 7-1

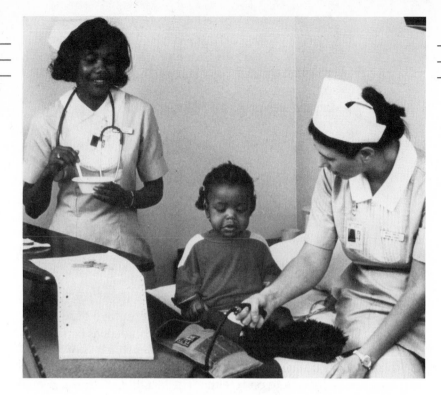

Courtesy of International Business Machines Corporation

3. *Disability income insurance* pays a portion of your salary when you are unable to work because of illness or injury. Policies will vary in several respects. These include the amount of income paid; how long the policy will be in effect (one year, two years, to age 65, lifetime); the waiting period required before payments begin; and the definition of disability. Therefore, the policy should be understood before disability insurance is taken.

The more Mr. Fernandez talked about insurance, the more Susan realized how important it is to understand the insurance contract, or policy. Everyone advises buyers to be sure to read the policy carefully. While that is certainly sound advice, it is not always easy to do. The policy is a legal document, however, enforceable in a court of law, so it is important to understand what you are buying. If you are totally confused by a policy or unsure of some provision, you may wish to seek legal advice. Have an attorney interpret the policy for you. If you cannot afford an attorney, check the legal aid society or a similar agency in the telephone directory. Many communities offer such legal assistance free or for a minimal fee.

Health insurance policies may include all kinds of *provisions*, but most will include the following: maximum coverage, renewability, deductibles, co-insurance premiums, exclusions, and other special limits.

Maximum coverage is the most money a company will pay a policyholder in benefits. Obviously, the higher the maximum coverage, the better. Usually an increase in the premium is small compared to the increase in coverage. For example, a $10-a-year increase in premiums may increase a $50,000 lifetime maximum to $150,000. Check to see if the maximum coverage applies to each illness. If you have $50,000 maximum coverage per illness, it is far more valuable than a $50,000 lifetime maximum. Some policies have *unlimited coverage* (no limit to the amount they will pay).

Renewability refers to the provisions for renewing a policy. *Guaranteed renewability* means that a policy will be renewed unless a person cancels the policy, gives false information on the application, stops paying the premiums, or the insurance company goes out of business. The least preferable provision is *optional renewability*, which means that a company can cancel a policy at a premium due date or at the end of a specified period for some reason.

Deductible refers to the amount of money a person must contribute before the insurance company will make any payments. Many companies have $100 to $500 deductible policies, which means the insured person pays the first $100 to $500 before the company makes any payments. The time limit before a person has to pay another deductible is called the *benefit period*, which is usually one year.

Be sure that you understand how the deductible works. Deductibles can apply to each separate illness, or they can be an annual amount. If you have to pay a $200 deductible for each illness, you are worse off financially than if you pay the $200 once each year.

Co-insurance means the policyholder must share in expenses above and beyond the deductible. The higher the deductible and co-insurance provisions, the lower the premiums.

The policy may include a 20 percent co-payment, which means the policyholder pays 20 percent of the medical costs. The insurance company pays 80 percent. As an example, suppose the charge for a one-day hospital visit comes to $400. If the insurance pays 80 percent above a $100 deductible, the out-of-pocket expenses would come to $160 ($100 deductible plus 20 percent of $300).

Premiums vary according to your age at the time you buy the policy, the area in which you live, the amount of your deductible, and the coverage of the policy. Your sex also affects the premium because men are hospitalized less often than women. In addition, premiums usually increase as the cost of hospitalization and medical care rises.

Exclusions refer to specific conditions listed in the policy for which the insurance company will not provide coverage. An example of an exclusion might be cosmetic surgery, except to remedy the results of an accident. Exclusions are often contained in clauses within the policy, which is another reason why the buyer should read the policy carefully and make sure it is understood.

Read the policy also for other *limits*, sometimes called *internal limits*. Some internal limits include a *ceiling* (limit) on how much will be paid for hospital rooms, operations, doctor's fees, and so forth. Some policies contain fixed dollar limits. This means that the insurance company will pay a fixed amount for certain medical procedures.

Good policies generally will take over the entire cost of an increasing medical bill. For example, after a $100 deductible, your policy may pay 80 percent of the bill up to $1,000. After your out-of-pocket expenses reach a total of $1,000, the insurance company pays 100 percent of any additional expenses.

Mr. Fernandez gave the following advice about buying a health insurance policy.

1. Always be truthful on health application forms. If you lie about a past medical problem, such as diseases in the family (heart, cancer, diabetes, etc.), the company considers this to be *concealment* (unlawful withholding of information). A future claim may be rejected, or your policy may be canceled.

2. Be aware of any riders in the policy. A *rider* is a specific exclusion in certain types of policies. If you have a history of drug or alcohol addiction, the insurance company may add a rider to your policy excluding coverage for any loss resulting from these conditions. Or the company may include the coverage and raise your premiums.

3. Be cautious about dropping a policy for another one. It is far better to do your homework on health insurance companies before you take out a policy. If you switch policies, you may pay higher premiums.

4. Check to see if group insurance is available for you. *Group policies* are offered to members of a group working for the same organization or belonging to the same association. Group policies are usually cheaper and offer more coverage. The one disadvantage of group insurance is that it ends when you leave the group—when you resign or retire. A person should investigate whether a group policy can be converted to an individual policy and at what expense.

Mr. Fernandez mentioned three other aspects of health protection that he thought members of the seminar would be interested in: dental insurance, workers' compensation, and health maintenance organizations.

Dental care insurance has become a common feature of health protection. *Dental insurance* pays for dental care such as routine examinations, x-rays, fillings, as well as major dental work. Dental plans differ: some pay the entire bill, but most require a deductible and co-insurance.

Workers' compensation is health insurance provided by the state government for employees who suffer injuries or illness as a result of their working conditions. Under state workers' compensation laws, most employers are required to pay for job-related accidents and illnesses.

The benefits provided through workers' compensation vary from state to state. Some states pay all medical expenses; others have a limitation to what they will pay. There is usually a waiting period before the employee receives benefits, just as there is with private disability income insurance.

If the employee is unable to return to work, a proportion of his or her wages are paid as benefits. The amount paid is usually about two-thirds of the employee's normal wages. Benefits are also paid to dependents (spouse and children) if the employee is killed on the job. Benefits for death or injury of a worker are generally paid regardless of whether the employer or employee was at fault.

Because of rising medical costs, alternative sources of health care have developed, such as health maintenance organizations (HMOs). *HMOs* are organizations made up of doctors, nurses, lab technicians, and other medical professionals, and are generally associated with particular local hospitals. Members of HMOs are charged a set monthly fee (sometimes less than the monthly premiums of conventional health insurance policies). In addition, part of the fee is frequently paid by employers.

Illustration 7-2

There are two basic types of HMOs: group and individual practice. Group HMOs use a central medical center where members go for all types of treatment: shots, x-rays, routine checkups, etc. Members of individual practice HMOs go to their individual doctors for treatment and to locations outside HMO centers for x-rays, prescriptions, therapy, and so forth. In both cases, one monthly fee covers all medical costs.

One of the often-cited advantages of HMOs is the emphasis they put on preventive medical care. Because they do not have to pay extra for office visits, regular checkups, or x-rays, members are inclined to use these services on a regular basis and, therefore, tend to avoid unexpected serious illness. Keeping people out of the hospital is good business for HMOs and good health for its members.

Another advantage of HMOs is the convenience. For some plans, you may go to only one health center for treatment. And then, you only show your HMO membership card, rather than fill out endless insurance forms.

One word of caution: In the mid-1970s HMOs were accused of scrimping on health care in order to save money. As a result, the federal government has set up controls regarding HMOs as well as all of the health-care industry. Still, you should check out the plans in your area before joining any HMO.

STUDENT ACTIVITY A

1. Match each term below with the appropriate definition.

_____ 1. rider

_____ 2. premium

_____ 3. disability income insurance

_____ 4. loss ratio

_____ 5. major medical insurance

_____ 6. deductible

_____ 7. benefit period

_____ 8. co-insurance

_____ 9. claim

_____ 10. coverage

a. formal request for payment

b. the amount paid for insurance coverage

c. provides payments when a person is unable to work

d. a specific exclusion in certain policies

e. time span before a person pays another deductible

f. items or circumstances for which insured is promised payment

g. the amount a person must pay before the company makes payments toward expenses

h. percentage of premiums that an insurance company pays on all claims

i. policyholder must share in expenses above the deductible

j. coverage for serious and costly accidents and illnesses

2. Three basic types of health insurance coverage, along with special provisions, have been described. In the cases below, name the coverage (and any special provision) that was needed in each situation.

a. Ann Stumpf was the leading forward on her basketball team. In the championship game she fell and seriously injured her spine. She was hospitalized for two months and still returns weekly for physical therapy. What type of insurance would have paid for most of her care?

_____

b. Skipper Schmidt, 25, said he was too young to have health insurance. One night Skipper Schmidt thought he was dying with a pain in his side. As it turned out, Skipper was not dying, but an emergency appendectomy forced him to take out a loan to pay for the operation. What kind of coverage would have paid for Skipper's operation?

_____

c. Tonia Treadaway's husband died, leaving her with three children to support. He had a $50,000 life insurance policy, so she felt reasonably secure. Last year Tonia had an accident at work which paralyzed her completely. What type of insurance would have helped Tonia?

_____

d. After 20 years of carrying health insurance with Company B, Ted Hennessy had a heart attack. After paying for medical expenses of $20,000, Company B canceled Ted's policy. What provision in the policy should Ted have checked?

_____

3. Answer *true* or *false* to the following statements.

_____ a. All reputable insurance plans include dental insurance.

_____ b. HMOs are sometimes less expensive than conventional health insurance.

_____ c. Workers' compensation is health insurance provided by the federal government.

_____ d. To join an HMO you must always be willing to give up your family doctor.

_____ e. Benefits through workers' compensation are the same throughout the United States.

BUYING LIFE INSURANCE

The second type of insurance Mr. Fernandez discussed was life insurance: "Even though you may have no intention of buying a life insurance policy at your age, you still need to know about it because you will be approached about life insurance sooner than you think."

Mr. Fernandez said that before buying any type of insurance, a person should take the time to identify one's needs. Unfortunately, when it comes to life insurance, many people just assume they need it. There are several factors, however, that should be considered when deciding on the need for life insurance.

1. What are my family's future financial obligations? Are there young children who have to be supported and educated? Will my spouse be supported if I die? Are my family's financial obligations greater now than they will be 20 years from now?

2. What are my present assets? How much do I have in a savings account? Do I own a home? A car? How will my home be paid for if I should die before it is paid for? Do I own any other property?

3. Will a rise in living costs make financial independence difficult for my family?

4. What might be the benefits from social security? *Social security* that provides income for a spouse and children of a deceased person if the deceased contributed to social security as a wage earner. Most social security benefits are far from adequate if not supplemented by other income. See additional information about social security on page 145.

Mr. Fernandez said that after determining the need for life insurance, the next step is to decide what type of life insurance you want. The basic choice is between a *term-insurance policy*, which provides protection only, and a *cash-value policy*, which combines protection plus savings.

Term insurance, as the name implies, insures your life for a specified number of years, such as five or ten years. If the insured person dies within the stated term, the *beneficiary* (a person named in the policy) receives the amount designated in the policy. If a person lives beyond the term of the policy and wants continued coverage, the policy must be renewed for another term. Term policies do not provide for savings; you cannot accumulate cash with a term policy as you can with a cash-value policy. With term policies, you pay for protection only.

There are variations within term policies. The *convertible term policy* can be converted into a cash-value policy. After a time period, some companies allow a term policy to be converted into a cash-value policy without a new medical examination. The buyer should read the policy carefully for this provision. Other variations include *level term policies*, whereby your premiums and your dollar coverage remain the same the entire time the policy is in effect. With a *decreasing term policy*, your premiums remain the same but the dollar coverage of the policy gets smaller each year.

A term policy should be examined for renewability. Is *guaranteed renewability* one of the provisions of the policy, or is the option of renewal entirely up to the insurance company? If renewability is not guaranteed and you develop a serious illness, you might not be able to buy a life insurance policy from the same company after the term has expired.

The premiums for term policies are usually much lower than the premiums for an equivalent amount of cash-value insurance. Low premiums are one of the attractions of term insurance for some people. Often a young family with a limited income can more easily afford the premiums of a term policy. By the time the premiums increase, the family income has usually increased.

There are different types of *cash-value* life insurance policies. The most common is *whole life*, often called *straight life* or *ordinary life*. It is a policy for which you pay the same premium your entire life. If you are still alive at age 100, the policy ends, and you receive the *cash value* of the policy. The cash value at age 100 would equal the face value of the policy. In other words, if you purchased a $50,000 policy and you are still alive at 100, you will receive $50,000, the face value or full amount of the policy. The cash value grows slowly and eventually becomes as large as the face value. If you die before age 100, the beneficiary of the policy receives $50,000.

There are variations in the whole life policies. One common variation is *limited-payment life*, sometimes referred to as *paid-up whole life*. With limited-payment policies, the insurance protection lasts for life, but the premium payments stop at a certain age, such as 65. Naturally, the shorter the payment period, the higher the payments.

Another variation is *modified whole life*. This is typically a cash-value policy in which the premiums are lower in the early years of payment on the policy and increase later, rather than remain level or constant throughout the life of the policy.

The *endowment* plan is another form of cash-value life insurance, which protects the insured for a stated number of years. At the end of the time period, the full amount (face value) of the policy is paid to the policyholder, and the insurance ends. If the insured dies before the end of the period, the full amount is paid to the beneficiary when a claim is filed. The endowment plan is the most expensive form of life insurance from the standpoint of the cost of premiums.

One of the major advantages of cash-value policies is that in addition to protection, the policy is building cash value annually. *Cash value* is the amount of money that will be paid to the policyholder if the policy is terminated. If the cash value of your policy is $2000 after five years, you will receive that amount if you cancel the policy. In contrast, if you cancel a *term* policy for any reason after five years, you will receive no money. However, remember that the premiums for cash-value policies are higher than those of term policies. Therefore, you will have put more money into a cash-value policy in five years than you will have put into a term policy.

Cash-value policies offer other advantages as well:

1. *Low-interest loans.* The policyholder can borrow from the insurance company an amount equal to the cash value of the policy. The interest rate will be much lower than if you borrowed the money from a bank or savings and loan association. The amount borrowed, however, is subtracted from the total amount received if the insured dies. In other words, the cash value of the policy is reduced.

2. If you fail to pay a premium, the company will probably pay it for you out of the available cash value of your policy. This special provision is called an *automatic premium loan.* As with any loan, interest must be paid.

3. If you cancel a policy, you can collect the accumulated cash value of the policy.

Mr. Fernandez compiled a chart that summarized the advantages and disadvantages of term and cash-value policies.

	Term			*Cash Value*	
	Advantages	*Disadvantages*		*Advantages*	*Disadvantages*
	1. Cheapest premiums	1. Offers protection only; no savings		1. Offers life-long protection	1. Not until 2d or 3d year does policy acquire cash value
	2. More afford-able during years when protection is most needed and income is lowest	2. Sometimes not renewable without a med-ical examina-tion		2. Low-interest loans	2. Interest is earned at low rate on cash value

(continued next page)

Term		Cash Value	
Advantages	*Disadvantages*	*Advantages*	*Disadvantages*
3. Usually, option of renewability and conversion to whole life policy		3. Cash-value payment if policy is canceled	3. Face amount of policy cannot be increased in many cases

Mr. Fernandez told Susan's class about a special type of life insurance that is a combination of term and cash-value insurance. It is called *universal life*. Here is how it works. The premiums paid are put into a fund from which the insurance company charges for insurance protection—in this case, term insurance—and for certain fees and expenses in administering the policy. After these charges are deducted, the money remaining in the fund earns interest for the policyholder, usually at a rate higher than that paid on traditional cash-value insurance policies.

Universal life has the following advantages over other types of policies:

1. The policyholder can vary premium payments as long as a certain minimum is contributed.

2. The interest rate is disclosed and generally better than cash-value policy rates.

3. The policyholder can withdraw the accumulated cash value and borrow against the policy without discontinuing it.

4. The face value of the policy can be raised or lowered without the writing of a new policy.

To close his discussion of life insurance, Mr. Fernandez gave three general rules to follow with regard to buying life insurance:

1. *Assess your need for life insurance at each stage of the life cycle.* For example, most college students do not need life insurance. However, if you are married and have a child, you probably do. When you are 65 and your spouse can be guaranteed a good source of income if you should die, you may need little or no life insurance.

2. After determining your need for life insurance, decide on the amount needed. A general rule is to *buy about five times your net income.* If you take home $15,000 a year, you should buy about $75,000 worth of life insurance in order for your spouse and/or family to live comfortably after your death. As your income increases, you will periodically need to assess the amount of coverage your policy provides.

3. As a general rule, *do not use life insurance for investment purposes.* Life insurance is for the protection of dependents (those left behind after your death). You can save money by buying term insurance and investing the money saved on lower-cost term insurance.

STUDENT ACTIVITY B

Mr. Fernandez listed the basic forms of life insurance policies as follows: (a) term, (b) whole life, (c) limited payment, (d) modified whole life, (e) endowment, and (f) universal life. Place the letter(s) for the correct form of life insurance before the statement below.

_____ 1. costs less than the other types of insurance

_____ 2. cheapest form of cash-value insurance

_____ 3. premiums can be raised or lowered

_____ 4. premiums paid for a stated number of years, after which the policy is paid for life

_____ 5. face amount of policy can be lowered or increased without discontinuing the policy

_____ 6. premiums lower in early years of payment on the policy

_____ 7. when policy matures, the policyholder is paid the full amount of the policy

_____ 8. offers protection and savings

_____ 9. has no cash value

_____ 10. interest rate is disclosed

KNOWING ABOUT PROTECTION THROUGH SOCIAL SECURITY

Before concluding the session on health and life insurance, Mr. Fernandez told the students about social security. In 1935 the United States government started the social security system as a relatively simple program for retired workers, their survivors, and the unemployed. Since the 1930s, the program has been expanded to include disability insurance and health insurance.

To support the system, employees pay part of their wages into a special fund (employers contribute an equal amount to the fund). The government acts as "trustee" of the fund and pays benefits to eligible persons when they qualify for their share of the money. In essence, workers of today contribute money into the fund, and the money is paid out in benefits to retired persons who contributed their money years ago. When today's workers retire, they'll be supported in turn by payments coming from the next generation of contributors to social security.

Retirement Income. Social security is probably best known for its retirement program. The amount of benefits a retiree receives depends on his or her age at retirement and the amount of earnings covered by social security during working years. Reduced benefits are paid for early retirement at age 62. At age 65, a person can retire and receive full benefits. When a retired worker continues to earn wages after retirement, benefits are reduced or eliminated. If a retiree's wages exceed a certain limit, ben-

Illustration 7-3

efits are reduced by $1 for every $2 of earnings above the limit. After age 72, the retired worker can earn any amount of money without having social security retirement benefits reduced.

Mr. Fernandez emphasized that social security should not be the primary source of income for retirement years. The social security retirement program should be considered supplementary retirement income at best. As soon as a person begins to work, one should become aware of alternative sources of retirement income, such as company-sponsored pension plans, IRAs, and the like.

Disability Insurance. In 1954 disability insurance was added to the social security program. If you have paid into the system long enough to qualify and can prove that you are physically or mentally incapable of work, you are qualified to receive the same benefits you would receive at age 65. Also, dependents (spouse and children under 18) may receive the same benefits they would receive if the disabled individual were 65 years old.

Unemployment Insurance. Under the Social Security Act of 1935, each state must have an unemployment insurance program. The program is operated in cooperation with the federal government. Each state sets up its own eligibility requirements and determines the amounts to be received as benefits. Employers, rather than employees, must contribute to the state unemployment fund. To qualify for unemployment benefits in most states, a worker must fulfill certain requirements:

1. Be unemployed through no fault of his/her own.

2. Register at a public employment office for a job.

3. Make a claim for unemployment benefits.

4. Be able and available for work.

5. Be employed for the minimum length of time specified by state law.

6. Have been employed in occupations covered by the unemployment law.

Health Insurance. In 1965 health insurance was added to the social security system. There are two forms of social security health insurance: (1) *Medicare* for persons 65 and over, and (2) *Medicaid* for individuals who are unable to pay for medical expenses, regardless of age. The federal government shares with states the cost of providing health care to needy people.

Medicare has restrictions, which change from time to time, on how much the government will pay. In addition, there are deductibles and time limits on hospital stays. Again, Mr. Fernandez stressed that total dependence on Medicare in old age could be disastrous. Possible illness in one's later years should be supplemented by a private health insurance plan.

Life Insurance or Survivor's Insurance. If a worker covered by social security dies, two types of benefits are paid: (a) a lump-sum of $255 for burial, and (2) monthly payments to the surviving spouse and/or children. To receive the lump payment, you have to file within two years of a person's death. If there are no surviving children or spouse, no one is eligible for the benefit.

Monthly payments are made to the following survivors:

1. Unmarried children who are full-time elementary or secondary students and who have not attained age 19. Unmarried children 18 or older in college are not eligible.

2. Unmarried children 18 or over who are disabled before age 22 and are still disabled.

3. Widow or widower 60 or older.

4. Widow, widower, or surviving divorced mother caring for worker's child under 16.

5. Widow or widower 50 or older who becomes disabled not later than 7 years after worker's death or within 7 years after he or she stops getting checks for worker's children.

6. Dependent parents who are 62 or older.

To conclude his discussion of social security, Mr. Fernandez asked the students who have social security cards to raise their hands. Susan had a card with her number on it because she had to apply for one when she went to work at Connie's Cafe. Mr. Fernandez asked Susan for her card so he could show it to the class (see Figure 7-1).

Figure 7-1:
**Social Security
Card**

"Notice Susan's social security number consists of nine digits," Mr. Fernandez said. "You may have exactly the same name as someone else, but your social security number is always unique—it is yours for life. The Social Security Administration records, under that number, all your earnings and the amount you paid into the system throughout your working life. The amount you or your survivors will receive in benefits when you die, retire, or become disabled is determined by your contributions. Also, the Internal Revenue Service (IRS) uses your social security number as a taxpayer identification number for processing tax returns."

"Is everyone eligible for social security benefits?" Susan asked.

"No," Mr. Fernandez answered, "only those who have worked and paid into the system for ten years or more (a minimum of 40 calendar quarters) are eligible for full social security benefits."

"How do you get a social security number?" another student asked.

Susan knew the answer. She explained that you can acquire one at a Social Security Administration office or ask your employer for one.

Mr. Fernandez added that when applying for a social security card, you will be asked to produce two documents: (1) one showing age and citizenship; for example, a birth certificate, and (2) one showing identification; for example, driver's license or school I.D. card. He showed them a copy of the application form for a social security number—Form SS-5 (see Figure 7-2).

Mr. Fernandez suggested that everyone keep track of his or her contributions to social security in case an error has been made. You can keep a record of your contributions to social security by examining the W-2 forms issued by your employer every year. Contributions to social security are listed under FICA (Federal Insurance Contributions Act) on your paycheck and on Form W-2. About every three years you should request from the Social Security Administration a statement of earnings (see Figure 7-3).

Figure 7-2:
Application
Form for Social
Security
Number

DEPARTMENT OF HEALTH AND HUMAN SERVICES
SOCIAL SECURITY ADMINISTRATION

Form Approved
OMB No. 0960-0066

FORM SS-5 — APPLICATION FOR A
SOCIAL SECURITY NUMBER CARD
(Original, Replacement or Correction)

MICROFILM REF. NO. (SSA USE ONLY)

Unless the requested information is provided, we may not be able to issue a Social Security Number (20 CFR 422-103(b))

INSTRUCTIONS TO APPLICANT ▶ Before completing this form, please read the instructions on the opposite page. You can type or print, using pen with dark blue or black ink. Do not use pencil.

		First	Middle	Last
NAA	NAME TO BE SHOWN ON CARD			
NAB	FULL NAME AT BIRTH (IF OTHER THAN ABOVE)	First	Middle	Last
ONA	OTHER NAME(S) USED			

1

2 | STT | MAILING ADDRESS | (Street/Apt. No., P.O. Box, Rural Route No.) |

CTY	CITY	STE	STATE	ZIP	ZIP CODE

3 CSP CITIZENSHIP (Check one only)

☐ a. U.S. citizen

☐ b. Legal alien allowed to work

☐ c. Legal alien not allowed to work

☐ d. Other (See instructions on Page 2)

4 SEX / SEX

☐ MALE

☐ FEMALE

5 ETB RACE/ETHNIC DESCRIPTION (Check one only) (Voluntary)

☐ a. Asian, Asian-American or Pacific Islander (Includes persons of Chinese, Filipino, Japanese, Korean, Samoan, etc., ancestry or descent)

☐ b. Hispanic (Includes persons of Chicano, Cuban, Mexican or Mexican-American, Puerto Rican, South or Central American, or other Spanish ancestry or descent)

☐ c. Negro or Black (not Hispanic)

☐ d. Northern American Indian or Alaskan Native

☐ e. White (not Hispanic)

6 | DOB | DATE OF BIRTH | MONTH | DAY | YEAR | AGE **7** PRESENT AGE | PLB **8** PLACE OF BIRTH ▶ | CITY | STATE OR FOREIGN COUNTRY | FCI ☐ |

9 | MNA | MOTHER'S NAME AT HER BIRTH | First | Middle | Last (Her maiden name) |
| FNA | FATHER'S NAME | First | Middle | Last |

10

PNO a. Has a Social Security number card ever been requested for the person listed in item 1? ☐ YES(2) ☐ NO(1) ☐ Don't know(1) If yes, when: ▶ | MONTH | YEAR |

b. Was a card received for the person listed in item 1? ☐ YES(3) ☐ NO(1) ☐ Don't know(1) **If you checked yes to a or b, complete Items c through e; otherwise go to Item 11.**

SSN c. Enter Social Security number assigned to the person listed in item 1. ☐☐☐ — ☐☐ — ☐☐☐☐

NLC d. Enter the name shown on the most recent Social Security card issued for the person listed in item 1. | PDB | e. Date of birth correction (See Instruction 10 on page 2) ▶ | MONTH | DAY | YEAR |

11 DON TODAY'S DATE ▶ | MONTH | DAY | YEAR | **12** Telephone number where we can reach you during the day. Please include the area code. | HOME | OTHER |

ASD **WARNING:** Deliberately furnishing (or causing to be furnished) false information on this application is a crime punishable by fine or imprisonment, or both.

13 YOUR SIGNATURE

14 YOUR RELATIONSHIP TO PERSON IN ITEM 1
☐ Self ☐ Other (Specify)

WITNESS (Needed only if signed by mark "X") | WITNESS (Needed only if signed by mark "X")

DO NOT WRITE BELOW THIS LINE (FOR SSA USE ONLY)	DTC	SSA RECEIPT DATE
SSN ASSIGNED ☐☐☐ — ☐☐ — ☐☐☐☐	NPN	

			BIC	SIGNATURE AND TITLE OF EMPLOYEE(S) REVIEWING EVIDENCE AND/OR CONDUCTING INTERVIEW
DOC	NTC	CAN		
TYPE(S) OF EVIDENCE SUBMITTED			☐ MANDATORY IN PERSON INTERVIEW CONDUCTED	DATE
				DATE
		IDN ITV	DCL	

Form **SS-5** (1-84) Destroy prior editions   3

Figure 7-3:
Statement of
Earnings

FOLD HERE AND STAPLE

- -

	FOR SSA USE ONLY	
REQUEST FOR STATEMENT OF EARNINGS (PLEASE PRINT IN INK OR USE TYPEWRITER)	**AX**	●
	SP	●

I REQUEST A SUMMARY STATEMENT OF EARNINGS FROM MY SOCIAL SECURITY RECORD

NH | Full name you use in work or business
First | Middle Initial | Last

SN | Social security number shown on your card | | Your date of birth
DB | Month | Day | Year | **A**

MA | Other Social Security number(s) you have used | ● **SX** | Your Sex
☐ Male ☐ Female

AK | Other name(s) you have used (Include your maiden name)

Specifications for This Form Were Secured From the Social Security Administration

FOLD HERE

- -

PRIVACY STATEMENT

The Social Security Administration (SSA) is authorized to collect information asked on this form under section 205 of the Social Security Act. It is needed so SSA can quickly identify your record and prepare the earnings statement you requested. While you are not required to furnish the information, failure to do so may prevent your request from being processed. The information will be used primarily for issuing your earnings statement.

I am the individual to whom the record pertains. I understand that if I knowingly and willingly request or receive a record about an individual under false pretenses I would be guilty of a Federal crime and could be fined up to $5000.

Sign your name here: (Do not print) | Date

I AUTHORIZE YOU TO SEND THE STATEMENT TO THE NAME AND ADDRESS BELOW: *(To be completed in all cases)*

PN | Name of the addressee

AD | Street number and name

City and state | **ZP** | Zip Code

Form **SSA-7004 PC** OP 1 (9-82) Previous Editions are Obsolete

---

STUDENT ACTIVITY C

A. Name five areas in which social security provides benefits for the eligible worker.

1. _____

2. _____

3. _____

4. _____

5. _____

B. Answer *true* or *false* to the following statements.

_____ 1. Retired workers support the social security system with their payments or contributions to the fund.

_____ 2. At age 62, you can retire and receive full benefits.

_____ 3. If you have paid into the system long enough and can prove that you are physically or mentally unable to work, you can receive the same retirement benefits as you would at age 65.

_____ 4. Joan is 21 and still in college; therefore, she is eligible for monthly social security benefits because of her father's death.

_____ 5. In order to receive unemployment benefits, you have to have lost your job through no fault of your own.

C. Follow the instructions on page 149 and fill out the application for a social security number card (Figure 7-2).

D. Fill out the card, Request for Statement of Earnings (Figure 7-3).

FURTHER DISCOVERY

Ask your parents or other adults if you can examine their health insurance or life insurance policies. Compare the terms of the policies with the types of coverage and special provisions discussed in this unit. Give a report on your findings to the class.

CHECKLIST

If you have completed all the student activities in this unit, you should have mastered the skills below. Check off the skills you know, and review the ones you are not sure of.

( ) Terms related to health and life insurance

( ) How to shop for health insurance coverage

( ) The types of health insurance coverage

( ) The special provisions of health insurance

( ) The differences in coverage provided by dental insurance, workers' compensation laws, and health maintenance organizations

( ) The differences between term, cash-value, and universal life policies

( ) The advantages and disadvantages of term and cash-value life insurance

( ) Guidelines for buying life insurance

( ) The benefits offered by the social security system

( ) How to fill out an application for a social security card and a request for a statement of earnings

If you have checked all of the above, ask your teacher for the Susan Thompson Test on Insurance: Health/Life/Social.

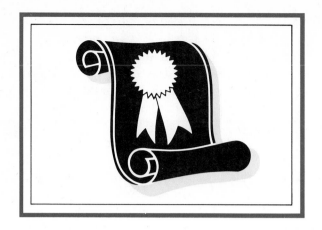

UNIT 8
INSURANCE: AUTO AND HOME

SKILL 1 **Buying Auto Insurance**

SKILL 2 **Buying Home and Property Insurance**

Further Discoveries

BUYING AUTO INSURANCE

As much as Susan enjoyed Mr. Fernandez's seminar on health, life, and social insurance, she was really looking forward to a discussion of auto insurance. She had just spotted a red sports model in Casey Motors downtown showroom window.

"Before taking any serious steps to buy a car, you should have some idea about the cost of auto insurance for the particular model you're considering," Mr. Fernandez said.

"I just want the basics," Susan said.

"The 'basics' is a rather broad term when it comes to auto insurance," Mr. Fernandez pointed out. "The cost of auto insurance differs greatly depending upon several factors; namely: the community in which a policyholder lives; age, sex, and marital status; driving record and habits; the year, model, and make of the car; limits of protection, amount of deductibles; and claims history."

"You mean if you and I have the same model car with the same amount of coverage, I might have to pay more for my auto insurance because of my age!" Susan asked.

"More than likely," Mr. Fernandez said. "You see, insurance rates are based on risks. If you're a bigger risk than I am, you are required to pay more for your coverage. In other words, statistics show that drivers in your age group have more accidents than drivers in my age group."

There are many factors determining the cost of auto premiums. The following discussion will explain these factors in greater detail.

The community in which a policyholder lives affects the price of premiums because each state is divided into *rating territories*. A rating territory can be a city, a section of a large city, or a rural area. Insurance companies examine statistics of claims connected with cars registered in each territory. The greater the number of claims from a territory, the higher the insurance rate. If you move from Rome, Georgia, to Los Angeles, California, your insurance premiums may go up simply because you live in a territory with higher rates, even though you have never had an accident in your life.

Another major factor in determining insurance rates is *driver classification* (age, sex, and marital status). Groups of drivers are classified according to their safety record. Certain categories of drivers tend to be involved in more accidents and have a greater number of serious traffic violations. The highest rates are paid by unmarried young males who own or are the principal operators of automobiles. If you are a 25-year-old single male, you will probably have to pay a relatively high premium even though you have a good driving record. In many states, female drivers between ages 30 and 65 pay lower rates because they are considered low-risk drivers. The driver classification with the lowest rates is a family with no male driver under 25 years of age and with a car not used for business. There are a few states, however, that now prohibit insurance companies from considering sex, age, and marital status as factors in determining insurance rates.

Your *personal driving record and habits* also affect rates. If you and everyone in the household who drives your car has a clear driving record, your rates will be lower than if one of you has a poor driving record. The purpose for which a car is driven and the miles it is driven also affect insurance rates. Cars driven for business purposes are driven more miles in a year than cars driven for pleasure and, therefore, are more likely to be involved in an accident.

The *year, model*, and *make* of a car affect rates. Generally, the newer and more expensive your car, the more you will have to pay for insurance. The older the car, the lower the rate. Older cars cost the insurance company less to replace if totally demolished in an accident. Also, your car's damageability—that is, how costly it is to repair—will affect the rate paid. Some cars, such as sports cars, get into wrecks more often, are costly to repair, and tend to be stolen more often; therefore, they command higher rates.

Your *claims history* affects auto insurance rates. The more claims you make, the higher your rates are likely to be. There are cases where insurance companies have dropped the insured altogether because of too many claims. If you do get dropped, it will be difficult to get another company to insure you.

If you have been dropped by an insurance company because of a poor driving record, you may end up in your state's Automobile Insurance Plan as an "assigned risk." If you are placed in the assigned risk category, you will not be able to choose your own auto insurance company. Instead,

Illustration 8-1

you will be assigned a company, and be charged very high rates—often two to three times more than you would ordinarily pay.

On the other hand, if you establish a good driving record, you will be able to choose your own company. Yet, if you feel you have been unjustly categorized as an assigned risk, contact your state insurance department and ask that your case be reconsidered.

Two other factors that affect the premium are *deductibles* and *limits of protection*. The higher the deductible, the less the premium because the policyholder pays a greater portion of the repair costs for a damaged car. Limits of protection or amount of coverage affect premiums in proportion to how much the policyholder buys. The more coverage the policyholder has, the higher the possible claims the insurance company will have to pay.

Susan's next major concern was how much protection to buy. Most automobile policies offer six types of coverage: bodily injury, property damage, collision, comprehensive physical damage, medical payments, and uninsured motorist protection. A policyholder can buy one or more of these types of coverage.

Before buying insurance, or even driving a car, one should understand the concept of liability. *Liability* means that a person may be held legally responsible for any damage that occurs as a result of an accident in which that person is at fault. If you run a stop sign and cause $2,000 damage to the other car, you are responsible for the costs of the damage. If you have *property damage liability* insurance, the company will pay the cost of the damage to the other person's car or property minus the deductible. If you injure someone in an accident in which you are at fault, the *bodily injury liability* covers expenses up to the limits of the policy. If you are sued because of bodily injury or death caused by an accident in which you are at fault, the liability coverage may pay up to the limits purchased. Liability insurance on a car also covers those who drive the insured car with permission.

The amount of money an insurance company will pay to cover the costs of injury and damage depends on the limits in the policy. Some automobile policies are written on a *single-limit basis*, which means there is one amount the company will pay for any one accident. Other policies are written on a *split-limit basis*, which means that separate limits are set for different categories. For example, if the coverage limit reads 25/50/10, up to $25,000 will be paid for bodily injury for one person; $50,000 bodily injury for more than one person; and $10,000 property damage. The insurance company will pay no more than the limit set for each category. Considering the costs of repairs and medical services today, buyers of automobile insurance would do well to consider how much increased coverage would cost. A $50,000 coverage may be increased to $100,000 for very little more a year.

Collision insurance covers damages to your car only. The insurance company will pay for repairs to your car when you collide with any object, turn your car over, or are hit by an uninsured motorist. It is the most expensive coverage because the risks of damaging a car through an accident are great. Most buyers reduce the cost of the premium by buying a policy with a deductible (often $100 or $250), which means that the policyholder pays the first $100 or $250 of repair costs. The smaller the deductible, the higher the premiums. As the car gets older and its value decreases, many car owners believe that it is foolish to pay for collision insurance if the car is not worth much. Collision insurance does not provide for payment of damages greater than the actual cash value of the car.

Comprehensive physical damage coverage protects the insured motorist against possible loss when the car is damaged in any way through no fault of the owner, or when the car is stolen. Causes of damage include fire, storms, flood, vandalism, or other causes listed in the policy. If a car is totally destroyed, or a stolen car is never recovered, the amount paid to the policyholder is equal to the estimated value of the car at the time of loss.

Medical payment coverage pays medical expenses incurred within one year after an accident. Usually it covers all members of the family and any guests riding in the car. Limits on medical payments are listed in the policy.

Uninsured motorists protection insures a person against hit-and-run drivers and motorists who have no insurance. If you are involved in an accident that is the fault of an uninsured motorist, your insurance company will pay you for bodily injury up to certain limits. If you are injured by a hit-and-run driver while crossing the street, your policy will pay the medical costs. In most states, uninsured motorists protection covers bodily injury only. Collision insurance must be carried to cover damage to the car by uninsured motorists.

STUDENT ACTIVITY A

1. Examine the following auto insurance cases and give your solution.

Case A: Tien Noschang's new car was stolen only five months after she bought it. It was never found. Since the car was insured for comprehensive coverage, Tien filed a claim for the purchase price of the automobile. The insurance company offered to pay her what they called the actual cash value of the car, which was considerably less than the amount Tien requested.

Who is legally correct?

_____

Explain. _____

_____

Case B: Ernest Gonzalez lost control of his car one night, crashed through the wall of a corner house, and landed in the living room. No one was seriously hurt, but there was considerable property damage. What coverage does Ernest need to pay the cost of the damage?

_____

Case C: Randy Covert didn't bother buying liability insurance. While on vacation he ran a red light and permanently disabled the motorist in the other car.

Is Randy in trouble?

_____

Explain. _____

_____

Case D: While crossing a busy intersection, Madelene Herbert was struck by a car and seriously injured. The driver never slowed down. What type of insurance would pay for Madelene's medical expenses?

_____

Case E: Karen Cave has all six types of coverage on her ten-year-old Chevy. Should she drop any part of the coverage?

_____

If so, which ones?

_____

Explain. _____

_____

Case F: Wayne Punch was furious because after moving to another state, his insurance premiums increased considerably. Wayne had never had an accident in his life, and he didn't think this was fair. Can you explain why Wayne's rates went up?

_____

_____

Case G: Arnel Pettigrew was comparing her automobile policy with her neighbor's. She couldn't understand why her premiums were so much higher than her neighbor's, since they had identical coverage from the same insurance company. What factors may have accounted for the difference in the costs of the two policies?

_____

_____

Case H: Tyrone Loar was sued by the Livingston family because Mr. and Mrs. Livingston were injured in an accident in which Tyrone was speeding. Tyrone's liability coverage was 25/50/10. The court awarded Mr. Livingston $25,000 and Mrs. Livingston $10,000 for bodily injury. Was Tyrone's coverage adequate to pay the costs?

_____

Explain. _____

_____

2. Mr. Fernandez showed his students a copy of his auto policy renewal notice from his insurance company. See page 159. You should study the form carefully and know the coverages and the limits contracted for. Answer the following questions.

a. What model car is covered?

_____

b. The auto is covered by insurance from

   (date) _____ to _____

c. How many autos are covered by this policy?

_____

d. What is the collision deductible?

_____

e. What is the deductible for a loss other than collision?

_____

f. On how many drivers in the household are the rates based?

_____

g. What is the amount of Mr. Fernandez's total premium?

_____

h. What are the limits of liability insurance for Auto No. 1?

_____

_____

_____

_____

THE INSURANCE COMPANY

Our Towne, California

Your insurance covering the automobile(s) listed below expires on

This notice contains information about your renewal policy. Any changes you have noted will be made on the effective date of the renewal policy unless an earlier date is requested. Your renewal policy will be prepared as shown below if this notice is not returned.

NAMED INSURED AND ADDRESS (No., St., Apt., Town or City, State, Zip Code)

R.E. Fernandez
2236 San Pedro Blvd.
Our Towne, CA 95551-1440

Previous Policy No.   930717-2014

County   OUR COUNTY

★ The auto(s) or trailer(s) described in this policy is principally garaged at the above address unless otherwise stated.

Occupation of the named insured is   COUNSELOR
LOSS PAYEE: (Name and Address)

Final Due Date

POLICY PERIOD: 12:01 A.M., STANDARD TIME From   JULY 1, 19--   to   JULY 1, 19--

DESCRIPTION OF AUTO(S) OR TRAILER(S)	AUTO NO. 1					AUTO NO. 2				
	YEAR 1978	TRADE NAME—MODEL CHEVROLET 8 MONTE CARLO S COUPE				YEAR	TRADE NAME—MODEL			
	VIN 1H57V6R447431					VIN				
	PURCHASED 12/78 NEW	FOB	COST 5247	SYM	AGE	PURCHASED	FOB	COST	SYM	AGE

THE PREMIUMS SHOWN ARE RENEWAL RATES AND ARE QUOTED SUBJECT TO ANY CHANGE IN THE RATE SCHEDULE.

COVERAGES	LIMIT OF LIABILITY AUTO NO. 1		LIMIT OF LIABILITY AUTO NO. 2		PREMIUM AUTO NO. 1	PREMIUM AUTO NO. 2
A. LIABILITY	$ 100,000	Each Accident	$	Each Accident	$ 318.00	
B. MEDICAL PAYMENTS	$ 10,000	Each Person	$	Each Person	$ 27.00	
C. UNINSURED MOTORISTS	$ 50,000	Each Accident	$	Each Accident	$ 32.00	
D. DAMAGE TO YOUR AUTO	ACV means Actual Cash Value					
1. Collision Loss	ACV Minus $ 200	Deductible	ACV Minus $	Deductible	$ 130.00	
2. Other than Collision Loss	ACV Minus $ 50	Deductible	ACV Minus $	Deductible	$ 50.00	
TOWING AND LABOR COSTS	$	Each Disablement	$	Each Disablement		

TOTAL PREMIUM $ 557.00

ENDORSEMENTS

RATES ARE BASED ON FOLLOWING DRIVERS IN HOUSEHOLD

SAFE DRIVER PLAN
CHARGEABLE POINTS -- NONE

Driver	Date of Birth			Male or Female	Married or Single	Operator under 21 with Driver Training	Owner or principal operator is male under 30 or single female under	Student away at school over 100 miles and auto not at school
	Mo	Day	Year					
1	01	04	32	M	M			
2	01	13	40	F	M			
3								
4								
5								

AUTO	USE OF AUTO
1	PLEASURE
2	

IF THE DATA ABOUT DRIVERS IN HOUSEHOLD OR USE OF AUTO SHOULD BE CHANGED IN ANY WAY, KINDLY ADVISE:
★ If garage location has changed, please give details—is the auto garaged indoors at night at the new location?....................................
....

Please Sign Here ....

PLEASE DO NOT FORWARD CHECK UNTIL YOU RECEIVE POLICY AND BILL.

Unless advised to the contrary we shall renew and forward your policy.

i. How much is Mr. Fernandez paying for $100,000 coverage on each accident?

_____

j. How much is Mr. Fernandez paying for $10,000 medical coverage on each person?

_____

"Does my auto insurance company have to pay regardless of who caused the accident?" Susan asked.

"Good question," Mr. Fernandez said. "Lots of time and money have been spent in court proceedings trying to determine who was at fault in auto accidents. The results are often expensive and brutally painful to all parties concerned. To avoid the problem, many states have adopted some form of no-fault insurance. *No-fault insurance*, pure and simple, means that your insurance company pays for bodily injuries to you and your passengers no matter who caused the accident.

"However, no state has adopted a pure no-fault law. There are variations in the no-fault laws for each state. Before buying an insurance policy, you should find out whether or not you live in a no-fault state and just what the particulars are regarding the law in your state.

"If you live in a no-fault state, you must buy wage-loss coverage. *Wage-loss coverage* reimburses the insured for income lost because of an auto injury. In states without no-fault, wage-loss coverage is optional.

"Many no-fault states require *substitute-service coverage*, which is coverage for services that you cannot perform for yourself because of an auto-related injury. For instance, your insurance company will pay for a cook or sitter for a specified period of time. Substitute-service coverage is not required in all no-fault states."

"If you live in a no-fault state, does that mean that people can't sue you for injuries?" Carlos asked.

"You can still be sued for *big* claims," Mr. Fernandez said, "but no-fault does eliminate the need to go to court for small claims. Probably the biggest advantage of good no-fault insurance is that the injured can receive immediate payment for injuries without waiting months for a court case to be settled.

"You bring up a good point, though. Medical expenses for the injured can amount to an enormous amount of money. The actual dollar amount can include everything from basic medical bills to compensation for pain and suffering, loss of income, and potential future earnings. You could lose everything in an automobile lawsuit."

Mr. Fernandez recommended a minimum of at least 100/300/25 under a split-limit plan, and $300,000 minimum under a single-limit plan. As he had explained, it is far better to cut back on small expenses than to risk possible injury suits that could cause financial disaster. In most cases, the increased coverage does not cost that much more per year.

Mr. Fernandez went to the board and jotted down ways to keep auto insurance down.

1. *Take higher deductibles.* Collision and comprehensive premiums are much less if you are willing to pay a higher deductible.

2. *Avoid "flashy" cars.* Susan may have fallen in love with the shiny, red sports car in the showroom window, but she should check with an insurance agent *before* purchasing the car to see how rates differ among models.

3. *Take advantage of discounts.* Insurance companies often offer special discount rates. For example, young drivers who have successfully completed a driver's education course usually get a discount. Drivers with good driving records can often get a safe-driver plan at a discount, and students with good grades sometimes get a discount.

4. *Eliminate duplication of coverage.* Your homeowners' insurance may cover personal property loss in your car. Your health insurance may cover medical expenses of passengers in your car as well as yourself. Be sure you understand what and how much is covered before you reduce your auto coverage, however.

5. *Shop around for the best insurance company for you.* As with everything else, the cost of auto insurance varies greatly. You may be able to get the same coverage at half the price. The cheapest company is not always the best, however. It's a good idea to check *Best's Insurance Reports*, an annual publication that evaluates the financial strength and stability of insurance companies.

STUDENT ACTIVITY B

Answer *true* or *false* to the following statements.

_____ 1. The cheapest auto insurance is the best auto insurance.

_____ 2. You do not need liability auto insurance if you live in a state requiring no-fault insurance.

_____ 3. The higher the deductible, the lower the premium.

_____ 4. You cannot be sued in states with no-fault insurance laws.

_____ 5. Discounts are usually offered to drivers with a good record.

BUYING HOME AND PROPERTY INSURANCE

Mr. Fernandez told his seminar the story of his Uncle Julian, who was furious because his insurance company had refused to pay for damages to his pipes caused by a freeze. Uncle Julian had taken out a basic home insurance policy that did not cover frozen plumbing.

"I'm changing companies," exclaimed Uncle Julian. "Imagine not covering frozen plumbing! For fifteen years I've been paying this company, and now they tell me they don't cover frozen plumbing. Why there's not a winter that goes by when we don't have an ice storm."

"No need to switch companies," I told him, "unless you're dissatisfied with the company for some other reason. What you need to do is to make sure you understand the coverage in your policy."

Mr. Fernandez explained to the seminar that homeowners' insurance includes two kinds of protection: property protection and liability protection. *Property protection* pays for losses to the house and other property. It may include everything from payments to cover the illegal use of lost credit cards to living expenses if your house burns down. The amount of property protection you get depends on the policy you buy. Most policies cover property damage caused by fire, windstorm, lightning, explosions, riots, aircraft, vehicles, vandalism, and theft.

Illustration 8-2

© Dave Wendt 1981

Liability protection usually covers bodily injury caused to others, damage to property of others, and medical payments to a person injured on your property. With full liability insurance coverage, you would be protected if someone tripped on your stairs and was injured.

There are six standard forms of homeowners' insurance: the basic form (HO-1); the broad form (HO-2); the special form (HO-3); the renters' form (HO-4); the comprehensive form (HO-5); and the form for condominium owners (HO-6). See Figure 8-1 for an outline of what each of these forms covers.

Generally, the coverage in most policies is for the contents (personal property) and the dwelling (real property). *Personal property* (or household property) includes furniture, clothing, appliances, etc. Homeowners' policies make a distinction between personal property and *real property*, which includes physical structures that are attached to the land, such as home, garage, fences, etc. Always study the coverage provided in insurance policies before signing the contract.

Figure 8-1:
Homeowners'
Policies

HOMEOWNERS' POLICIES — WHAT DO THEY COVER?

HO-1, *the basic form,* covers ten perils named in the policy: fire and lightning; windstorm or hail; explosion; riot or civil commotion; vehicles; aircraft; smoke; vandalism; glass breakage; theft.

HO-2, *the broad form,* covers the ten perils named for the basic form, plus falling objects; weight of ice, snow, or sleet; building collapse, leakage or overflow of water or steam from plumbing, heating, or air-conditioning systems; freezing of plumbing, heating, or air-conditioning systems; damage to appliances caused by electrical surges; discharge of steam or water.

HO-5, *the comprehensive form,* covers all-perils except those specified. Most all-perils policies exclude nuclear accident, flood, earthquake, war, and other events specified in the policy. The difference between an all-perils policy and a named-perils policy is the burden of proof when there's a question about the cause of damage. In a named-perils policy, it's up to the homeowner to prove that damage was caused by one of the perils listed in the policy. In an all-perils policy, it's up to the insurance company to prove the damage was caused by something excluded from the policy.

HO-3, *the special form,* provides the same protection for the dwelling as HO-5 but less extensive coverage for personal belongings.

HO-4, *the renters' form,* is for tenants in a house or apartment. It provides personal property protection and liability coverage. There's no coverage for the dwelling since that's the landlord's responsibility.

HO-6, *the condominium form,* covers only the space occupied. The condominium corporation usually insures the building itself.

Insurance companies recommend that homeowners insure their property for at least 80 percent of replacement cost in order to be fully paid at the time of a loss. If you have your $60,000 home insured for 80 percent of its replacement cost and a fire caused damages of $30,000, your insurance company would pay the full $30,000 minus a deductible. If the same home burned to the ground, the insurance company would pay 80 percent, or $48,000. It is assumed that 20 percent of the value of the home would be left in the land and the foundation if the house burned to the ground.

Furniture, appliances, and other personal property in the home are usually insured for the *actual cash value.* If your ten-year-old bedroom furniture is destroyed by fire, you will receive payment for its depreciated value, not the amount you originally paid for it or the current cost of replacing it.

Some insurance companies offer *replacement cost coverage* on personal property. In such cases, the insured receives the amount it takes to replace the property rather than the actual cash value. Since the cost of personal property adds up, replacement cost coverage is worth checking into.

Personal property, such as antiques, jewelry, and artwork, are often very valuable. Many people buy separate insurance specifically for these items through a *floater policy*. This insurance is tailored to each valuable and "floats" with the property wherever it goes. If your gold necklace is stolen in London while you're on vacation, it's covered. Floaters may be written as separate policies or as an *endorsement* (or addition) to a homeowners' policy. Floaters usually have no deductibles and provide coverage for the full value of the personal property insured.

To extend liability coverage, many property owners have *umbrella policies*. The standard homeowners' policy protects against claims only for bodily injury and property damage. Most umbrella policies also cover such things as libel, defamation of character, invasion of privacy, and the like. They also provide liability coverage above the limits set in both homeowners' and auto insurance policies. For about $100 a year, a person can have a million dollars of liability coverage.

STUDENT ACTIVITY C

1. Answer the following questions.

   a. What type of homeowners' insurance did Uncle Julian have?

   _____

   b. Why didn't the insurance company pay for the frozen pipes in Uncle Julian's home?

   _____

   _____

   _____

   c. What two kinds of protection does a homeowners' insurance policy include?

   _____

   _____

   d. List some reasons why a renter might need insurance on an apartment.

   _____

   _____

   _____

   _____

e. Define a floater policy.

_____

_____

f. Distinguish between personal property and real property.

_____

_____

_____

g. Explain the difference in coverage among the following forms: basic form, broad form, and comprehensive form.

_____

_____

_____

_____

_____

_____

_____

h. What is an "umbrella" policy?

_____

_____

2. Study the Renters' Insurance Renewal Statement, and answer the following questions.

a. List the coverage that John Smith included in his policy.

_____

_____

b. How much did he pay for the policy?

_____

c. Did he agree to pay a deductible?

_____

d. Which of the coverages listed on the policy do you think you would want if you had an apartment?

_____

_____

Explain. _____

_____

_____

_____

_____

POLICY TERM: 12 MONTHS FROM	MO-DAY-YEAR 1/19/--	TO	MO-DAY-YEAR 1/19/--	PRODUCER'S CODE 072430	POLICY NUMBER 426960890 634 1

NAME OF
INSURED AND
MAILING ADDRESS
OF INSURED
PREMISES

```
JOHN SMITH
707 TUPELO STREET
OUR TOWNE, CA 95551-1445
```

ADDITIONAL COVERAGES	LIMITS OF LIABILITY	PREMIUMS
PERSONAL PROPERTY	$ 10,000	$ 101
ADDITIONAL EXPENSES	$ 2,000	INCLD IN C
PERSONAL LIABILITY	$ 25,000	INCLD IN C
MEDICAL PAYMENTS TO OTHERS	$ 500	INCLD IN C

TOTAL PREMIUM
$ 101

POLICY EDITION	C2	Loss Deductible Amount
POLICY FORM	634	$ 1.00

Producer: Our Towne Insurance Agency

Declarations and any attached endorsements form a part of your "Policy Provisions" jacket bearing the policy edition and policy form number stated above. If a change number and effective date are entered at the top of this page, these declarations are made a part of your policy numbered above as of such date and all of the above entries supersede those on any previous declarations.

Agency At ___OUR TOWNE, CALIFORNIA___   ___A.C. DUNN___ Agent

Mr. Fernandez said that if you insure your personal property, you should always keep an inventory record of the property insured. An inventory record can be very helpful if property is damaged, especially in a fire. Most people have a difficult time remembering everything they own, not to mention the original cost and age of the furniture. Since personal property is usually insured according to actual cash value, an inventory record can be very helpful in settling claims. Figure 8-2 is an illustration of an inventory record form provided by an insurance company for a dining/kitchen area. A similar record should be kept for each room in the house or apartment.

Figure 8-2:
Inventory
Record Form

Dining/Kitchen Area

No. of Items	Item	When Purchased	Original Cost	Present Value
_____	Air conditioner	_____	_____	_____
_____	Bric-a-brac	_____	_____	_____
_____	Buffet	_____	_____	_____
_____	Cabinets,	_____	_____	_____
_____	Cabinet contents	_____	_____	_____
_____	Chairs	_____	_____	_____
_____	China	_____	_____	_____
_____	Clocks	_____	_____	_____
_____	Crystal	_____	_____	_____
_____	Curtains	_____	_____	_____
_____	Dishwasher	_____	_____	_____
_____	Electrical appliances	_____	_____	_____
_____	Floor covering	_____	_____	_____
_____	Foodstuffs	_____	_____	_____
_____	Freezer	_____	_____	_____
_____	Household utensils	_____	_____	_____
_____	Kitchen utensils	_____	_____	_____
_____	Lamps	_____	_____	_____
_____	Mirrors	_____	_____	_____
_____	Pictures, etc.	_____	_____	_____
_____	Radio	_____	_____	_____
_____	Refrigerator	_____	_____	_____
_____	Rugs	_____	_____	_____
_____	Silverware	_____	_____	_____
_____	Stove	_____	_____	_____
_____	Tables	_____	_____	_____
_____	Table linens	_____	_____	_____
_____	TV	_____	_____	_____
_____	Wall shelves	_____	_____	_____
_____	Window drapes/shades	_____	_____	_____

FURTHER DISCOVERIES

1. Do a survey of at least five students in your school who have been in automobile accidents or whose families have filed automobile insurance claims for any reason. In a written report describe the cases, and give the results of the claims made.

2. Visit two automobile insurance agents, and compare their rates. Make a form similar to the one below. Before you visit the agents, review Unit 8 to determine the kinds of coverage you want.

	Company A	Company B
Name of company		
Name of agent		
Types of Coverage	*Premiums*	*Premiums*
Liability Limits __/__/____		
Collision Deductible _____		
Comprehensive Deductible _____		
Medical Limit _____		
Uninsured-motorist		
Other coverages		
Total premium		

3. Ask a family member or friend if you may read his or her homeowners' insurance policy. Compare the coverage of the policy with the coverage explained in Figure 8-1. Do you think the policyholder has enough coverage? Write your comments about the coverage, and share your opinions with the class.

4. State laws requiring car owners to prove that they will be able to pay for damages caused in an accident are known as *financial responsibility laws*. A minimum amount of insurance coverage as determined by the state will fulfill this requirement. Investigate state laws regulating auto insurance to learn what types of coverage are needed to satisfy the law.

CHECKLIST

If you have completed all the student activities in this unit, you should have mastered the skills below. Check off the skills you know, and review the ones you are not sure of.

(   ) Terms related to automobile and homeowners' insurance policies

( ) How to determine the amount of auto insurance coverage to buy

( ) Why automobile insurance premiums vary

( ) The types of automobile coverage available

( ) How no-fault insurance works

( ) Terms used in homeowners' policies

( ) What types of coverage are available to a homeowner

( ) How to interpret a policy for renters' insurance

If you have checked all of the above, ask your teacher for the Susan Thompson Test on Insurance: Auto and Home.

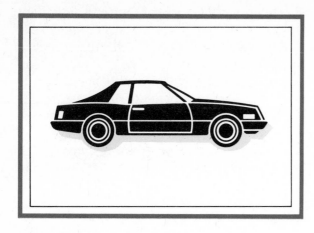

UNIT 9
OWNING AND OPERATING A CAR

SKILL 1 **Estimating Expenses**

SKILL 2 **Shopping for a Used Car**

SKILL 3 **Shopping for a New Car**

SKILL 4 **Applying for a Car Loan**

Further Discoveries

Many people are reevaluating the necessity of owning a car these days. Some have decided that public transportation is more convenient for their needs; others have decided that the maintenance and general costs of operating an automobile are too expensive; and others do not enjoy the hassle of driving in today's traffic. But many people still wish to own their own cars. Maxwell Ford, a participant in Mr. Fernandez's consumer seminar, was one of those people.

ESTIMATING EXPENSES

One day while sitting around the lunch table, Maxwell Ford came to a rather abrupt decision.

"I'm going to buy some wheels," said Max. "I'm tired of waiting in the rain for late buses."

"How about a motorbike," suggested Susan.

"I don't want to *ride* in the rain either," said Max. "I just don't know whether I can afford a car."

"Well, let's estimate the cost of owning and maintaining a car," said Susan. "The best way to decide whether you can afford something is to write the figures on paper. I learned that much from Mr. Fernandez."

That afternoon Susan and Max put their heads together and came up with the fixed and flexible expenses of owning and maintaining a car. They divided the costs into two categories: fixed expenses and flexible expenses. They considered *fixed expenses* to be those that remain essentially the same, whether you drive a car 5,000 or 30,000 miles a year. Under fixed expenses, they listed installment payments, insurance, license fees, etc. They listed expenses that vary under *flexible expenses*, which included gasoline, oil, regular tune-ups, tires, and so forth. Flexible expenses are directly related to the number of miles a car is driven.

Figure 9-1 is a chart that Susan and Max drew up as an estimate of the monthly and yearly cost of owning and maintaining a 1987 small automobile.

For the sake of simplicity, depreciation is excluded as an expense in Figure 9-1. *Depreciation* is a decrease in the value of property as it becomes older and starts to wear out. A new large-size car may depreciate approximately 30-40 percent the first year; 20 percent the second year, and at a decreasing percentage rate each year thereafter. Based on a 30 percent depreciation rate, a $13,000 car would probably sell for around $9,100 after the first year. A two- or three-year-old used car can be purchased for a considerably lower price than a comparable new model. If customers can be reasonably sure that the used car has been maintained well, they may be getting more value for their money than the new-car buyer.

Figure 9-1:
Average Cost of Operating a Small Car*

PERSONAL COSTS OF OWNING AND OPERATING AN AUTOMOBILE

	Cost per Month	Cost per Year
Fixed Expenses		
Installment payment	$141.33 (60 month Loan)	$1,695.96
Insurance		504.00
License fees (includes driver's license, inspection fee, license tag: fees vary from state to state).	paid once a year	30.00
Other (parking fees, etc.)		
Total fixed expenses	$141.33	$2229.96
Flexible Expenses		
Gasoline	80.00	960.00
Oil		25.00
Tires (should last 3 years or up to 40,000 miles)		
Maintenance (parts, repairs, tune-ups)		200.00
Total flexible expenses	80.00	$1185.00
Total fixed & flexible expenses	$221.33	$3414.96

* Depreciation is excluded for the sake of simplicity.

Adapted from the Money Management Institute booklet titled *Your Automobile Dollar*, published by the Money Management Institute of Household Finance Corporation, Prospect Heights, Illinois.

STUDENT ACTIVITY A

1. The Thompson family has been saving $100 a month for a car for the past two years, and they now have $2,400 in a savings account. They plan to withdraw $2,000 from savings for the down payment. The monthly installment payments for the new car will be $208.33 per month for 48 months. The estimated expenses for the car are:

Insurance	$600 a year
Gas	$100 a month on the average
Oil	$15 a year
Maintenance	$300 a year
License fees	$25 a year

Estimate the Thompson's monthly and yearly costs of owning and operating an automobile. Use the chart below as your model.

PERSONAL COSTS OF OWNING AND OPERATING AN AUTOMOBILE

	Cost per Month	Cost per Year
Fixed Expenses		
Installment payment	_____	_____
Insurance	_____	_____
License fees	_____	_____
Other	_____	_____
Total fixed expenses	_____	_____
Flexible Expenses		
Gasoline	_____	_____
Oil	_____	_____
Tires........................	_____	_____
Maintenance	_____	_____
Total flexible expenses	_____	_____
Total fixed & flexible expenses	_____	_____

---

2. a. Define depreciation.

_____

_____

b. If a car depreciates at an estimated 30 percent the first year and 20 percent the second year, how much would a $10,000 car be worth after one year?

_____

After two years?

_____

c. List any other factors that affect the rate of depreciation of a new car.

_____

_____

SHOPPING FOR A USED CAR

After estimating the cost of operating a car, Susan and Max decided to consider the possibility of buying a used car. Mr. Fernandez suggested that they pay a visit to Paddy O'Toole, who teaches Auto Shop at Our Towne High. Mr. O'Toole would have some helpful pointers on buying a used car, Mr. Fernandez said.

Illustration 9-1

"Where you buy a used car can be as important as what car you buy," said Mr. O'Toole.

Mr. O'Toole told them that used cars can be purchased from three major sources: a private party, used-car dealers, and new-car dealers. He elaborated on the advantages and disadvantages of each of these sources.

Private party. You can buy from a friend, an acquaintance, or an individual who advertises in the classified section of the newspaper. The advantage is a lower price, usually. The odds of your being sold a "lemon" are, of course, greater than if you bought from a reputable used-car dealer. There is usually no warranty, and the buyer may have to take care of expensive repairs. A *warranty* is a promise by a manufacturer or a dealer that a product is of a certain quality and that defective parts will be replaced within a certain period of time.

Used-car dealers. Used-car dealers offer a fairly wide variety of cars. They get the cars from private parties or new-car dealers. Prices are generally not excessive. Used-car dealers usually can provide financing, but other sources of financing are probably less expensive. If a warranty is offered, it is usually only a *limited* one. This means that the dealer will pay part of the total repair bill for covered systems that fail during the warranty period.

New-car dealers. New-car dealers usually have a large selection of late-model used cars that are in good condition. Warranties are sometimes better because a new-car dealership has its own service department to make the repairs. However, a used car from this dealer will generally be more expensive than one purchased from another source.

"Decisions about what kind of car you want and the price you should pay for it need to be made at home," said Mr. O'Toole. He recommended that they list cars which they are interested in buying. He mentioned the following sources of information about used-car prices:

1. *National Automobile Dealers Association Official Used Car Guide*

2. *Red Book Official Used Car Valuations*

3. *Automotive Market Report*

Mr. O'Toole said these guides can be found in banks, some savings and loan associations, and car dealerships. Most bank officers and car dealers will show you the guides they have. Mr. O'Toole warned that these guides only estimate the price of a car, since the condition of a car determines its ultimate price. Ads for used cars in newspapers may be useful in getting an estimate of current prices.

Sometimes the condition of a car can be detected by the buyer and sometimes it cannot be. The used-car salesperson can tell a knowledgeable buyer from a naive buyer, and the asking price will vary according to how well the buyer can evaluate the condition of a used car. A good source of general information about used cars is the *Guide to Used Cars* published by Consumers Union each year.

Mr. O'Toole said that the Federal Trade Commission ruling of 1985 has improved the chances of a buyer getting a good used car. The FTC requires used-car dealers to make sure that buyers know who will be responsible for payment of repairs after the sale. The ruling does not insure that a consumer will get a car without problems, but does let the consumer know who will pay for problems that might develop.

The rule requires that a "Buyers Guide" sticker, such as the one shown in Figure 9-2, be placed on all used cars. If the "As Is" block is

Figure 9-2:
Buyers' Guide
Sticker

BUYERS' GUIDE

IMPORTANT: Spoken promises are difficult to enforce. Ask the dealer to put all promises in writing. Keep this form.

Vehicle Make   Model   Year   ID Number

WARRANTIES FOR THIS CAR

☐ **AS IS — NO WARRANTY**

YOU WILL PAY ALL COSTS FOR ANY REPAIRS. The dealer assumes no responsibility for repairs regardless of any oral statements about mechanical condition.

☐ **WARRANTY**

☐ FULL ☐ LIMITED WARRANTY. The dealer will pay _____% of the total repair bill for the covered systems that fail during the warranty period. Ask the dealer for a copy of the warranty document for a full explanation of warranty coverage exclusions, and the dealer's repair obligations. Under state law, "implied warranties" may give you even more rights.

SYSTEMS COVERED: DURATION:

_____   _____

_____   _____

_____   _____

_____   _____

_____   _____

SERVICE CONTRACT. A service contract is available from _____ for $_____ extra. This service contract adds to the dealer's responsibilities under any warranty. If you buy a service contract within 90 days of the time of sale, state law "implied warranties" may give you additional rights.

PRE-PURCHASE INSPECTION. ASK THE DEALER IF YOU MAY HAVE THIS CAR INSPECTED BY YOUR MECHANIC EITHER ON OR OFF THE LOT

SEE THE BACK OF THIS FORM for important additional information, including a list of some major defects that may occur in used cars.

checked, the buyer must pay for all repairs. If "Warranty" is checked, the used-car dealer must pay for whatever items are listed for the length or time promised (duration). In some cases, a dealer may check "Full Warranty," in which case the dealer is responsible for all repairs for a designated amount of time.

"Verbal promises are difficult to enforce," warned Mr. O'Toole. "Ask the dealer to put all warranties in writing."

STUDENT ACTIVITY B

Marta Espanol was looking for a small used car under $5,000. When she priced used cars at one car lot, she discovered that a year-old Toyota with standard equipment was priced at $6,175 and a year-old Mercury, loaded with options, was priced only $835 higher, at $7,000.

1. Can you account for the similarity in price between two used cars that varied considerably in price when new? Give possible reasons.

   _____

   _____

   _____

2. If you were choosing between these two cars, what other points would you consider in making your choice?

   _____

   _____

3. Which of the two cars would you buy?

   _____

4. If a similar model Toyota were advertised for $4,500 in the newspaper by a private party, should Marta dash out and buy it?

   _____

   Explain. _____

   _____

Mr. O'Toole told Susan and Max that people who are not knowledgeable about the mechanical functions of a car can have trouble making distinctions between serious problems and less costly ones. Oil drips, for instance, explained by the seller as normal in an older car, may be a sign of costly trouble.

He said he would be happy to go with them to check out some used cars. First, he would discuss a few general items they should consider when looking at various models.

Check the body condition of the car. Generally, owners who took good care of the body of a car, probably took good care of the engine, too. You must check carefully, however, to see whether the car has been repainted in order to hide defects. Check under the hood or in the trunk to make sure the exterior body paint matches. You should also look for rust spots in areas which do not immediately catch your eye—such as around headlights. Don't forget to check the interior for signs of wear such as torn upholstery, worn brake pedals, or damaged accessories.

Check the odometer reading. The odometer measures the mileage. The sellers of used cars were notorious at one time for turning back the odometer to make a car appear less used. Since a federal odometer law was passed in 1972, the penalties for odometer tampering discourage most sellers from violating the law. Sometimes the buyer can tell if the odometer reading has been changed. If two or more digits do not line up, or if the tenths counter vibrates when the car is moving, the chances are that the mileage has been turned back. According to the law, the seller of a used car must give written confirmation of the actual mileage. When you buy a used car, ask for a signed statement that the odometer has not been altered in any way.

Another way to check car mileage is to look for oil change stickers on the inside of the door on the driver's side or to look at a state automobile inspection sticker on the windshield. Most reputable used-car dealers will give the name and address of the previous owner. If a dealer refuses, walk away. By talking with the previous owner, you can confirm the mileage figure and find out if the car had mechanical problems.

Consider the mileage on the car. Low mileage is not always an indicator of good car maintenance. You do not want to buy a car with 170,000 miles on it, yet, a two-year-old car with 30,000 or 50,000 miles may be better than a two-year-old car with 8,000 miles. A car can benefit from long-range driving. Driving a car only short distances can be hard on the engine; it results in the accumulation of acids and sludge in the lubrication system.

Get a mechanic to check the car. There is no sense in lifting the hood and staring blankly at an engine if you know nothing about it. It is worth the money it costs to get a mechanic to test a car thoroughly for possible needed repairs. Ask to have the car for an afternoon, and take it to a mechanic's shop to be tested.

If you buy from a stranger, ask to see the car's registration and title (proof of ownership). Check with the police or motor vehicles bureau to be sure the car is not stolen. If you buy a stolen car or one that is not paid for, you do not have legal title (or ownership) to the car. Title to a car cannot be transferred to another person until a car loan as been paid off. If you do not have a "clear" title to a car, the car can be taken from you, and you can lose a lot of money.

Mr. O'Toole showed Susan and Max a diagram (see Figure 9-3) that identified possible problem areas that a mechanic will be sure to check. He said they should always road test a used car and take a mechanic along if possible. The test drive should consist of more than a ride around the block. An adequate test drive takes between 30 and 45 minutes. The test drive should include the following:

- Drive up hills and on bumpy roads. Drive on highways with the window down so that noises can be detected. Do not test drive an automobile with the radio on. You can test the radio later.

- Run the car in all gears. An automatic transmission should shift without strain or slippage. The manual shift should not stick or slip.

- Accelerate. Test the speed of acceleration by passing a car on a highway or entering the highway from an access road.

- Test the brakes while driving slowly. If the car swerves or the brake time is too long, the car may be too dangerous to drive.

- Try the starter several times to see if it works properly.

- Listen for whines, irregular idling, and other noises when the engine is idling. Such irregularities may mean engine trouble.

- Drive a short distance with wet tires. If the tires leave four tire tracks instead of just two, the frame of the car may be bent.

- Park the car on a smooth, clean surface and check for oil or gas drips. Leaking transmission fluid is red; engine oil is black.

- Check interior and exterior lights, quality of air conditioning, heater, windshield wipers and washers, seat adjustments, locks, all doors and windows, mirrors, ash trays, and other accessories.

Figure 9-3:
Possible
Problem Areas

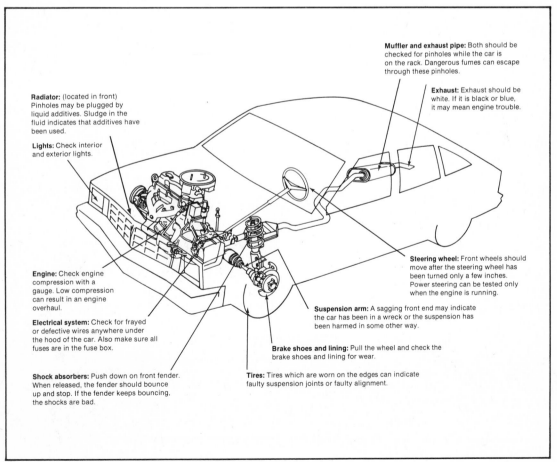

Muffler and exhaust pipe: Both should be checked for pinholes while the car is on the rack. Dangerous fumes can escape through these pinholes.

Exhaust: Exhaust should be white. If it is black or blue, it may mean engine trouble.

Radiator: (located in front) Pinholes may be plugged by liquid additives. Sludge in the fluid indicates that additives have been used.

Lights: Check interior and exterior lights.

Steering wheel: Front wheels should move after the steering wheel has been turned only a few inches. Power steering can be tested only when the engine is running.

Engine: Check engine compression with a gauge. Low compression can result in an engine overhaul.

Suspension arm: A sagging front end may indicate the car has been in a wreck or the suspension has been harmed in some other way.

Electrical system: Check for frayed or defective wires anywhere under the hood of the car. Also make sure all fuses are in the fuse box.

Brake shoes and lining: Pull the wheel and check the brake shoes and lining for wear.

Shock absorbers: Push down on front fender. When released, the fender should bounce up and stop. If the fender keeps bouncing, the shocks are bad.

Tires: Tires which are worn on the edges can indicate faulty suspension joints or faulty alignment.

Illustration Credit: General Motors Corporation.

Unit 9: Owning and Operating a Car

1. See the diagram below, and identify areas you would check before buying a used car.

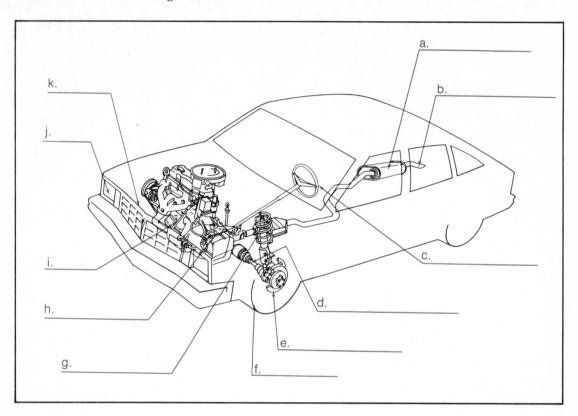

2. What might indicate that the car has been in a wreck?

_____

_____

3. What might tell you that the car has potential engine trouble?

_____

_____

4. What are some indications that the odometer has been tampered with?

_____

_____

SHOPPING FOR A NEW CAR

After discussing used cars, Susan and Max asked Mr. Fernandez about shopping for a new car. They had heard horror stories about customers being persuaded to buy cars they really did not want, or worse, could not afford.

"The best way to buy a new car," Mr. Fernandez said, "is to make most of your decisions at home, a safe distance away from shiny-car sales rooms."

Mr. Fernandez suggested that they go to the public library and consult some magazines. The librarian showed them *Consumer Reports*, especially the April issue, which is devoted almost entirely to car buying. *Motor Trend, Road & Track, Road Test*, and *Car and Driver* were also recommended. Other magazines available included *Gas Mileage Guide*, which gives a yearly report on gas mileage tests conducted on new model cars; and an auto-buying guide called *New Car Prices*. The librarian said that all libraries do not order the yearly copy of *Gas Mileage Guide* or *New Car Prices*. Generally, local car dealers have copies of the two publications and are usually willing to show them to customers.

Illustration 9-2

Photo location courtesy Public Library of Cincinnati and Hamilton County

As Susan and Max read through the magazines in the library, they learned many new things about buying a new car. Here are a few of the things they learned.

The *rate of depreciation* varies with the type of car. A large new car may depreciate more than a small car, depending on the demand of consumers for small cars. The small car is more in demand when gasoline prices are high because smaller cars get better gas mileage.

The cost of *auto repair and maintenance* is another item that should be considered before buying a new car. Small cars can be more expensive to repair than intermediates or even luxury cars. Also, in an accident the smaller car is often damaged to a greater degree than a larger, heavier car. Thus, damages to a smaller car can result in expensive repair costs.

If you have decided on a particular model before visiting the showroom, you need to concern yourself primarily with *price*. The price pasted on the window of the new car is generally referred to as the *sticker price.* The sticker price usually includes the *total price* (the price of the car with optional equipment, transportation, and dealer charges). *Options* include everything from air conditioning to fancy seats and upholstery, which increase the sticker price. Some consumers who decide on a smaller car for economic reasons often end up paying much more than they had planned because they select numerous options.

Always make an offer *below* sticker price. Dealers expect to sell most models below sticker price. Choose a *reputable dealer* because even though a new car is under warranty, the dealer is the one who must repair any defects. Before buying from a particular dealer, call the nearest Better Business Bureau to check for information on any complaints about the dealership; or you might visit the service department to listen to and talk with customers. Are customers generally satisfied with the service provided by the dealership?

When you have decided to buy a particular car, you will have to sign a *sales agreement*, which is a contract to purchase the car. The sales agreement may also be referred to as the *buyer's guide.* The terms of the sales agreement are negotiable until both the purchaser and the sales manager have signed the agreement.

A word of caution to the unsuspecting consumer: there are tactics used at times to encourage eager car buyers to sign a sales agreement. Two of the more frequently used tactics are *lowballing* and *highballing.* Lowballing is used by a salesperson who has no intention of selling the car at the low price offered. The tactic begins when a salesperson accepts an offer from a customer that is far below the sticker price of the car. Usually, after a customer has shown considerable interest, the salesperson will take the offer to the sales manager, who does not approve of the low sales price but agrees to sell the car at a higher price. By this time, the prospective buyer is often so attracted to the car that the higher price is accepted.

Highballing involves the trade-in of a used car on a new car. A salesperson will offer a high price for the car that the customer plans to trade-in. After the price has been agreed upon, the salesperson checks with the sales manager, who says that too much was offered for the trade-in. The customer, who is interested in the new car, often agrees to pay a higher price for the new car or to select a similar car with fewer options at the agreed-upon price. Either way, the dealer makes a profit.

Often you will do better if you sell an old car yourself rather than trade it in. Check an automobile-trade price book (often found in libraries, dealerships, and banks) for price information. Also, check newspaper ads for the asking price of other used cars similar to yours.

Before signing the sales agreement, be sure that you clearly understand all aspects of the *new-car warranty.* Many new-car warranties on American-made cars cover basically the same things, and are valid for 12 months or 12,000 miles—whichever comes first. The buyer should note the provisions that must be followed in order to benefit from the warranty. The buyer should concentrate on what the warranty does *not* cover. Tires are usually guaranteed by the tire manufacturer.

1. Sparky Karr had car fever. On his way home from work, he couldn't resist stopping at the new car dealership that had just opened last month. The salesperson saw Sparky eyeing the new red hatchback.

   Salesperson: You like that one?

   Sparky: Love it, but it's a little too high for my budget.

   Salesperson: You must be living right; it just so happens we're having an open-house sale this month. I can knock about $700 off that sticker price for you.

   Sparky: Now you're talking "cents!" Real cents for ole Sparky here! I'll bring the down payment tomorrow. Hold it for me.

   . . . . . .

   Sparky: I'm back. Where's the dotted line? I'm ready to sign.

   Salesperson: I apologize. The sales manager said that the $700 discount only applies to higher-priced cars. My mistake. But he said that since I've caused you this trouble, I can knock $200 off the sticker price.

   Sparky: Well, that's a car of a different color. If you know what I mean. I like the car though. Well, a deal's a deal. I'll take it.

   a. What is the name of the salesperson's sales tactics?

      _____

   b. Explain how this sales tactic works.

      _____

      _____

   c. List the mistakes Sparky made in shopping for a new car.

      _____

      _____

      _____

      _____

2. Answer *true* or *false* to the following statements.

   _____ a. New-car buyers should concentrate on what the warranty does not cover.

   _____ b. A new small car usually depreciates more than a new large car.

   _____ c. The sticker price of a car is the base price.

   _____ d. The reputation of a dealership is unimportant if you buy a new car under warranty.

   _____ e. The April issue of *Consumer Reports* is devoted almost entirely to car buying.

After Susan and Max read the magazines at the library, they decided to compile a checklist of options to consider before going to look at new cars. Max called the checklist the "What-I-want-is-not-necessarily-what-I-get-chart." Figure 9-4 is a copy of the chart Max filled out.

Figure 9-4:
Max's Chart of Car Options*

	What I want	What I need	What I can afford	What I get (results: 2 out of 3)
1. Automatic	✓		✓	✓
---or--- Standard transmission		✓		
2. Small car	✓	✓	✓	✓
---or--- Intermediate car				
---or--- Large car				
3. Sports car	✓			
---or--- Standard car		✓	✓	✓
4. 4 cylinder		✓	✓	✓
---or--- 6 cylinder	✓			
---or--- 8 cylinder				
5. Power steering	✓		✓	✓
---or--- Standard steering		✓		
6. Power brakes	✓			
---or--- Standard brakes		✓	✓	✓
7. Air conditioning	✓		✓	✓
---or--- No air conditioning		✓		
8. AM radio		✓	✓	✓
---or--- AM-FM radio				
---or--- AM-FM stereo radio	✓			

*The option with two check marks is what Max thinks he should buy.

The chart in Figure 9-4 is rather general. Large and small cars, for instance, can be subdivided more specifically. Small cars include *subcompacts* (the smallest of all) and *compacts* (somewhat larger and more expensive). Then there are *intermediates* and *large* (full-size or luxury) cars. The body types of cars are not limited to the standard car and sports car. There are four-door and two-door sedans, hatchbacks, station wagons, and convertibles.

Skills for Consumer Success

STUDENT ACTIVITY E

Complete the chart below for yourself. Consider the options you could afford if you were employed and a high-school graduate.

	What I want	What I need	What I can afford	What I get (results: 2 out of 3)
1. Automatic ---or--- Standard transmission				
2. Small car ---or--- Intermediate car ---or--- Large car				
3. Sports car ---or--- Standard car				
4. 4 cylinder ---or--- 6 cylinder ---or--- 8 cylinder				
5. Power steering ---or--- Standard steering				
6. Power brakes ---or--- Standard brakes				
7. Air conditioning ---or--- No air conditioning				
8. AM radio ---or--- AM-FM radio ---or--- AM-FM stereo radio				

APPLYING FOR A CAR LOAN

When consumers cannot pay for a new car in cash, they have to acquire a loan for a specified time period—12, 18, 24, 36, 48, or 60 months. If you have done extensive shopping for the best price on a new car and then take out a loan at an extremely high APR, you have defeated your purpose. The most convenient way to finance a car loan is through the car dealer, but it is not always the least expensive. A copy of an installment contract issued by a dealer is shown in Figure 9-5.

Figure 9-5:
Installment Contract

Undersigned Buyer agrees to buy the property described below (hereafter called "Collateral") and Buyer acknowledges receipt thereof. Buyer promises to pay Seller, the unpaid part of this contract (Line 8) in the consecutive monthly installments commencing on the date indicated in the Terms of Payment or, if no date appears, one month from the date of this contract. Buyer hereby grants to Seller a security interest in the below described Collateral including all parts, accessories, equipment and any other additions or accessions, now or hereafter attached to and used in connection with said Collateral, to secure the payment of the Total of Payments (Line 8) and any delinquency charges including interest, any expenses of repossession and resale including costs of storage.

PURCHASER(S): _Anthony Fernandez 202 Oriole Street OurTowne California_
(Print Full Name)   (No., Street or R.F.D.)   (City)   (State)

SELLER: _Our Towne Ford Co. 1012 Smith Street OurTowne California_
(Dealer's Name)   (Correct Legal Address)   (City)   (State)

Seller does hereby sell, transfer and delivery unto Purchaser under the terms and conditions set forth herein, the following described property, delivery and acceptance of which in good order is hereby accepted by Purchaser:

NEW OR USED	YEAR	MAKE	BODY TYPE	SERIAL NO.	ODOMETER READING	LICENSE NO.
New	19--	Ford Tempo 82	4 door	IB089AA130040	.5	

Cash Price (including Sales Tax) .... $ 8620 1
Down Payment
  (a) Cash (Down Payment) .... $ 2,000 ..
 1(b) Trade-In $ ....
      Less Amount Owed $ ....
      Net Allowance $ ....
      Total Down Payment .... $ 2000 2
Unpaid Balance of Cash Price .... $ 6620 3
Premiums for Property Insurance, if any, for a term
  of .... months........................... $ — 4
Documentary Fees .... $ — 5
Unpaid Balance, i.e., Amount Financed (Add lines 3, 4, 5) $ 6620 6

FINANCE CHARGE (Interest) .... $ 2,330.08 7

2**ANNUAL PERCENTAGE RATE** ___8.8__%
Total of Payments (Add lines 6 and 7) .... $ 8950.08 8

  TERMS OF PAYMENT: ......48...... successive
  monthly installments of $ ..186.46............
  and one final payment of $ ....
  commencing .... March 2 . 19 --

PROPERTY INSURANCE, if written in connection with this contract may be obtained by the Buyer through any person of his or her choice. If Buyer desires such insurance to be obtained through the Seller, the cost will be $_____ for the term of _____ year(s).

DEFAULT CHARGES: Seller shall be entitled to collect a delinquency charge on each installment in a default for a period of not less than 15 days of 5% of the unpaid amount of the installment. In the event Seller elects to accept delinquency and collection charges hereunder, all such payments from the Buyer shall be applied first to the current installment due, if any, then to delinquency charges, collection charges, and unpaid installments.

Buyer acknowledges reading and receiving a copy of this contract in its completed form.

Executed at Our Town, California, this ____17____ day of ____February____ 19--

Pat Roberts Salesmanager   _Anthony Fernandez_
(Seller)   (Buyer)

---

[1] A trade-in can be counted toward total down payment.
[2] In this case, the interest rate (8.8%) is low because the dealer is offering special financing.

Other sources of loans for a car are the same as those mentioned in Unit 4. Banks and savings and loan associations that offer auto installment loans require collateral. Your car is usually the collateral or security for a loan. Title to the car is held by the financial institution until the loan is repaid. A down payment—often 20 percent of the total cost of the car—is customary. Credit unions require large down payments, but the cost of financing the car may be less than for other sources. If you have a cash-value life insurance policy, you can obtain a loan up to the cash value of the policy. If you borrow from a consumer finance company, your car is usually security for the loan. Consumer finance companies specialize in loans to borrowers with weak credit ratings. Therefore, finance companies often charge higher rates of interest than other loan sources.

Your ability to get a loan at the lowest possible interest rate depends largely on the sources available to you and on your credit standing. Whatever the case, check the APR on the loan contract. Make sure you understand what the total finance charge is. According to the Truth-in-Lending Law, the total dollar cost of the loan must be stated in the contract.

STUDENT ACTIVITY F

1. After studying the installment contract (Figure 9-5) answer the questions below.

   a. The loan is based on APR of

   _____

   b. The finance charge is

   _____

   c. What is the amount of the down payment?

   _____

   d. The loan extends for a period of

   _____

2. Sometimes lending institutions advertise their APR in the newspaper. Below is an ad about new car loans.

   a. According to the car loan ad above, how much would your finance charge be on a $4,800 loan?

   _____

   b. What would be the total amount repaid after 36 months on a $4,800 loan?

   _____

   c. What are the monthly payments for a $4,800 loan?

   _____

   d. What is the APR for the same loan?

   _____

The Installment Plan

Amount Financed	Finance Charge	Total of Payments	36 Monthly Payments of	Annual Percentage Rate
$3,000.00	$655.80	$3,655.80	$101.55	12.95
3,300.00	719.04	4,019.04	111.64	12.91
3,500.00	760.96	4,260.96	118.36	12.88
3,800.00	824.20	4,624.20	128.45	12.85
4,000.00	866.48	4,866.48	135.18	12.84
4,300.00	929.36	5,229.36	145.26	12.81
4,500.00	971.64	5,471.64	151.99	12.80
4,800.00	1,034.88	5,834.88	162.08	12.78
5,000.00	1,076.80	6,076.80	168.80	12.76
5,500.00	1,182.32	6,682.32	185.62	12.74
6,000.00	1,287.48	7,287.48	202.43	12.72
6,500.00	1,392.64	7,892.64	219.24	12.70

FURTHER DISCOVERIES

1. Take a copy of the price comparison chart on page 189 with you to one or more new car dealers, and do your own comparison shopping of four cars of your choice. Fill out the chart, and prepare a report on your findings for the class.

2. Using your local school or local library, do a comparative study of new cars and used cars. Based on your findings, draw up a chart that shows the advantages and disadvantages of purchasing new and used cars.

CHECKLIST

Having completed all the *student activities* on buying a car, you should be able to perform the following skills. Check off the skills you know, and review the ones you are not sure of.

( ) How to estimate the cost of owning and operating a car

( ) Where to buy a used car

( ) Where to find information about used car prices

( ) Guidelines to follow when shopping for used cars

( ) Sources to consult for information about new cars

( ) Things to consider when shopping for a new car

( ) Where to shop for a car loan

( ) The form used for a car loan installment contract

If you checked all the skills listed above, ask your teacher for the Susan Thompson Test on Owning and Operating a Car.

Price Comparison Chart

	Car 1	Car 2	Car 3	Car 4
Name of Car/Model				
Base Price				
Options:				
8 cylinders				
6 cylinders				
4 cylinders				
Automatic transmission				
Power steering				
Power brakes				
Radial tires				
White sidewall tires				
Air conditioning				
Rear-window defogger . .				
Radio: AM				
AM/FM				
AM/FM Stereo				
Exterior trim stripes				
Custom interior				
Bucket seats				
Vinyl roof				
Clock				
Speed or cruise control				
Tinted glass				
Other:				
Delivery charges				
Total or list price of car including options				

Adapted from the Money Management Institute booklet titled *Your Automobile Dollar*, published by the Money Management Institute of Household Finance Corporation, Prospect Heights, Illinois.

UNIT 10
HOUSING

SKILL 1 **Determining Choices Available**

SKILL 2 **Understanding a Lease**

SKILL 3 **Buying a Home**

Further Discoveries

DETERMINING CHOICES AVAILABLE

When Susan first appeared in Mr. Fernandez's office several months ago, she had announced she wanted a job of her own and a place of her own. Mr. Fernandez was curious to see if there were any changes in Susan's outlook since the seminars began.

"Do you still want to run out and rent an apartment after graduation, Susan?" Mr. Fernandez asked.

"I'm not sure," Susan admitted. "My budget looks more fragile by the minute."

Mr. Fernandez laughed as he walked to the chalkboard. "A budget has a way of making us all go back to the drawing board," he said. "Still, at some point we do have to leave our parents' nest and make it on our own. As seniors about to graduate from high school, many of you have several options." He listed the options on the board and explained each of them.

1. *Live with parents.* Many young people just out of high school simply cannot afford to pay for their own housing. A full-time job, even if you have a high school education, does not always provide enough money at first for housing. If you choose to go to a local college, you may want to live at home while attending school. If you do stay at home, however, you should offer to share household expenses and responsibilities.

2. *Live in a dormitory.* Dormitories provide lodging for college and university students, and they are usually less expensive than other types of rental property. You will experience living away from home, usually with another student, which should teach you a lot about whether you want to share an apartment with someone else later.

3. *Rent an apartment or efficiency.* Whether now or later, most young people rent before they buy. The cheapest type of apartment is the *efficiency*—one room that serves as a living area, bedroom, and kitchen. Apartments vary in cost depending upon their size, condition, location, conveniences (central air, laundry facilities, pool, etc.), and whether or not they are furnished or unfurnished. Furnished apartments usually have necessary furniture such as a kitchen table and chairs, a bed and living room furniture.

4. *Buy a mobile home, condominium, or single-family house.* Few young people can consider such large purchases immediately after high school—few want to. Purchasing your own dwelling is a big financial step with a lot of responsibilities. See page 203 on buying a home.

"If you do decide to rent an apartment, certain steps should be taken beforehand," Mr. Fernandez said. "First, you need to decide whether or not you want to share the apartment with a friend. If so, discuss and agree on certain aspects of living together before looking for an apartment. A six-month planning period may be needed before moving to an apartment." Mr. Fernandez emphasized the following points:

1. *Discuss your responsibilities and living habits.* Nothing ruins a good high-school friendship faster than shared housing. Be sure to discuss how you will divide household responsibilities and expenses, including rent, utilities, groceries, telephone bills, etc. Discuss living habits: neatness, house guests, entertainment rules, quiet time.

2. *Make agreements in writing.* Agree in advance about arrangements for one partner moving out before the lease is up; what type of notice should be given; and how the cost of damages to the apartment are shared. It is advisable that each person keep an independent budget except for those items that must be shared: rent, utilities, groceries, and telephone bills. The *common budget* should be in writing.

3. *Look for and decide on an apartment together*, so that later on one partner does not blame the other for a poor choice of dwelling.

"Secondly," Mr. Fernandez suggested, "if you haven't already, you should start collecting items needed for apartment living: lamps, pillows, dishes, silverware, cooking utensils, etc. These household items will cost a bundle if you have to buy them all at once."

Many young people do not plan for the initial expenses of renting. In addition to monthly rent, the following expenses should be included in the first month's budget:

1. *First and last month's rent.* Some rental contracts require that the first as well as the last month's rent be paid. In this way, owners are protected against renters who might leave without notice or payment of rent due.

2. *Security or damage deposit.* Find out to what extent you are held responsible for possible damage to the apartment. If the apartment is in the same condition as when rented, the deposit must be returned.

3. *Gas and/or electric utility service.* A fee is often charged for initial hookups.

4. *Telephone installation and service.* The fee varies according to your requirements; that is, rotary or push-button phone, Touch-Tone service, number of wall jacks, etc.

5. *Water and garbage services.* Arrangements may have to be made for water usage and garbage pick-up.

"How would you go about looking for an apartment?" asked Mr. Fernandez. Several students in the seminar had suggestions. Mr. Fernandez summarized their suggestions on the chalkboard.

Family and friends often know about a place to rent before the place is advertised in the newspaper. Owners frequently like to rent to people they know or to those referred by trustworthy acquaintances. You may get a better deal as a result.

The classified section of your *local newspaper* will give you a good idea of the cost of various types of apartments in different sections of the city.

Some *real estate agencies* have apartment listings. Usually the agent's fee is paid by the owner of the building, so the assistance is of no cost to you. Real estate agencies are a big help when moving to a city you're unfamiliar with.

Illustration 10-1

Photo location courtesy of Fath Management Co., Torrence Lane Apartments, Cincinnati, Ohio

One possibility is to walk to the door of the *apartment manager* and ask the following questions.

- What is the monthly rent? initial deposit?
- What does the rent include? utilities? laundry facilities? repairs?
- Is there a lease? (Leases are discussed in detail on page 196.)
- What type of building security is provided?
- What parking provisions are provided?
- What are the rules and regulations regarding the complex (pets, quiet times, etc.)?

Then, of course, take a careful look at the apartment.

"Before deciding on an apartment, talk to the *tenants* (the people who live in the apartment building)," Mr. Fernandez suggested. "Ask them about their experiences as tenants. For example:

- How good is security?
- Is the place noisy?
- How often is the rent raised?
- Are repairs to the apartment made quickly?
- Is the building well kept?

STUDENT ACTIVITY A

1. After high school graduation, what four options might you consider as a place to live?

    a. _____

    b. _____

    c. _____

    d. _____

2. Name three topics which should be discussed and agreed upon before renting an apartment with someone else.

    a. _____

    b. _____

    c. _____

3. What five expenses should be accounted for in the first month of renting?

    a. _____

    b. _____

    c. _____

    d. _____

    e. _____

4. What are five sources of information about apartments?

a. _____

b. _____

c. _____

d. _____

e. _____

5. With a job paying $4 an hour for a 40-hour week, determine what type of apartment you can afford. First, figure your monthly income. Remember you are figuring gross income, *not* take-home pay. Take-home pay will amount to even less. Second, make a list of needed materials and their costs. Third, list expenses directly related to renting an apartment. Use the following chart for your calculations.

Gross income
($4 × 40 hours per week × 4) $_____

Household items   Costs
(Check with family and friends for accurate estimates)

_____   _____

_____   _____

_____   _____

_____   _____

_____   _____

_____   _____

_____   _____

_____   _____

_____   _____

_____   _____

                                        Total $ _____

Initial apartment expenses   Costs
(Check averages for your area)

Security deposit   _____

Gas/electric utilities   _____

Water and garbage services   _____

Telephone installation/service   _____

Last month's rent   _____

                                        Total $ _____

6. Conclusions:

   a. How much should you have in savings before renting an apartment?

   _____

   b. How much can you afford to pay each month for an apartment?

   _____

   c. If earning $4 an hour for a 40-hour week, would you move into an apartment?

   _____

   If not, what other options do you have?

   _____

UNDERSTANDING A LEASE

Having discussed housing choices, Mr. Fernandez explained the concept of a lease to his students.

"A *lease* is a written contract allowing use of the owner's property for a specified time period," Mr. Fernandez said. "It is possible to rent property through an oral or written agreement for an indefinite time period, but such an agreement has built-in problems. In such cases, the owner, called the *landlord* or *landlady*, has the right to raise the rent or ask you to leave at any time (unless state law requires a 30-day notice). On the other hand, you—the renter or tenant—have the right to leave the apartment, with 30-days' notice, since you are not under contract for a definite period."

Mr. Fernandez advised a lease in most cases, unless you plan to stay in one place for a very short period of time. Most landlords/landladies require some type of written agreement.

"Before signing a lease, you should thoroughly inspect the apartment and carefully read the lease," Mr. Fernandez said. "As I mentioned before, you will probably have to put down a deposit for possible damage to the apartment. Therefore, you want to take note of any damage already done so that you won't have to pay for someone else's damage. One way to avoid any disagreement when the time comes for you to move is to fill out a checklist before signing the lease. Have the landlord/landlady sign it and you sign it. *There is nothing like a written agreement!*"

Figure 10-1 is a copy of the condition report (checklist) Mr. Fernandez gave his seminar. This report is for an unfurnished apartment. If the landlord/landlady does not supply such a sheet, use the one in Figure 10-1. If the apartment is furnished, include all furnishings in the report.

"You may be asked to sign a *rental application* before you receive a lease," Mr. Fernandez said. "A rental application usually asks for your employer's address and phone number, and credit references. If you are approved as a tenant, you will be offered a lease."

**Figure 10-1:
Apartment
Condition
Report**

CONDITION REPORT OF APARTMENT _____

	Dirty		Damaged	
	Yes	No	Yes	No
General Condition				
Walls	_____	_____	_____	_____
Floors	_____	_____	_____	_____
Ceilings	_____	_____	_____	_____
Ceiling Fixtures	_____	_____	_____	_____
Carpet	_____	_____	_____	_____
Drapes/Curtains	_____	_____	_____	_____
Door Key/Lock	_____	_____	_____	_____
Windows	_____	_____	_____	_____
Window Screens	_____	_____	_____	_____
Mailbox	_____	_____	_____	_____
Thermostat	_____	_____	_____	_____
Kitchen				
Stove	_____	_____	_____	_____
Refrigerator	_____	_____	_____	_____
Garbage Disposal	_____	_____	_____	_____
Kitchen Cabinets	_____	_____	_____	_____
Dishwasher	_____	_____	_____	_____
Bathroom				
Towel Racks	_____	_____	_____	_____
Medicine Cabinet	_____	_____	_____	_____
Tub/Shower	_____	_____	_____	_____
Toilet	_____	_____	_____	_____

_____ Date: _____
Signature of Tenant

_____ Date: _____
Signature of Landlord

Illustration 10-2

Photo location courtesy of Fath Management Co., Torrence Lane Apartments, Cincinnati, Ohio

Mr. Fernandez showed the class a copy of his nephew's lease. He explained that both the landlord/landlady (*lessor*) and the tenant (*lessee*) are bound by all the terms agreed upon in the lease. He warned the class never to rely on oral agreements because the lessor is not legally committed to any agreements that are *not* in writing.

Figure 10-2:
Apartment
Lease

APARTMENT LEASE

Date _February 10, 19--_

Parties

Thomas T. Lentz (hereinafter referred to as Lessor) hereby leases to _Roberto Ortique_ (hereinafter referred to as Lessee) the following described property:

Premises

Apartment No. _3_ at _301 Green Street_ in _Our Towne, CA_ for use by resident as a private residence only.

Term

This lease is for a term commencing on the _1_ day of _March_ 19 _----_ , and ending on the last calendar day _February_ , 19 _----_ .

Automatic Renewal

If Lessee, or Lessor, desires that this lease terminate at the expiration of its term, he or she must give to the other party written notice at least 30 days prior to that date. Failure of either party to give this required notice will automatically renew this lease and all the terms thereof except that the term of the lease will be for one month. This provision is a continuing one and will apply at the expiration of the original term and at the expiration of each subsequent term.

Rent

This lease is made for and in consideration of a monthly rental of _($320)_ _Three Hundred Twenty_ Dollars per month payable in advance on or before the 1st day of each month at _1001 Maple Street_ ____ . If the rent is paid by the 5th of the month, Lessee shall be entitled to a deduction of _($20) Twenty_ Dollars per month or a net rental of _($300) Three Hundred_ Dollars per month; provided however that any monthly rental payment not received by the 5th of the month shall be considered delinquent. If Lessee pays by check and said check is not honored on presentation for any reason whatsoever, Lessee agrees to pay an additional sum of $10.00 as a penalty.

In the event that the rent is not paid by the 10th of the month, Lessee shall be deemed to be in default; and Lessor shall have the option to cancel this lease effective on midnight of the 14th of the month. On or before the termination date, Lessor shall deliver written notice of Lessor's election to cancel this lease to Lessee's premises.

Lessor acknowledges receipt from Lessee of the sum of _($300) Three Hundred_ Dollars which is pro-rated rental for _30_ days from the date of commencement of this lease to the first day of the following month.

Security Deposit

Upon execution of this lease contract, Lessee agrees to deposit with Lessor, the receipt of which is hereby acknowledged, the sum of $ _(150) One Hundred Fifty_ . This deposit, which is non-interest bearing, is to be held by Lessor as security for the full and faithful performance of all the terms and conditions of this lease. This security deposit is not an advance rental and Lessee may not deduct any portion of the deposit from rent due to Lessor. This security deposit is not to be considered liquidated damages. In the event of forfeiture of the security deposit due to Lessee's failure to fully and faithfully perform all the terms and conditions of the lease, Lessor retains all of his or her other rights and remedies. Lessee does not have the right to cancel this lease and avoid his or her obligations thereunder by forfeiting the said security deposit. Deposit refund will be mailed.

Lessee shall be entitled to return of the said security deposit within 30 days after the premises have been vacated and inspected by Lessor provided said lease premises are returned to Lessor in as good condition as they were at the time Lessee first occupied same, subject only to normal wear and tear and after all keys are surrendered to Lessor. Lessor agrees to deliver the premises broom clean and free of trash at the beginning of this lease and Lessee agrees to return same in like condition at the termination of the lease.

Notwithstanding any other provisions expressed or implied herein, it is specifically understood and agreed that the entire security deposit aforesaid shall be automatically forfeited as liquidated damages should Lessee vacate or abandon the premises before the expiration of this lease, except where such abandonment occurs during the last month of the term of the lease, Lessee has paid all rent covering the entire term and either party has given the other timely written notice that his lease will not be renewed under its renewal provisions.

Occupants

The leased premises shall be occupied by the following persons only:
<u>Roberto Ortique</u>

Pets

No pets allowed to live on the premises at any time. However, this provision shall not preclude Lessor for modifying any lease to allow pets by mutual written agreement between Lessor and Lessee.

Sublease

Lessee is not permitted to post any "For Rent" signs, rent, sublet or grant use or possession of the leased premises without the written consent of Lessor and then only in accordance with this lease.

Default or Abandonment

Should the Lessee fail to pay the rent or any other charges arising under this lease promptly as stipulated, should the premises be abandoned by Lessee or should Lessee begin to remove furniture or any substantial portion of Lessee's personal property to the detriment of Lessor's lien, or should voluntary or involuntary bankruptcy proceedings be commended by or against Lessee, or should Lessee make an assignment for the benefit of creditors, then in any of said events Lessee shall be *ipso facto* in default and the rent for the whole of the expired term of the lease together with the attorney's fees shall immediately become due. In the event of such cancellation and eviction, Lessee is obligated to pay any and all rent due and owing through the last day said premises are occupied.

In the event that during the term of this lease, or any renewal hereof, either the real estate taxes or the utility costs, or both, should increase above the amount being paid on the leased premises at the inception of this lease, the Lessee agrees to pay his or her proportionate share of such increase and any successive increases. Such payment or payments by Lessee shall be due monthly as increased rent throughout the remainder of Lessee's occupancy; and all such sums may be withheld from Lessee's security deposit if not fully paid at the time Lessee vacates the premises. A 30-day notice will be given to Lessee before any increase is made.

Other Conditions

A temporary visitor is one who inhabits the property for no more than ten (10) days.

_____

_____

Executed in duplicate at
<u>301 Green St., Our Towne, CA</u>

this <u>10</u> day of <u>February</u>,

19_____

Thomas T. Lentz
Lessor

Roberto Ortique
Lessee

STUDENT ACTIVITY B

Read the lease in Figure 10-2 carefully, and answer the following questions.

1. Who is the lessor?

   _____

2. Who is the lessee?

   _____

3. What must Roberto do if he wishes to move out of the apartment by the expiration date on the lease?

   _____

   _____

4. How much rent does Roberto owe if he pays before the 5th of the month?

   _____

5. What is the penalty if Roberto writes a check not honored by his bank (a "bad" check)?

   _____

6. What right does the lessor have if the lessee does not pay the rent by the 10th of the month?

   _____

7. What was the amount of Roberto's security deposit?

   _____

8. Is Roberto entitled to the return of his security deposit?

   _____

   a. When?

   _____

   b. Under what provisions?

   _____

   _____

   _____

9. Can Roberto keep a cat in the apartment?

   _____

10. Is Roberto permitted to rent (sublet) the apartment to anyone if he temporarily moves out of his apartment for the summer?

    _____

11. Can Roberto move out during the term of the lease without notifying the lessor?

    _____

12. Can the lessor raise the rent during the designated term of the lease? Explain.

_____

_____

13. If you were renting, what other provisions would you want included in the lease?

_____

_____

Mr. Fernandez reemphasized how important it is to take time to read the apartment lease carefully before signing. You should take note of the following:

1. Requirements for the return of the security deposit;

2. Conditions of the lease;

3. Legal rights of both the lessor and the lessee if any violations of the lease occur:

4. Party responsible for repairs and maintenance; and

5. Oral agreements not contained in the lease.

STUDENT ACTIVITY C

Chita and her friend Marta have fallen in love with the window boxes on the front of an apartment house. They could not wait to move in. It was their first experience at renting on their own. The landlady had been very friendly and had charged them only $250 a month, which they thought was reasonable. They had noticed, however, that the refrigerator and bathroom fixtures looked old. When they mentioned it, the landlady promised she would take care of any needed repairs. They signed the lease quickly and moved in.

Two weeks later the refrigerator in Chita and Marta's apartment is not working. The bathroom toilet overflows. When they complain to the landlady, she says she will take care of the problem. They checked their lease, and it says nothing about repairs.

1. What is wrong with Chita and Marta's approach to renting an apartment?

_____

_____

2. Can they be assured of ever getting the refrigerator and toilet fixed?

_____

Explain.

_____

_____

BUYING A HOME

"Buying a home is one of the largest purchases most of us make in a lifetime," Mr. Fernandez said. "In fact, buying a home is considered an investment—and a good one—if the time and place is right for us.

"Most of you will not be financially able to buy a home in the near future. Indeed, many young couples with combined salaries cannot afford a home. The average cost of a home in the mid-1980s was $75,000, and that does not include other expenses associated with buying and owning a place to live. Still, owning your own home is part of the American dream, and most of us have such a goal in our financial picture. One way to determine how much you can afford to spend on a home is to multiply your annual net income by 2.5. You should be able to afford a home that is two and one-half times your annual income.

"There are advantages and disadvantges to buying a home. Let's look at the advantages first," said Mr. Fernandez.

Illustration 10-3

"Without question, one of the biggest advantages of owning your own home is the *privacy and freedom* it affords. Apartments are often noisy, and you are not free to make improvements without the permission of the landlord/landlady. Then, improvements become the property of the lessor, unless prior agreements to the contrary are made. Improvements on your own home increase the value of the property.

"Home ownership provides you with equity. *Equity* is the difference between the value of your home and the amount you owe. So, if you own a $100,000 home and owe $30,000 on a home loan, you have equity of $70,000. To put it another way, if you sold the property for $100,000 you would have $70,000 after paying off your $30,000 debt. Also, lending institutions often lend money to borrowers who wish to use their home equity as collateral. See page 84 of Unit 4, "Credit," for information on collateral.

"Owning a home can be a *tax savings*. You can deduct the interest paid on a home loan from your income tax. Because most lending institutions use the Rule of 78's, you pay more interest during the early years of your loan. (See Rule of 78's, Unit 4, "Credit," p. 86.) The more interest you can deduct, the less income tax you have to pay. Therefore, you are saving on taxes while gradually increasing your equity," Mr. Fernandez said.

"If that's the case, why doesn't everyone buy instead of rent?" Susan asked.

"Because it's not as easy as it looks," Mr. Fernandez said. "Let's examine a few of the disadvantages—or difficulties—involved when buying a home. First of all, when you sink your money into a home, you automatically reduce your mobility. You can't just give a 30-day notice and move to another spot. You are stuck with the house until you sell it. So if you don't intend staying in one place for two or three years, you probably shouldn't buy.

"Secondly, when you buy a home, you automatically incur a lot of costs, and many of them have to be paid immediately." Mr. Fernandez then discussed the costs associated with the purchase of a home.

You usually have to make a down payment when buying a home. A *down payment* covers a percentage of the purchase price, usually 10 or 20 percent. So for a $75,000 home, you might be required to pay a 10 percent down payment or $7,500. The larger your down payment, the less you have to borrow, and the less your monthly house payments. You don't want to exhaust your savings on a down payment, however, because you will have closing costs to pay. Also, you should always have six-month's salary in savings in case of an inability to work or because of unemployment.

A *mortgage* is a loan in which the principal (amount borrowed) is repaid to the lender with interest. Mortgage payments are usually made monthly over a 15- to 30-year time period. For example, a $60,000 loan at 14 percent, amounts to $8,400 in average yearly interest. Multiply $8,400 by 30 years (the length of the loan), and you get $252,000—the total interest you will pay over the length of the loan. Many people do not realize that they are paying far more than the purchase price of the home. Few of us, however, can afford to pay cash for a home.

The last step in buying a home is the completion of the sale, or closing. Closing costs include fees for services required to transfer ownership of the property from one person to another. Closing costs usually include a *title search*, which is an investigation to see if the *title* (evidence of ownership) is clear. A title search should reveal whether or not the property to be sold has any *liens* or debts against it. A person who buys property with a lien against it is obligated to pay the creditors (those who hold the lien and are owed money). Therefore, it is important to have a title search and be assured of a clear title to the property.

Closing costs may also include the attorney's fees, the recording fee, the loan origination fee, and the appraisal fee. In all, fees may range from $1,000 to $5,000. According to the Real Estate Settlement Procedures Act of 1974, the lender should provide an estimate of settlement costs within three days after a mortgage application is made and provide all the necessary information about closing costs at least one business day before closing.

"So when you decide you want a cute little home with red shutters, remember, there's more to it than the monthly payments," Mr. Fernandez said. "You should begin saving money for a home as soon as you get a full-time job because it takes a good while to build up enough cash for the down payment. When it comes time for you to buy, you should figure what you can afford on paper before looking around. That will prevent you from tempting yourself with a disastrous financial situation."

"Suppose I want to buy the house with the red shutters," Susan said, "how would I go about it?"

"Well," Mr. Fernandez laughed, "the first thing you need to do is ask yourself a few questions *before deciding* on the red-shutter house." Below are some of the questions Mr. Fernandez suggested one ask:

1. What are my needs now, and later? Do I plan to own a home for a long period of time?

2. What can I afford for a down payment? monthly payments?

3. How important are the following to me?

   a. neighborhood

   b. shopping convenience

   c. nearness to work

   d. property taxes

   e. resale value of property

   f. construction of the house, inside and out (make a checklist of things to examine)

4. What are the sources of mortgage loans?

   a. *Savings and loan associations* make loans primarily for home purchases.

   b. *Commercial banks* commonly provide home loans.

   c. If you have a life insurance policy, you might consider the *life insurance company* as a possible source for a loan.

   d. *Mortgage companies* share an important role in home financing in many communities. There is a great lack of uniformity in the policies and procedures of these companies.

   e. *Private lenders* often include relatives or the seller of the property. Private lenders are free to operate as they please as long as they stay within the bounds of state laws on lending.

5. What are the costs associated with buying a home?

a. down payment

b. mortgage payments

c. settlement on closing costs such as:

- *Property taxes*—the seller may be entitled to a refund for a portion of the year for which property taxes were paid.

- *Attorney's fees*—for preparing and checking legal documents covering the sale and the mortgage.

- *Loan origination fee*—some lenders charge fees or commissions for granting the loan. This fee is often charged as a small percent of the amount borrowed.

- *Title search*—examination of title is an investigation of ownership to make certain there are no claims to the property by others.

- *Recording fee*—for the deed to the property. A *deed* is written evidence of the ownership of a piece of property and serves as a means of conveying the title from one person to another.

- *Appraisal fee*—the charge for examining and determining the value of the property. The lender will usually request an appraisal of the property.

- *Title insurance*—a policy which protects the lender's interest in the property against the claims of others when the claims were not disclosed by the title search or examination.

- *Termite inspection*—many lenders request that the property be checked for harmful pests before granting a loan.

d. *Mortgage redemption insurance:* A form of life insurance whereby the balance of the loan is paid by the insurance company if the borrower should die before the loan is repaid.

e. *Moving expenses.* What will be the cost of having furnishings and households goods moved by a professional mover as compared to doing it yourself?

f. Other expenses, often unexpected:

- repair and upkeep costs, especially on an older home

- initial utility costs, such as phone installation

- appliance purchases, such as the purchase of a refrigerator or washing machine

Once you have decided to buy a certain home, you should make an offer somewhat below the asking price. The owner may accept your offer or make a *counter offer*; that is, agree to sell the property at a price above your offer. Once you and the owner come to an agreement on the price and other terms relating to the sale, you sign an agreement to buy the home at a stated price and offer *earnest money* (usually $1,000 to $5,000) which proves you are seriously interested in buying the home. Of course, this earnest money is deducted from the selling price of the home at closing. If you fail to meet the terms of the agreement, you may lose the earnest money, so you should always include a clause in the agreement saying the sale is not definite until you get financing (loan approval).

After the agreement is reached, a neutral third party called an *escrow agent* arranges for the closing. (The escrow agent is often an officer of a bank or a savings and loan association.) The closing date is usually 30 to 60 days after an agreement is reached to sell a home. At the closing, the buyer, seller, real estate brokers, lender, and lawyers meet to sign and deliver all legal papers. The seller is also paid for the home at this time. If there is a mortgage loan, the lender and the buyer together pay the lender, and the mortgage goes into effect.

STUDENT ACTIVITY D

1. When Mr. Fernandez finished talking about all that was involved with buying a home, Susan thought of her cousin Lou. When she was over at Lou's house last Saturday night, Lou and his wife were talking about buying a home. The conversation went something like this.

    Louis: I'm sick of this apartment. I want to buy our own home. I'm tired of giving our money to the landlord. I want something we can call our own.

    Angie: But, Lou, we only have $3,000 in savings. How can we buy a home?

    Louis: Easy, you and I are both working. We can borrow from this friend of mine whose father owns a mortgage company. We'll sink the $3,000 into the house and borrow the rest.

    Angie: What house?

    Louis: I saw this house for sale on the corner. Looks really fine. I called the real estate agent. They want $60,000. I say we jump at it.

    Angie: But I heard you had to put 20 percent of the cost down in cash. And how much is the interest rate at the mortgage company?

    Louis: Who cares! Look, you work, and I work. We can handle it. Don't you like the house?

    Angie: Well, yes, but it's so quick. . . .

    a. What is wrong with Lou's approach to buying a home? List any mistakes.

    _____

    _____

    _____

    _____

    _____

    _____

b. With $3,000 in savings, are Lou and his wife able to put 20 percent down on a $60,000 home?

_____

How much would they need in addition to the $3,000 in savings?

_____

c. What costs is Lou forgetting?

_____

2. Susan had several terms on her list of considerations for buying a home. Match each term below with the appropriate definition.

_____ 1. real estate mortgage

_____ 2. down payment

_____ 3. closing costs

_____ 4. appraisal fee

_____ 5. title

_____ 6. mortgage redemption insurance

_____ 7. deed

_____ 8. equity

_____ 9. earnest money

_____ 10. escrow agent

a. policy in which the balance of the loan is paid by the insurance company if the borrower should die before the loan is repaid
b. part of the property price that is paid in cash at the time of purchase
c. proof of ownership of property
d. contract between the borrower and lender for the purpose of buying property
e. neutral third party who handles the closing
f. proof of interest in buying a home
g. difference between the value of a home and the amount owed on a mortgage
h. charges for taxes, recording of deed, examination of title, etc.
i. charge for examining and determining value of property
j. written evidence of the ownership of a piece of property

FURTHER DISCOVERIES

1. Look for newspaper ads of apartments for rent requiring a lease. Choose two apartments in a neighborhood in which you would like to live. Use the checklist provided at the end of the unit to help you examine the apartments. Also, examine a copy of the rental agreement or lease. Write a report about the similarities and differences in the apartments.

2. Having read about renting an apartment and buying a home, list the advantages and disadvantages of renting and buying. You may have noticed some advantages and disadvantages by observing experiences of your family and friends.

Renting

Advantages	Disadvantages
_____	_____
_____	_____
_____	_____
_____	_____
_____	_____
_____	_____
_____	_____
_____	_____

Buying a Home

Advantages	Disadvantages
_____	_____
_____	_____
_____	_____
_____	_____
_____	_____
_____	_____
_____	_____
_____	_____

3. Check newspaper ads of homes for sale. List five homes of similar size and quality (brick, frame, etc.) in various neighborhoods of your community. Prepare a chart that compares the five homes on the basis of shopping convenience, property taxes, location in the community, school system, construction, and price. Figure out the monthly mortgage payments with the present interest rates and a 20 percent down payment.

CHECKLIST

If you have completed the student activities in this unit, you should have mastered the skills below. Check off the skills you know, and review the ones you are not sure of.

(   ) What to consider before renting

(   ) How to interpret a rental agreement or lease

(   ) What to consider before buying a home

(   ) Sources of loans for home buyers

(   ) Terminology commonly used in buying a home

(   ) The various costs and procedures involved in purchasing a home

If you have checked all of the above skills, ask your teacher for the Susan Thompson Test on Housing.

RENTERS' CHECKLIST

	Apt. 1	Apt. 2
Address		
Is the apartment close to public transportation?		
What is the monthly rent?		
How many rooms?		
Is it furnished or unfurnished?		
What is the length of lease?		
Options for renewal?		
Can you sublet?		
What is the amount of the security deposit?		
Who pays utilities?		
Average monthly cost?		
Who pays heat?		
Average monthly cost?		
Are pets allowed?		
Are there extra fees for:		
Storage space?		
Air conditioning?		
Parking space? (outdoor, indoor, covered)		
Use of swimming pool?		
Use of tennis courts?		
Is there a resident manager or superintendent?		
What are the garbage disposal facilities?		
Is there laundry equipment in the unit?		
Is the laundry room safe?		
Are laundry room hours assigned?		
What are the provisions for mail and parcel delivery?		

(continued next page)

RENTERS' CHECKLIST (cont'd)

What are the security provisions? .... _____

    Are the stairs well-lighted? .... _____

    Are there safe fire exits? .... _____

    Is there a smoke detector system? .... _____

Is the general layout of the unit good? .... _____

Is the bathroom clean? .... _____

Is there adequate hot water? .... _____

Will the unit be painted or decorated before you move in? . . _____

Are there "house rules"? (e.g., no TV or stereo at
certain times) .... _____

Is there adequate closet space? .... _____

Is there a dead-bolt lock on the door? A peephole? .... _____

Can you install your own lock? .... _____

Is the kitchen clean? .... _____

    Adequate cupboard space? .... _____

    Appliances included? .... _____

    Exhaust fan? .... _____

Are drapes included? carpeting? .... _____

Are there sufficient (2-3 per room) electrical outlets? .... _____

Is there adequate ventilation? .... _____

    Can windows be opened? .... _____

    Are there screens? .... _____

    Are there storm windows? .... _____

    Will the outside of the windows be cleaned by building
    maintenance? .... _____

What are the other tenants like? (age, children) .... _____

Other (comments, impressions) .... _____

© 1982, *Current Consumer & Lifestudies.*
Reprinted by permission of Curriculum Innovations, Inc., Highland Park, IL.

UNIT 11

CONSUMER PROTECTION

SKILL 1 **What You Should Know About Your Rights as a Consumer**

SKILL 2 **How to Use Consumer Publications**

SKILL 3 **How to Handle Complaints as a Consumer**

SKILL 4 **How to Interpret Legal Agreements and Warranties as a Consumer**

Further Discoveries

WHAT YOU SHOULD KNOW ABOUT YOUR RIGHTS AS A CONSUMER

Susan was enjoying her Saturday, for a change. She was reading and relaxing on the porch. Everything was quiet, so she could listen to her favorite radio station without being disturbed.

She noticed an ad about "miracle belts" in the magazine she was reading. According to the ad, Susan could lose as much as three pounds a day. Susan was painfully aware of the extra flab that had mysteriously gathered around her waistline. The gadget was expensive, but it sounded worth the money.

She was on the verge of writing for the miracle belt when she remembered two things. One, her bank account was painfully low; and two, Carlos had ordered a muscle-builder last year that did less than great things for him. Susan decided to show the article to Mr. Fernandez.

"If you haven't learned already, you need to become aware that you are a consumer," Mr. Fernandez told the class, holding up Susan's article for everyone to see. "Whenever you buy a product or a service, you are acting as a *consumer*. The people in the marketplace depend on you to buy their products. In recent years, consumers have become more aware of their influence on the types of products and caliber of products being sold. Before 1962, consumers had little recourse when they got stuck with a 'lemon.' Today, if consumers do not protect themselves against unsatisfactory products, it is their own fault because there are consumer protection laws that cover just about every area of the marketplace."

Mr. Fernandez went on to say that if you are to be a smart consumer, you need to know your rights and responsibilities. Most of your rights are protected by federal and state laws; unfortunately, many people are uninformed about consumer protection laws.

In his State of the Union Address of 1962, President John F. Kennedy proposed a consumer bill of rights that included the following:

1. *The right to safety*—protection against the sale of products that are dangerous to life or health.

2. *The right to choose*—protection against practices that result in uncompetitive prices for goods and services available to the consumer.

3. *The right to be informed*—protection against fraudulent and misleading advertising.

4. *The right to be heard*—assurance of consumer representation in the formation of government policy and enforcement of consumer protection laws.

Since 1962, many consumer protection laws have been passed dealing with door-to-door sales, junk mail, credit costs, land sales, unordered merchandise, vocational schools, mail-order purchases, leasing, eyeglasses, franchises, hobbies, fabric labels, and advertising, to name only a few areas.

STUDENT ACTIVITY A

1. Why do you think Carlos's muscle-builder experience caused Susan not to send for the miracle belt?

   _____

   _____

2. If Susan's belt was advertised to perform miracles and didn't, which one of the bill of rights was the advertiser ignoring?

   _____

3. Name other deceptive mail-ads that often appear in teenage or adult magazines.

   _____

   _____

HOW TO USE CONSUMER PUBLICATIONS

Mr. Fernandez told his students that one way to keep informed as a consumer is to read consumer magazines. There are several magazines that can help you shop more wisely. Two of them have the word *consumer* in the title—*Consumer Reports* and *Consumers' Research Magazine*. Both magazines are published by nonprofit organizations which have their own laboratories and testing facilities. These magazines rate products that have been tested. Another magazine that provides information for the consumer is *Changing Times.*

Magazines like *Consumer Reports, Consumers' Research Magazine,* and *Changing Times* save shopping time. For instance, if you wish to buy an auto receiver cassette player, you might have to go to five or six stores in order to see all the major brands. This type of shopping takes a considerable amount of time. Besides, if you do not have time to check everywhere, the dealers you see may tell you only about the brands they sell. Although most dealers are honest, there are some who may convince you that a certain cassette player is the best simply because they carry the brand. Some dealers are unfamiliar with brands they do not carry.

Before you go into the store to buy a cassette player, you should know what you want in the product. Do you know which brands have the best power, frequency response, and sensitivity? Would you have even considered these features before buying a cassette player? There is no need to waste money on a bad purchase because you do not know what to look for. In March 1985, *Consumer Reports* rated twenty-one brands of auto receiver cassette players. Time spent reading the article could help you narrow your choices to three or four models before leaving home to shop. Figure 11-1 is a rating chart on auto receiver cassette players from the March 1985 issue of *Consumer Reports.*

STUDENT ACTIVITY B

Study the ratings in Figure 11-1, and answer the following questions.

1. Are the models listed in alphabetical order or according to the best overall quality?

   _____

2. Which brand-model is rated the best?

   _____

3. Which brand-model is rated the worst?

   _____

4. What does (◉) symbolize?

   _____

5. What does (●) symbolize?

   _____

Figure 11-1:
Auto Receivers and Cassette Players

Ratings

Better ● ◑ ○ ◐ ● Worse

Auto receivers/cassette players

Listed in order of estimated overall quality. Differences in overall score of 8 points or less were judged not significant. Prices are approximate retail; discounts are usually available.

Brand and model	Price	Power at 4/8 ohms (watts)	Overall score	Cassette player — Cassette score	Flutter	Frequency response	Dynamic range	Receiver — Receiver score	FM multipath handling	FM front-end overload	FM selectivity	FM capture ratio	FM sensitivity	AM sensitivity	Advantages	Disadvantages	Comments
Chrysler RAN	[1]	12/9	84	87	●	◑	◑	87	○	●	◑	◑	●	◑	◑	B,E,H,I,K	f	A,C
Kenwood KRC3100	$199	3.5/2.5	82	78	◑	○	◑	91	●	●	◑	◑	●	◑	◑	A,E,F,H,I,J	i	C
J. C. Penney Cat. No. 8520306	250+	13/7.5	82	82	◑	◑	○	87	◑	◑	◑	●	◑	●	●	B,E,J	—	A,C
Jensen ATZ100	320	3.5/2.5	81	79	◑	◑	○	83	◐	●	●	◑	◑	○	◑	A,B,D,E,F,H,I,J,L	—	A,B,F
Sony XR65B	330	3.5/2.5	80	79	◑	◑	◑	86	●	●	◑	◑	●	◑	◑	A,D,E,H,J,L	h,i	—
Craig T860E	290	3.5/2.5	79	83	◑	○	◑	83	●	◑	◑	○	◑	◑	◑	B,E,F,J,K	b,c,g	A
Clarion 6900RT	199	4/2.5	78	82	◑	○	◑	83	●	◑	◑	◑	●	◑	○	E,F	c,i	—
Pioneer KEA630	280	3.5/2.5	77	79	◑	◑	◑	79	●	●	●	○	○	◑	●	C,D,E,H,I,J,K,L	i	B
Realistic 121905	250	6.5/5.5	77	73	◑	◐	○	85	●	◑	◑	◑	◑	◑	●	A,E,F,H,L	b,l	C,H
Sparkomatic SR315	350	14/9	77	80	○	◑	●	80	●	○	◑	●	○	◑	◑	B,E,G,I,J	f,i	A,C
Ford 586	[2]	15/9	77	81	◑	◑	○	77	◑	●	◑	◑	◐	◑	●	D,E,F,H,I,K,L	—	C
Delco UU7	[3]	10.5/7.5	76	72	○	●	○	86	◑	◑	◑	◑	◑	◑	●	E,F,H	a,c	C
Hi-Comp HCC1050	230	3.5/2.5	75	82	●	◑	○	76	○	◑	●	◑	○	○	◑	C,I,J	a	B
Concord HPL122R	280	5/3	72	81	◑	◑	◑	75	◑	●	◑	◑	○	◑	◑	E,J	a,f	A,C
Sanyo FTE25	300	6/5	72	79	◑	◑	●	72	◐	●	◑	●	○	◑	●	B,H,I	—	A,B
Alpine 7154	330	3.5/2.5	71	84	●	○	◑	75	●	◑	◑	○	◑	○	◑	F,I,L	a,d,e,g	C
Panasonic CQS804	250	3.5/2.5	71	73	○	◑	◑	79	●	◑	◑	○	○	○	◑	E,H	b,c,l	E
Sears Cat. No. 50029	200+	13.5/8	70	79	◑	◑	●	70	○	◑	◑	◑	○	●	◑	I,J	g	B,D
Blaupunkt Aspen SQR24	320	4/2.5	68	72	○	○	◑	70	◐	○	◑	◑	○	◑	◑	E,H,I	i	C,G
Kraco ETR1089	380	7/5	68	75	○	●	◑	69	◐	●	●	●	◐	●	◑	E	a	C,D
Audiovox AVX3500	280	7.5/5	61	76	◑	◑	◑	61	◐	◑	◑	◑	◐	◑	○	—	c,g	D

[1] 1984 factory equipment. Lists for $389 on Turismo/Horizon, $389 on Reliant, Gran Fury, Voyager, and Fifth Avenue, $299 on Laser, $424 on LeBaron, E Class, and New Yorker, and $139 on Executive Sedan/Limousine. Price includes 4 speakers, antenna, and installation. 1985 model has AM stereo and DNR instead of Dolby noise reduction.

[2] 1984 factory equipment. Lists for $396 on LTD, Thunderbird, Escort, GL, and EXP (Escort and EXP price varies depending on trimline); $310 on Crown Victoria. Price includes 4 speakers, antenna, and installation. 1985 model has tape-search feature.

[3] 1984 factory equipment. Lists for $277 on 1984 Chevrolet Celebrity or Cavalier. Price includes 4 speakers, antenna, and installation. 1984 models replaced by new version in 1985 cars.

Specifications and Features

All have: • FM stereo indicator light. • Locking fast-forward and rewind controls. • Automatic tape stop or play after fast-forward or rewind. • "Motorola-type" antenna jacks. • Tone controls.
Except as noted, all have: • Well-lighted controls.

Key to Advantages

A – Can play tape without radio on.
B – Cassette is easy to insert and eject.
C – Can skip weak stations in seek mode.
D – Seek mode works both up and down band.
E – Tone controls are easy to set.
F – Tone controls are hard to disturb.
G – Has bass-boost switches.
H – Good control layout.
I – Well-lighted controls.

J – Control settings are easy to check.
K – Panel brightness is adjustable with headlight switch.
L – On/off switch is separate from volume control.

Key to Disadvantages

a – Cassette is difficult to insert or eject.
b – Tuner is susceptible to front-end overload and has no "local" switch to ameliorate problem.
c – Tuner makes noise when changing stations.
d – Has small slide controls, which are difficult to adjust.
e – Tone controls difficult to set.
f – Tone controls are easy to disturb.
g – Controls poorly laid out.
h – Has poor AVC (automatic volume control).

which compensates for varying signal strength on AM.
i – Installation instructions judged sketchy.

Key to Comments

A – Cassette ejects automatically when power is turned off.
B – Has liquid-crystal display with backlight.
C – Has lighted-segment numeric display.
D – Includes device to check wiring-harness installation.
E – Has "ambience" switch, which is claimed to expand the stereo effect.
F – Display lights go on when ignition is on.
G – Has "Automatic Radio Information" feature (see story).
H – According to company, model has been discontinued.

6. Which brand-models are rated the best on flutter?

_____

7. Which brand-model has the best overall score?

_____

8. How are the advantages and disadvantages indicated on the chart?

_____

_____

_____

Susan liked *Consumer Reports* because it was written in simple language and raised many questions that she had not thought about. She wondered, however, if she should depend on the ratings in *Consumer Reports*. She asked Mr. Fernandez about it. Mr. Fernandez told Susan that *Consumer Reports* is very dependable. He said that the magazine is published by Consumers Union of United States and is one of the oldest consumer magazines in existence. Consumers Union does not allow companies to quote from articles in the magazine for the purpose of advertising, including companies to whom they give the highest ratings.

Mr. Fernandez cautioned the class that even a good product may have an occasional bad item, so *Consumer Reports* is not a guarantee of a good buy. But Susan could see that choices for making a good purchase were improved by consulting a consumer magazine such as *Consumer Reports*.

STUDENT ACTIVITY C

1. Is *Consumer Reports* the only magazine offering guidance about shopping wisely?

_____

2. Name some consumer publications other than *Consumer Reports*.

_____

_____

3. Who publishes *Consumer Reports*?

_____

4. What is *Consumer Reports* policy regarding the advertisement of products the magazine recommends?

_____

_____

5. If you buy a product recommended in *Consumer Reports*, are you guaranteed it will always work properly?

_____

Why or why not?

_____

_____

Since the class seemed particularly interested in *Consumer Reports*, Mr. Fernandez showed them how the magazine was organized. He explained that *Consumer Reports* is published monthly, January through November of each year. The issues are numbered 1 through 11. Many libraries bind these eleven issues into one volume at the end of the year. For the consumer's convenience, each issue contains an index to articles in the preceding eleven issues. Every December there is a special issue called the *Buying Guide*. The *Buying Guide* is dated for the following year. For example, the December 1986 issue is dated as the *Buying Guide Issue, 1987*.

The *Buying Guide* is different in appearance from the other issues of *Consumer Reports*. The *Buying Guide* looks like a thick paperback book instead of a magazine. Somewhat condensed versions of the most important articles in issues 1 through 11 of *Consumer Reports* are included in the *Buying Guide*, which has its own index. The *Buying Guide* is handy because it is only one volume, and it often contains updated information that was not contained in the preceding issues of *Consumer Reports*. Some people who do not buy the regular issues like to purchase the *Buying Guide* to use for quick reference. If you are interested in a product about which you know little, however, issues 1 through 11 of *Consumer Reports* offer more detailed explanations of the product.

In addition to summary articles from issues 1 through 11, the *Buying Guide* contains other items of interest. One such item is a list of addresses to which you can send complaints about products.

STUDENT ACTIVITY D

1. Does your school library subscribe to *Consumer Reports*?

_____

If so, what is the call number?

_____

2. What issue of *Consumer Reports* contains summaries of articles appearing in the past eleven issues?

_____

3. If you are interested in finding an article in one of the last eleven issues of *Consumer Reports*, what would be your guide?

_____

4. If you want to read about a topic or subject unfamiliar to you, would you use the *Buying Guide* or a regular issue? Explain your answer.

_____

_____

HOW TO HANDLE COMPLAINTS AS A CONSUMER

Mr. Fernandez told the class that in addition to consumer magazines, there are many different agencies that provide services to consumers. Many of the agencies send out free pamphlets upon request. He took the class to the library. The card catalog in the library had information on any number of agencies and organizations. There was consumer literature from the Consumer Federation of America, the Department of Commerce, National Consumers League, Environmental Protection Agency, Federal Trade Commission, Food and Drug Administration, and the Office of Consumer Affairs, to name only a few.

Illustration 11-1

Photo location courtesy Public Library of Cincinnati and Hamilton County

As Susan flipped through the card catalog, she noticed there was information on everything from how and where to borrow money to complaints about defective automobile tires. She could hardly believe how much consumer information was available. She discovered federal, state, and local agencies as well as private organizations to which a person can complain about almost anything, as the chart on page 221 shows.

The librarian told the class that there are many good consumer books on the market, in addition to consumer magazines. "Several of them are very helpful," she said. "Just look under 'consumer' or 'consumerism' in the card catalog. Also, the local newspaper usually carries articles that are beneficial to consumers. Get in the habit of reading consumer-related articles. You never know when the information may come in handy."

"Bought a lemon lately?" Mr. Fernandez asked the class. "Almost everyone has bought a bad product at some point in their lives, but to buy a bad product from someone who refuses to repair or replace it is a sour experience indeed. When that happens, you need to know how to complain successfully.

"To complain successfully, you need to know *how* and *where* to complain. Some people complain by displaying bumper stickers. The people may feel better, but bumper stickers do not accomplish much.

"Before complaining, be sure you are right and make sure you have the documentation to support your complaint. Otherwise, complaining will be a waste of time."

Where To Complain

Mr. Fernandez gave the class some tips on where to complain.

1. *First state your complaint to the local dealer.* Ask to speak to the manager. Salespersons have little authority to do anything about your complaint unless it's a simple matter of returning an obviously defective product. There is no need to get emotional. State your case and be sure to have your sales receipt with you and the warranty if there is one.

2. *If the problem is not resolved, contact the manufacturer in a letter.* Again, don't get emotional in your letter. State the facts. Don't exaggerate or be dishonest. Include *copies* (not the original) of your sales receipt and warranty in your letter. Let the manufacturer know what you want (replacement, repair, or refund). The addresses of manufacturers can be found in the *Thomas Register of American Manufacturers.* Corporations and their presidents can usually be found in *Standard and Poor's Register of Corporations, Directors and Executives.* Both publications are available in most public libraries. Never use threats or sarcasm in a letter of this nature.

3. *If you still get no results, contact a consumer interest group to find out where to get aid.* The list below will give some idea of the organizations available to complainants.

Where to Complain	*What to Complain About*
City and county consumer protection agencies	Gyps, frauds, false advertising, complaints about merchandise
Local Media Programs — Action Line	Unsatisfactory products/services
Local Food and Drug Administration office	Adulterated food, drugs, cosmetics and mislabeling of products
Regional office of Federal Trade Commission	Deceptive advertising, packaging, and selling
Local Better Business Bureau	Fraudulent business practices and advertising
Council of Better Business Bureaus 1150 Seventeenth Street, N.W. Washington, DC 20036	Same as above
State consumer office	Any type of consumer problem
State Office of Attorney General	Sales or business fraud

National Highway Traffic
  Safety Administration
Office of Public Affairs and Consumer
  Services
400 Seventh Street, S.W.
Washington, DC 20590
	Safety problems with cars and car accessories

Consumer Advocate U.S. Postal Service Rm. 5920, L'Enfant Plaza West, S.W. Washington, DC 20260	Postal service complaints, such as lost or damaged mail or packages
Consumer Product Safety Commission Washington, DC 20207	Defective or unsafe products
Office of Consumer Affairs Civil Aeronautics Board 1825 Connecticut Avenue, N.W. Washington, DC 20428	Complaints related to air travel and shipments
U.S. Office of Consumer Affairs Dept. of Health and Human Services 300 Seventh Street, S.W. Washington, DC 20004	Any type of consumer problem
Major Appliance Consumer Action Panel 20 N. Wacker Drive Chicago, IL 60606	Major appliance repair problems if dealer and manufacturer have not responded

Mr. Fernandez told the class that part of complaining successfully is knowing how to write an effective *letter of complaint.* The letter should clearly state what action is required in order to resolve the problem successfully. It should include all the essential facts: your name, address, and telephone number; name and model number of the product; place and date purchased; nature of the problem; clear description of previous efforts to resolve the problem, and responses from the dealer or manufacturer. Be sure to include a copy of your receipt and know your warranty coverage. The letter should be simple, direct, and complete. Mr. Fernandez showed the class an effective letter of complaint from a friend of his in Santa Rosa, California.

Figure 11-2:
Letter of
Complaint

---

789 Pioneer Trail
Santa Rosa, CA 95405-1622
April 7, 19--

Ms. Angelica Herrera, Manager
Boats Unlimited
10 Lakewood Drive
Lower Lake, CA 92225-2089

Dear Ms. Herrera:

On May 14, 19--, I purchased one of your 16-foot boats, the
Nautilus 242, from your Santa Rosa dealer. The boat is certainly
one of the easiest to handle that I have ever owned. Its appearance and styling are far superior to any other boat on the market
in its class and price range.

During the year that I have owned the boat, leaks have appeared
in various places under normal use. The fiberglass seems to be
extremely brittle, and it cracks at the slightest bump or scrape.
I have taken the boat in for repairs on three occasions. However,
the problems keep recurring, and your Santa Rosa dealer suggested
that I contact you.

I would like to take the boat to your Lower Lake plant to let
your engineers determine the cause of the leaks and the reason for
the brittle nature of the fiberglass. If the problem cannot be
resolved, I will expect a replacement boat under the provisions of
your full warranty for the Nautilus 242.

Because of the good reputation of your firm in manufacturing boats,
I am sure you will want to resolve this problem for me right away.

Sincerely yours,

Miss Mary Lee Vaughn

Miss Mary Lee Vaughn

STUDENT ACTIVITY E

1. Study the chart on page 221, and answer the following questions.

   a. To which agency might you report a defective ice-maker in your new refrigerator if you received no response from the manufacturer or dealer?

   _____

   b. Where might you report a company that sold you a $500 membership to a health club that does not exist?

   _____

   c. To whom would you report a lost package mailed to a friend in Iceland?

   _____

   d. Which organization can you contact when you have a consumer problem but are not sure about whom to contact?

   _____

2. List at least five consumer pamphlets available in your school or public library.

Consumer Pamphlet	Publisher
_____	_____
_____	_____
_____	_____
_____	_____
_____	_____

3. Check your local telephone directory, or one from a larger city nearby, and list the name, address, and telephone number of consumer agencies in your area.

   _____

   _____

   _____

   _____

A business-sponsored agency that handles a great number of consumer complaints is the *Better Business Bureau (BBB)*. Many cities have Better Business Bureaus, which are a part of the national organization called the Council of Better Business Bureaus. The Better Business Bureau functions for the consumer in the following ways: by informing the consumer about the reliability of a business in dealing with customers; by assisting the consumer in resolving any disputes if satisfaction is not received from the business or manufacturer; and by providing consumer information (the BBB prints numerous tip sheets, fact books, and information pamphlets).

Susan was not familiar with most of the organizations Mr. Fernandez had talked about, but she knew about the BBB. She was the proud owner of a set of stereo speakers that had a lot of static when played. Admittedly, she could occasionally hear a song in the distance, but mainly she heard static. Susan tried to return the speakers to Central Stereo, where she had bought them, but was told that sale items could not be returned. She asked them to repair the speakers. They agreed to do so and took the speakers, but Susan did not hear from them for one month. When she called, they could not find the speakers. To make matters worse, Central Stereo had changed managers. Susan called the BBB.

The BBB had several complaints on file for Central Stereo. Customers had complained that Central took too long to perform repairs. The Bureau told Susan that Central Stereo had refused to straighten out complaints when informed of them by the BBB. When Susan asked what to do, the Bureau told her that they do not take legal action against a company, but they would help in handling her complaint.

STUDENT ACTIVITY F

1. Name three functions of the Better Business Bureau.

   a. _____

   b. _____

   c. _____

2. What should Susan have done before buying the stereo speakers?

   _____

   _____

3. Now that she owns a pair of faulty speakers which cannot be found, what can she do about it?

   _____

   _____

4. Does the Better Business Bureau take legal action against a business?

   _____

"Susan should have checked with the BBB about Central Stereo *before* buying the speakers," Mr. Fernandez said. "Now that the deed is done, she has two choices.

"When two parties have failed to settle their dispute by other means, the BBB can arrange for a third party to help settle the matter voluntarily. A voluntary settlement through the help of the BBB is an alternative to taking the dispute to court.

"As you know, there are times when legal action against someone who has treated you unfairly is necessary. One means of taking legal action is through *small claims court*. Most larger communities have a small claims court, which operates for the purpose of handling only smaller claims, usually $1,000 or less in most states. Suing someone in small claims court has several advantages:

1. You do not need a lawyer.

2. Legal costs are relatively low. Court filing fees are around $15.

3. Most cases are settled quickly; however, if you win the case, it is up to you to collect the judgment.

"You simply go to the courthouse with your complaint, and they will tell you the procedure. You should have certain information with you, such as:

1. Name and address of the person or company you are suing.

2. Product brand name, model number, year of purchase, warranty coverage if complaining about a product.

Illustration 11-2

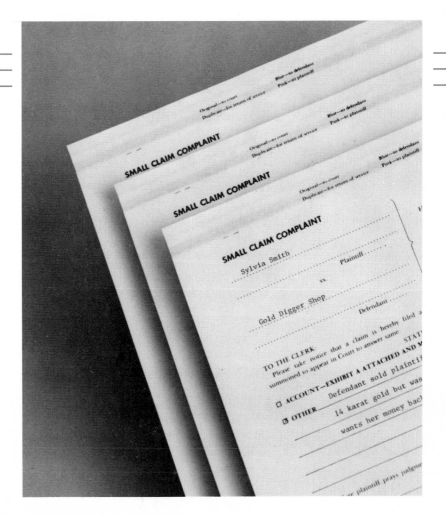

3. Proof of purchase (sales or charge slip, bill, or canceled check).

4. History of your complaint (previous action taken with names, dates, any written correspondence, brief description of the situation, and results of the complaint, if any)."

Susan was familiar with small claims court because her friend, Sylvia, had gone to small claims court to take legal action against the Gold Digger Shop. The $100 "gold" chain she bought for her boyfriend turned green.

Sylvia won her case, but, as she told Susan, going to small claims court should be the last resort. She had to gather every piece of evidence she could find: the receipt for the chain, the ad saying the chain was supposed to be 14-karat gold, her canceled check paid to the shop, the chain itself. She even had to drag her boyfriend into court to testify that the chain had indeed turned green.

Sylvia said she had to leave school to go to the courthouse and appear in court, and so did her boyfriend. But it was worth it for Sylvia. She had tried every other means she knew to get her money back or have the chain replaced with a genuine gold chain. The dealer would only repeat that her chain was genuine.

Susan had been impressed with Sylvia's ability to take care of herself. But Sylvia warned that a person should consider using small claims court only in the following instances:

- The claim can be awarded in money. You cannot go to small claims court seeking to recover property or to require somebody to perform a specific act.

- There is some particular person or company responsible for causing your complaint.

- All other means of getting satisfactory results have been exhausted, such as direct complaints to the person or company involved, the BBB, or a consumer protection agency.

STUDENT ACTIVITY G

You have read about consumer agencies, the BBB, and small claims court. If any one of the following experiences happened to you, what would you do to protect your rights as a consumer?

1. After informing your landlord three times that the back door would not lock properly, someone discovered the problem and entered your apartment. About $500 worth of jewelry was stolen. When you told the landlord, he apologized but refused to pay for the cost of replacing the stolen jewelry. What would you do?

_____

_____

_____

_____

_____

_____

_____

_____

2. You entered a contest in which you were supposed to name the capitals of Arkansas, Rhode Island, California, Texas, and North Carolina. Because you are a whiz in geography, you felt you were sure to win. You did not mind sending the $15 entrance fee. After all, the winner had a chance to win $50,000. You never heard from the company again. What would you do?

_____

_____

_____

_____

_____

_____

HOW TO INTERPRET LEGAL AGREEMENTS AND WARRANTIES AS A CONSUMER

Although there are consumer protection laws and consumer groups to assist you if you have been treated unfairly, a person should take precautions to be dealt with justly in the first place. Most people are not out to swindle the consumer, although there are some who make a business out of cheating others. There are times, however, when the consumer is swindled by not being alert to the terms of an agreement. An alert consumer is always aware of the terms and conditions of a contract. " 'An ounce of prevention is worth a pound of cure,' " Mr. Fernandez said.

Legal agreements are usually in the form of some kind of contract. A _contract_ is an agreement between two or more people that establishes a legal obligation. All agreements are not contracts. If Susan promises to marry Carlos in the summer and changes her mind on May 31, she has not violated a contract. There must be five basic elements in a contract for it to be legal:

1. There must be an offer and acceptance of the offer.

2. The persons involved must be competent (capable of understanding the terms of the contract).

3. The purpose or subject of the agreement must be legal (enforceable in a court of law).

4. There must be consideration (payment for product or service performed).

5. The agreement must be in a legally acceptable form.

Each time Susan sold a meal at Connie's Cafe, she was, in a sense, carrying out a contract. The customers knew the meals were offered to anyone willing to pay for them. Most customers were aware of what they were paying for, and selling meals is a legal operation. In the case of Connie's Cafe, the agreement between the cashier and customer is oral.

Contracts can be either *oral* or *written*. Usually an oral agreement is sufficient for transactions involving a small amount of money; and even then, the customer ordinarily gets a receipt as evidence of the transaction. Oral contracts can be risky when the terms of the contract are complex or the amount of money involved is significant. If there is a disagreement between individuals (parties) involved in an oral contract, witnesses to the terms of the agreement have to be provided. Otherwise, little can be done to enforce the contract legally.

Susan's father was living proof that someone can be cheated on an oral contract. He paid a contractor $200 to repair part of his roof, only to find a puddle in the middle of his living room floor after the first heavy rain. The contractor had moved on to other projects and could not be contacted. Furthermore, Susan's father had no written evidence of the contract.

A written contract can range from a short and simple agreement to a lengthy agreement with clauses, restrictions, and specifications. Basically, a written contract should include the following:

1. The date and location of the agreement

2. The identification of the parties entering into the agreement

3. A statement of the terms agreed upon

4. The signatures of both parties or their legal representatives

5. The signatures of witnesses if required

Figure 11-3 is a copy of Mr. Fernandez's contract with his electrician.

A *bill of sale* is another type of written contract. A bill of sale is not simply a receipt. It includes the name of the item or service purchased and the signatures of the seller and buyer. A bill of sale is usually written at the time ownership is transferred.

Possession of goods does not imply ownership. Stolen goods cannot be transferred. The right to transfer property to another person involves more than the mere possession of property. Always ask for verification of ownership, such as the bill of sale, before buying goods from another person. A bill of sale, which is a document signed by the seller giving evidence of transfer of title to the buyer, legally allows one to assign or transfer property. A thief or finder cannot transfer property to another person. A person who purchases stolen goods, even in good faith, must return the property to the owner.

Skills for Consumer Success

Figure 11-3:
Contract for
Electrical Work

> This AGREEMENT is made on May 14, 19--, between
> Edison, Inc., 1200 Howard Avenue, Our Towne, California,
> the party of the first part, and Anthony Fernandez,
> 207 Oriole Street, Our Towne, California, the party of
> the second part.
>
> The party of the first part agrees to rewire the home
> of the party of the second part at 207 Oriole Street,
> Our Towne, California, by September 30, 19--, in
> accordance with the specifications attached hereto.
> In consideration of which the party of the second part
> agrees to pay the party of the first part $2,001.76
> upon satisfactory completion of the work.
>
> *Thomas Edison*
>
> *Anthony Fernandez*

STUDENT ACTIVITY H

Are the following contracts legal? If not, which element of a legal contract is missing?

1. Juan Rodriguez signed a contract for a home-study extension course entitled "English as a Second Language." Juan cannot read a word of English and told the salesperson who had come to his home that he was unable to read the contract. The salesperson assured Juan everything was okay, showed him where to sign, and took Juan's tuition check for $500. Juan did receive some materials in the mail, but he could not read them. Is the contract legal?

   _____

   Explain. _____

   _____

   _____

2. Joe knows a place, The Pawn Shoppe, where second-hand merchandise that looks like new can be purchased very inexpensively. In fact, the goods cost so little that Joe had often wondered if everything was legitimate at The Pawn Shoppe. Last week The Pawn Shoppe was raided, and the owner was arrested for selling stolen goods. The police found Joe's bill of sale for a TV, stereo, and an oak table. The police went to Joe's

apartment to pick up the goods. Was Joe's contract (bill of sale) with the owner legal?

_____

Explain. _____

_____

3. Stella insisted that her electrician was to install two outside lights. The electrician claimed that no such provision was made in the contract for lighting work. But Stella reminded him that he had told her he would put up the lights as an extra service, even though it was not in the written contract. Is the electrician legally bound to install the lights?

_____

Explain. _____

_____

4. Uncle Wilbur suffered head injuries in a car accident and could not think clearly, so his two nephews wrote a will for him, making themselves the sole inheritors of his money. Uncle Wilbur signed the will. Is the will legal?

_____

Explain. _____

_____

Frequently, a sales contract includes a warranty or guarantee. A *warranty* is a promise regarding the service or quality of an item sold. Warranties may be either *express warranties* or *implied warranties. Express warranties* are usually written and include specific promises about a product or service, including statements to the customer about replacement or repair of a product that does not work properly. If the warranty promises are not fulfilled, the customer has the legal right to sue as a last resort.

Even though there may be no written warranty on a product, most states require unwritten or *implied warranties* on all products sold to the public. The implied warranty means.

- That a product will do what it is supposed to do. (A popcorn popper should pop popcorn.)

- That a product does all special functions for which it is bought. (A carving knife blade cuts through frozen meat without chipping.)

Warranties should be read carefully by the consumer *before* the product is purchased. The following are questions that might be considered before purchase:

1. *What* does the warranty cover? parts and labor? certain parts and not others?

2. Are there any conditions under which the warranty is void or useless?

3. Do you have to mail in a card confirming the date of purchase in order to be eligible for the warranty?

4. Whom do you contact if the product is defective?

STUDENT ACTIVITY I

Below is a copy of a warranty. Read it, and answer the following questions.

1. When will the warranty end?

_____

2. If the product is defective, who will replace it or repair it?

_____

3. Will the company replace or repair the product in all circumstances?

_____

Explain. _____

_____

_____

4. If the product is defective, how do you get it repaired or replaced?

_____

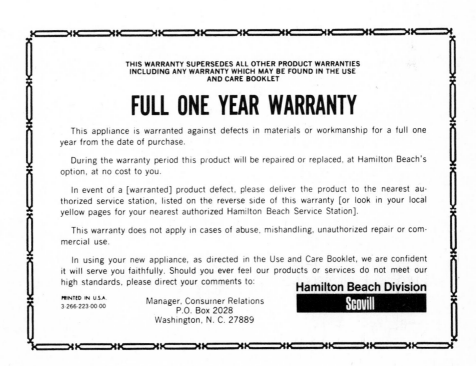

THIS WARRANTY SUPERSEDES ALL OTHER PRODUCT WARRANTIES INCLUDING ANY WARRANTY WHICH MAY BE FOUND IN THE USE AND CARE BOOKLET

FULL ONE YEAR WARRANTY

This appliance is warranted against defects in materials or workmanship for a full one year from the date of purchase.

During the warranty period this product will be repaired or replaced, at Hamilton Beach's option, at no cost to you.

In event of a [warranted] product defect, please deliver the product to the nearest authorized service station, listed on the reverse side of this warranty [or look in your local yellow pages for your nearest authorized Hamilton Beach Service Station].

This warranty does not apply in cases of abuse, mishandling, unauthorized repair or commercial use.

In using your new appliance, as directed in the Use and Care Booklet, we are confident it will serve you faithfully. Should you ever feel our products or services do not meet our high standards, please direct your comments to:

PRINTED IN U.S.A.
3-266-223-00-00

Manager, Consumer Relations
P.O. Box 2028
Washington, N. C. 27889

Hamilton Beach Division
Scovill

Reprinted with permission of Hamilton Beach Division: Scovill.

Under the Magnuson-Moss Warranty Act of 1975, a warranty must be designated either "full" or "limited" if the product costs at least $10. A *full warranty* must provide the following:

- Repair within a reasonable time and without charge

- Coverage not only to initial purchasers of a given product but also to anyone who buys the product second-hand during the period the warranty is in effect

- No unreasonable conditions for service, such as requiring shipping to the factory or mailing of warranty card in advance

- Replacement of the defective product or a full refund if the product is still defective after a reasonable number of attempts to fix it

A *limited warranty* means anything less, such as:

- Coverage for parts but not labor

- Partial refunds instead of full refunds on a defective product

- Coverage for the first owner only

- Charges for shipping and handling a product sent to the manufacturer for repair

While a product is under warranty, you should be sure to keep the receipt confirming the date of purchase and a copy of the warranty. Both will be needed if you intend to have warranty service.

FURTHER DISCOVERIES

1. The consumer magazine, *Changing Times,* usually includes information on gyps and frauds (*gyps* meaning, in this case, a swindle to cheat the consumer). Review the December index of *Changing Times* for the last few years to identify some common gyps. Read three articles about gyps and frauds, and write a report on your findings.

2. Many products carry a "seal or label." Among the best known are Underwriter's Laboratory, Good Housekeeping, and Parents' Magazine. Make a list of various products that carry a "seal or label." Investigate what these "seals or labels" indicate. Write a report on your findings.

3. If you have *Consumer Reports* in your school or local library, look up the topics listed below and indicate whether or not they were included as articles in the last twelve issues. If they were, give the month and year the article was published. (Clue: The long way to complete this activity is to search through all the magazines. What is the easy way?)

Topics	Yes/No	Month/Year
Automobiles		
Job market		

Topics	Yes/No	Month/Year
Consumer protection	_____	_____
Frauds	_____	_____
Budgeting	_____	_____
Insurance	_____	_____
Credit	_____	_____
Warranties	_____	_____
Investments	_____	_____
Buying a home	_____	_____

Read two articles of interest, and write a brief summary on each article.

4. On page 214 several areas are mentioned in which consumer legislation has been passed. Using your school or local library, see what you can find about laws passed at the federal level in any of the areas mentioned. Write a one paragraph summary about each law you discover.

CHECKLIST

Having performed the student activities in this unit, you should have mastered the skills below. Check off the skills you know, and review ones you are not sure of.

( ) Rights and responsibilities as a consumer

( ) How to research products through the proper use of consumer publications, especially *Consumer Reports*

( ) How to locate agencies for consumer protection in my community

( ) The services provided by the Better Business Bureau

( ) How to use small claims court

( ) What determines a legal contract

( ) The basic legal requirements of a contract

( ) How to interpret a warranty agreement

If you have checked all of the above, ask your teacher for the Susan Thompson Test on Consumer Protection.

INDEX

agencies, employment, 10–12
agreements, legal, how to interpret, 227–228; sales, for new car, 182
American Stock Exchange, 121
annual percentage rate (APR), 79; new cars, 185–187
application, letter of, 19–21; contents of, 20
appraisal fee, 206
assets, defined, 85
automatic teller, 67–68
automobile, owning and operating, 171–185
automobile insurance, bodily injury liability, 155; buying, 153–156; collision, 156; comprehensive physical damage, 156; deductibles, 155; liability, 155; limits of protection, 155; medical payment coverage, 156; no-fault, 160; property damage liability, 155; single-limit basis, 156; split-limit basis, 156; substitute-service coverage, 160; uninsured motorists protection, 156; wage-loss coverage, 160

bank statement, defined, 48; how to interpret, 48–53; how to reconcile with checkbook balance, 51–53
bankrupt, defined, 85
Better Business Bureau (BBB), 14, 223–226
bill of sale, 228
blank endorsement, 45
bonds, defined, 124; types of, 124–125
broker, defined, 120
budget, defined, 99; estimated, 105; expenditures, 102–104; fixed expenses, 102–103; guidelines, 108.
Buying Guide, 218

canceled checks, 48
capacity, and credit standing, 77
capital, 77
capital gain, defined, 120
car options, 181–184
careers, 3–13; abilities, determination of, 4–15; centers for, 9; choice of, 4–9; counseling for, 9–12; defined, 3; training for, 9–13; types of, 8–11;
cash value, defined, 85
cash value, of life insurance policies, 143
Changing Times, 126, 215
character, and credit standing, 76
charge accounts, understanding, 92–96
check, 41–44; how to write, 43–44; special, 71; stop payment order, 44
checkbook, 41; defined, 41

checking account, 35–55; account number, 38; balance forward, 42; bank number, 38; bank statement, 48–49; checkbook, 41; checks, 41–44; check register, 41; check stub, 41–44; deposits, 42; economy, 39; how to deposit money in, 44; how to open, 37–39; individual, 38; interpreting bank statement and reconciling checkbook balance, 50–53; joint, 38; minimum balance, 39; reconciliation statement, 48–51; regular, 39; service charge, 39; share draft, 36; signature card, 38
check records, keeping accurate, 41–44
check register, 42
check stubs, 41–43
closing costs, 205
co-applicant, defined, 85
co-insurance, defined, 137
collateral, 84
commission, broker's, defined, 120
complaint, letter of, 221–222
complaints, agencies which deal with, 219–221; how to handle, 219–226
compound interest, how to calculate, 60–63
concealment, on insurance policy, 138
consumer, defined, 214
consumer bill of rights, 214
consumer credit laws, 79
consumer finance companies, 82
consumer publications, how to use, 215
Consumer Reports, 126, 181, 215–218
consumer rights, 212–214
Consumers' Research Magazine, 215
contract, defined, 227
co-owners, defined, 86
cosigner, defined, 85
credit, 75–97; applying for, 92; guidelines for, 95–96; line of, 94; requirements for buying on, 76–78; three C's of, 77
credit bureaus, 79
credit insurance, 91
credit references, defined, 85
credit standing, 77
credit union, 36; as source of loans, 82
credit worthiness, 77
creditor, defined, 86

data sheet, 15–19; appearance of, 16; defined, 15; information on, 16–19; references, listed on, 16; style of, 17–19
debt balance, defined, 85
deductions, from pay, 101
default, defined, 86
dependents, defined, 86

deposit, in checking account, 44
depreciation, of cars, 172
disclaimer, defined, 92

earnest money, 206
economy account, checking, 39
electronic transfer of funds, 67–69
employment agencies, placement firms, 10; private, 10; state office, 10; temporary-help, 12
endorsement, blank, 45; in full, 47; restrictive, 46
Equal Credit Opportunity Act, 79
Equal Employment Opportunity Act, 26
equity, defined, 203
escrow agent, 207
expenditures, 100

Fair Credit Billing Act, 79
Fair Credit Reporting Act, 79
Fair Debt Collections Practices Act, 79
Federal Deposit Insurance Corporation (FDIC), 36
Federal Insurance Contributions Act (FICA), 148
Federal Savings and Loan Insurance Corporation (FSLIC), 36
finance charge, 79
floater policy, 164

garnishment, defined, 91
gross pay, 100
guidelines for budgeting, 108

health insurance, 134–140; basic hospital/surgical/physician, 135; benefit period, 137; ceiling, 137; deductible, 137; disability income, 136; exclusions, 137; limits, 137; major medical, 135; maximum coverage, 136; premiums, 137; renewability, 137
health maintenance organizations (HMOs), 139
highballing, 182
home, advantages vs. disadvantages, 203–204; buying a, 203–207; costs of buying, 203–207; mortgage, 204–207
homeowners' and renters' insurance, types of, defined, 163
housing, choices available, 191–192; expenses, 193–195; rent vs. buy, 209

income taxes, 28–30
individual account, checking, 38
installment contracts, 88–92; credit insurance, 91; default payment clause, 91; deficiency clause, 91; down payment, 88; finance charge, 88
insurance, health, 134–140
insurance premiums, 135
interest, 57–63; compound, how

to calculate, 60–63; defined, 57–58; how to figure, 57–60; rate of, 58–63

interview, job, guidelines for, 23–25; follow-up for, 27; questions asked, 25–26

investing, defined, 119

investment club, defined, 128

investment opportunities, 119–131

investment publications, listing of, 130

job market, 1–33; availability in, 9–12; sources of information for, 9–12; training for, 9–13

jobs (see also careers; job market), applying for, 15–23; defined, 3; choice of, 4–9; discrimination on, 26; full-time, sources of, 15; income, tax of, 28–30; interviewing for, 23–26; part-time, benefits of, 12; sources of, 8–15; training for, 9–13 (see also vocational schools)

joint account, checking, 38

joint applicant, defined, 85

landlady or landlord, defined, 196

lease, defined, 196; understanding, 196–200

letter of application, 19–21

letter of complaint, 221–222

letter of inquiry, 20

liabilities, defined, 86, 155

liability protection, 162

life insurance, 141–144; beneficiary, 142; buying, 141–144; cash-value policies, 142; convertible term policy, 142; guaranteed renewability, 142; level term policy, 142; term policy, 142

life insurance company, as source of loan, 143

loan origination fee, 206

loan shark, defined, 83

loans, 81–86; collateral for, 84; cost of, 84; finance charge, 84; installment, 84; interest rate, 84; obtaining, 81–85; personal, 81; promissory note, 84; secured, 84; signature, 84; single payment, 83; sources of, 81–82; terminology, 85–86; types of, 83–84; unsecured, 84; usury laws, 83

loss ratio, for insurance companies, 135

lowballing, 182

mortgage, defined, 85, 204

mortgage holder, defined, 85

mortgage redemption insurance, 206

mutual fund, defined, 126

net pay, 100, 109

new cars, buying, research on, 181; depreciation of, 172; fixed expenses, 172; flexible expenses, 172; obtaining a loan,

185–187; options, 182–184; rate of depreciation, 181; repair and maintenance, 181; sales agreement, 182; shopping for, 180–184; warranty, 182

New York Stock Exchange, 121

NOW (negotiable order of withdrawal) account, 39

Occupational Outlook Handbook, 9

outstanding checks, 50

overdrafting and overdrawing, 53

part-time job, benefits of, 12; sources of, 8–15; training for, 9–14

passbook, 64–65

pawnbroker, defined, 83

paycheck, 101; stub, 101

percentage, conversion to decimal, 58–59

personal property, defined, 162

premiums, for health insurance, 137

principal, 58

proceeds, defined, 86

promissory note, 84

property protection, 162

property taxes, 206

provisions, in health insurance policies, 136

rate of interest, 58, 62, 64

real estate, defined, 85

real property, defined, 162

reclaim, defined, 86

reconciliation statement, 48–51

recording fee, 206

regular checking account, 39

regular passbook savings account, 64–65

replacement cost coverage, 164

repossess, defined, 86

restrictive endorsement, 46

resume (see data sheet)

riders, on insurance policy, 138

Rule of 78's, defined, 86

savings account, 63–66; deposit slip, 65; investing money in, 64–65; liquidity of, 64; NOW (negotiable order of withdrawal) account, 65; regular passbook account, 64; special time-period accounts, 65; withdrawal slip, 66

savings and loan associations, 36

secured loan, 84

securities, 120; defined, 85; unlisted, 121

service charge, for checking account, 39

share draft accounts, 36

signature card, for checking account, 38

signature loan, 84

simple interest, how to figure, 58–59

single payment loan, 83

small claims court, 225

Social Security Act, 146

social security card, filing for, 148–149

social security system, disability insurance, 146; health insurance, 147; life (survivor's) insurance, 147; retirement income, 145; unemployment insurance, 146

special time-period savings accounts, 65

stale check, 47

statement, bank, for checking, 48

statement of earnings, 150

statement, reconciliation, 48–51

stocks, dividends, 122; listings, 122; types of, 122

stop payment order, checking, 44

taxes, income, 28–30, (see also tax return); Form W-2, 29; Form W-4, 28; Internal Revenue Service (IRS), 29; refund of, 29; reporting of, 28–30; terminology of, 28–30; understanding of, 28–30; withholding of, 28–29

tax return, filing of, 29–30; forms, types of, 29; preparation of, 29–30

tellers, 37

term life insurance, 141–144

time, in figuring simple interest, 58

title, 204

title insurance, 206

title search, 204

total income, how to determine, 100

Truth-in-Lending Act, 79

umbrella policies, 164

unsatisfied judgment, defined, 85

unsecured loan, 84

used car, buyers guide, 175; dealers, 175; obtaining a loan, 185–187; possible problem areas, 178–179; shopping for, 174–185

usury laws, defined, 83

vita (see data sheet)

vocational schools, 13–14; as adult education programs, 13; benefits of, 13–14; at community colleges, 13; to determine interests and abilities, 13; government sponsored, 13; high-school, 13; training programs in, 13–14

wage assignment, defined, 91

Wall Street Journal, 126

warranty, express, 230; full, 232; implied, 230; limited, 232; new car, 182

withholding tax, 101

work-study programs, 9

yearly budget, how to prepare, 115–116

yield, in savings plans, 63